DATE			

Moving through Whitman's career four times from four different perspectives, this book investigates several major American cultural developments that occurred during Whitman's lifetime—the development of American dictionaries, the growth of baseball, the evolution of American Indian policy, the development of photography and photographic portraits—and tracks the ways these cultural actions became essential components of Whitman's innovative poetics. Resisting the usual critical temptation to present a totalized, one-dimensional Whitman, this study views him instead as multiple and contradictory, a gatherer of discordant tones and clashing approaches from a variety of surprising cultural arenas. From Webster's and Worcester's continually expanding dictionaries, Whitman learned about the possibilities of an unbounded and infinitely absorptive language, out of which a new kind of expansive poetics could emerge. In baseball, he saw the inception of national sport, one that had a rhythm, movement, and ethos distinctively American, and he saw in this game the possibilities for democratic crowds and camaraderie that he would celebrate in his poetry. From the time of the Great Removal when he was a boy on through to the massacre at Wounded Knee just before his death, Whitman saw in American Indians an autochthonous otherness that he tried to absorb even as it vanished under the imperialistic hand of his expanding nation. And in photography, he found the technological counterpart of his poetics of wholeness and inclusiveness, offering the possibility of turning the world and his life into an endless series of cluttered representations. In such cultural activities, Whitman found not his poetic subjects so much as his poetic tools and techniques. These cultural actions taught him how to make native representations.

CAMBRIDGE STUDIES IN AMERICAN LITERATURE
AND CULTURE

Walt Whitman's Native Representations

Cambridge Studies in American Literature and Culture

Editor
Eric Sundquist, University of California, Los Angeles

Founding Editor
Albert Gelpi, Stanford University

Advisory Board
Nina Baym, University of Illinois, Champaign-Urbana
Sacvan Bercovitch, Harvard University
Albert Gelpi, Stanford University
Myra Jehlen, University of Pennsylvania
Carolyn Porter, University of California, Berkeley
Robert Stepto, Yale University
Tony Tanner, King's College, Cambridge University

Continued on pages following the Index

Walt Whitman's Native Representations

ED FOLSOM
The University of Iowa

CAMBRIDGE
UNIVERSITY PRESS

Published by the Press Syndicate of the University of Cambridge
The Pitt Building, Trumpington Street, Cambridge CB2 1RP
40 West 20th Street, New York, NY 10011-4211, USA
10 Stamford Road, Oakleigh, Melbourne 3166, Australia

First published 1994

Printed in the United States of America

Library of Congress Cataloging-in-Publication Data
Folsom, Ed, 1947–
Walt Whitman's native representations / Ed Folsom.
    p.   cm. — (Cambridge studies in American literature and
culture ; 80)
Includes bibliographical references (p.) and index.
ISBN 0-521-45357-7
1. Whitman, Walt, 1819–1892—Knowledge—America. 2. Whitman,
Walt, 1819–1892—Knowledge and learning.   3. Literature and
anthropology—United States—History—19th century.   4. Indians of
North America in literature.   5. Lexicography in literature.
6. Photography in literature.   7. Baseball in literature.
8. Poetics.   I. Title.   II. Series.
PS3242.A54F65   1994   93-29689
811'.3—dc20   CIP

A catalog record for this book is available from the British Library.

ISBN 0-521-45357-7 hardback

To Pat and Ben

Contents

Illustrations

Preface: Walt Whitman and . . .

Walt Whitman is the poet of the grand conjunction, the singer of "and."
His catalogs, indeed his whole poetic fabric, are woven with that conjunction. He is the poet of conjoining, of singing the parts of the world
into a massive juxtaposition. He forges a vision of wholeness out of disparate parts held together by his adhesive voice. It is not surprising that
so many of our books and essays about him echo that conjunctive impulse: *Walt Whitman and the Civil War, Walt Whitman and Science, Walt
Whitman and Opera, Walt Whitman and the Body Beautiful, Emerson, Whitman and the American Muse,* "Whitman and the American Idiom," "Walt
Whitman and German Thought"—the list goes on and on. Of course,
many writers have been studied in conjunction with another subject, but
Whitman's work has a particularly intimate relationship with its cultural
surroundings, and these titles reflect the critical consensus that Whitman
is best understood contextually, as a writer who absorbed many aspects
of his culture into his work, a writer we best read by moving from the
poetry out into the world that the work was woven from, a writer best
understood in juxtaposition to just about any aspect of the culture we
can name. Ezra Pound paid no greater homage finally to his "pig-headed
father" than when he began his own song of himself, his open-ended
Cantos, with "And," then ended the first canto with that dangling, endlessly active conjunctive desire "and . . ." When E. M. Forster looked to
Whitman to find a name for his novel of shattered East–West conjoin-
ings, his ironic use of *Passage to India* was undercut with the Whitmanic
message of adhesive hope that hovers beneath the book, a message he
expressed in another novel as "Only connect."

The English language's sign of connection—"and"—is Whitman's poetic sign; one of his favorite concepts is "adhesiveness," a term he takes
from phrenology and applies to a wide range of emerging democratic
friendships that he would come to call "camaraderie." As he searched for
and invented names for this necessary adhesive quality of strong demo-

cratic affection, he found its grammatical equivalent in the English conjunction indicating adhesion. His notebooks and letters are punctuated
with his idiosyncratic ampersand, a distinctive shorthand sign of adhesion, a ubiquitous small scripted knot tying his observations together.
"And" allowed the voice to bind the parts of the world and eventually
to blend them, and it served Whitman well in creating what C. Carroll
Hollis has demonstrated to be a remarkably metonymic vision, a poetry
that creates its world by naming things next to each other instead of
naming things like each other (as the much more common metaphorical
visions do).

This book is a kind of metonymic criticism; like Whitman's represen-
tatively random catalogs, my chapters—"Whitman and Dictionaries,"
"Whitman and Baseball," "Whitman and American Indians," "Whitman
and Photography," "Whitman and Photographs of the Self"—could go
on indefinitely. They form a set of expanding cultural essays, each one
cycling through Whitman's writing career and casting his artistic activity
in a new light. The cycles get wider as the cultural activities under investigation get more pervasive. I hope to show not only how Whitman had
significant and surprising reactions to some areas and events in American
cultural history that we do not usually associate with him, but also how
he worked hard to turn those events to poetic action, to discover how
almost any cultural activity could help him form his poetry and enable
him to define a distinctive American poetics. I will be demonstrating,
then, an isomorphic relationship between Whitman's poetry and various
key facets of his culture.

All of us who write criticism wonder at some point about the autobiographical connections, the ways in which our scholarly investigations
reveal our own passions, fears, loves. So perhaps it is not inappropriate
to reveal that my own long and convoluted interaction with Whitman
began when I was eight years old and encountered him on a baseball
card. It was in the mid-1950s, and celebrations of the centenary of *Leaves
of Grass* were going on in many places and receiving a good deal of pub-
licity, though I of course was unaware of any of it. My attention that
year was for the first time focused fully on baseball, and my major occupation was purchasing and trading baseball cards. Most were the standard Topps bubble gum issue, but there were countless variations—cards
cut from the backs of cereal boxes, from the sides of milk cartons, from
the wrappers on hot dog packages. In what now seems like an intricately
significant moment in my childhood, but what then seemed a mundane
and vaguely disappointing fact of life, I somehow one day ended up with
a Walt Whitman card, an old man with a bushy beard wearing a baseball
cap. He was then, and still remains, a mystery. He entered my card collection like a visitor from another planet; the card was no doubt some

parodic commemorative memento of a centenary celebration that I was oblivious to, and so it represented a collision of worlds. The card showed a man too old to be a player; my first thought was that he must be a manager or a coach, but the card stated that he was a New York Yankee from "out of left field." I knew all the Yankee outfielders, and even Enos Slaughter didn't look *that* old. Confused, I tucked the card away and eventually coerced a younger kid into a trade, convincing him that Walt Whitman was a Hall of Famer. It's a trade that only recently I have begun to regret, for it's a card the significance of which I have only recently— while writing this book—begun to appreciate.

That card played on an association between the Great American Poet and the Great American Game, an association that in fact has a substantial basis in Whitman's life, as I demonstrate in Chapter 2. But the card also played on another association, that of Whitman and photography. The baseball card joke works better with Whitman than with other nineteenth-century writers in part because we so fully associate Whitman with photographs: he is the most photographed of all the writers who died before the twentieth century began. He was also, in part because of photography, one of our first celebrity writers; his striking physiognomy made him a favorite of photographers, and his cabinet card portraits were sold by well-known photographers like Napoleon Sarony, George C. Cox, and Frederick Gutekunst. ("My head gets about: is easily recognized," Whitman said.) These were the photographers who were creating the modern notion of "celebrity," helping to manufacture personalities who were instantly recognizable precisely because of the widespread availability of their photographic images. Cabinet card portraits of politicians, military heroes, actors, and writers were available in many studio stores, and by the 1870s thousands of people collected these celebrity cards. Whitman's portrait was a popular favorite, and he occasionally collected royalties on the sale of his image. In his own lifetime, he had already appeared on the nineteenth-century equivalent of baseball cards. His awareness of the importance of having a widely familiar image was one of the things that attracted him to photography and allowed him to see the democratic possibilities that the new mode of representation offered.

All of the events, actions, and processes that I will be tracing in this book—an evolving dictionary of American words, the development of a national sport, a changing policy toward American Indians, and the emergence of a new way to record vision—were part of the American cultural weave for Whitman. They were strands of the material that formed, as he said, "one man's—the author's—identity, ardors, observations, faiths, and thoughts" (*LG* 563). Whitman once claimed that the very subject of *Leaves of Grass* was "the now ripening Nineteenth Century" (*LG* 564). Things were forming—words, actions, attitudes, identities—that would ripen into America and democracy. *Leaves of Grass* was forming with them; if the book could also be formed *out* of these things, Whitman believed it would become a native representation. What "has not yet appear'd," he said, and what he sought to bring into language and thus into being, was "native American individuality" (*LG* 571). That individuality, and the poems that expressed it, would be woven out of the threads spinning from multiple cultural spools.

The cultural spools that I focus on here have been, as my bibliographic notes indicate, the subjects of many innovative and illuminating studies of American culture in the past few years. Americans are actively redefining themselves through careful reexaminations of their shifting attitudes toward language, sport, race, and art. Whitman, it turns out, set out a century and a half ago to define the nation by examining those same cultural realms as they were in the process of formation. He read the originating texts and applied their lessons to his own emerging text, a text he hoped would be native and democrative, definitive, filled with words that no dictionary could yet express, as accurate as a photograph: a whole new ball game.

Acknowledgments

Much of this book is about the language Whitman used and the cultural sources from which he took, crafted, aligned, and created the words that form his poetry and prose. It is, in that sense, a book about some of the sources of his speaking and singing, the cultural origins of his voice. In thinking and writing about Whitman's culturally rich lexicon (and the various real and figurative dictionaries from which it derives), I have been acutely aware that my own critical lexicon has *its* sources in teachers and critics too numerous to mention. The words of this book are themselves taken, crafted, and aligned out of their books: significant critical texts quickly become a kind of dictionary, sourcebooks of terms and definitions and etymologies that we use to increase our own vocabularies, so that we can push our sense of discovery a little further into discourse. We all speak with each other's words, and it is with a sense of gratitude that I acknowledge here a few of the critical "dictionaries" from which I have garnered definitions and words and origins that I had not previously known. My book often speaks in their terms as it seeks its own definitions.

I was lucky enough to be introduced to American literature through the careful and lucid words of Benjamin T. Spencer, whose books *The Quest for Nationality* and *Patterns of Nationality* are model inquiries into the development of the idea of a distinctly American literature. Gay Wilson Allen's work, especially *The Solitary Singer* and the *New Walt Whitman Handbook,* has served three generations of Whitman scholars and is so definitive that I sometimes suspect that all subsequent work on Whitman forms what might be thought of as a lengthy annotation to Allen's formidable structurings of Whitman's life and work. C. Carroll Hollis's work has taught me to explore the less obvious roads, the engaging detours that eventually lead to major destinations; his own work, particularly *Language and Style in Leaves of Grass,* has investigated meticulously the journalistic and oratorical origins of Whitman's style and vocabulary, and I have learned invaluable lessons from it. Harold Aspiz's *Walt Whitman and the Body Beautiful* and M. Wynn Thomas's *The Lunar Light of Whitman's Poetry* are two extraordinary books that use surprising cultural contexts—nineteenth-century medicine and the decline of Jacksonian artisanal culture—to read Whitman's work in fresh and illuminating ways. All of these Whitman scholars have generously offered me advice over the years. In my bibliographical notes, I record many other debts, other books whose language and ideas have furnished lexicons that helped me form my own.

Jerome Loving and Brooks Landon are friends and colleagues to whom I owe the endless debts associated with agreeing to read and listen to a project that had no discernible conclusion. This book would still be in its early stages had it not been for the support of the Center for Advanced Studies at the University of Iowa; Jay Semel, the director, has generated and nurtured more scholarly activity than anyone I know, and he is a master at creating the ideal environment in which that activity can flourish. I'm also grateful to the University of Iowa for a Faculty Scholars Award that allowed time for much of my research.

Parts of this book appeared in earlier versions in various journals: parts of Chapter 2 appeared in the *Iowa Review* and in *Arête: The Journal of Sport Literature;* part of Chapter 3 appeared in *Etudes Anglaises;* and part of Chapter 4 appeared in the *Mickle Street Review*. I thank the editors of those journals—David Hamilton, Lyle Olsen, Roger Asselineau, and Geoffrey Sill—for their good critical eyes and for their permission to offer revised and expanded versions of that work in this book. At Cambridge University Press, Albert Gelpi, Julie Greenblatt, Janis Bolster, and Robert Racine offered valuable advice, and I'm grateful to them all. The participants in my graduate Whitman seminars over the past fifteen years have so enlivened my own encounters with Whitman's work that this book would have been unthinkable without them.

My wife, Pat, and my son, Ben, have been incomparable company on various trips associated with the writing of the book, including numerous evening research jaunts to watch the Cedar Rapids Reds play their nostalgic brand of minor-league baseball, evenings as reminiscent of the nineteenth century as any that I can imagine.

Abbreviations

AP	Horace Traubel, ed., *An American Primer by Walt Whitman* (1904; rpt. Stevens Point, WI: Holy Cow!, 1987).
BG	Sculley Bradley and John Stevenson, eds., *Walt Whitman's Backward Glances* (Philadelphia: University of Pennsylvania Press, 1949).
C	Edwin Haviland Miller, ed., *The Correspondence*, 6 vols. (New York: New York University Press, 1961–77).
CW	Richard Maurice Bucke, Thomas B. Harned, and Horace Traubel, eds., *The Complete Writings of Walt Whitman*, 10 vols. (New York: Putnam, 1902).
DBN	William White, ed., *Daybooks and Notebooks*, 3 vols. (New York: New York University Press, 1978).
EPF	Thomas L. Brasher, ed., *The Early Poems and Fiction* (New York: New York University Press, 1963).
GF	Cleveland Rodgers and John Black, eds., *The Gathering of the Forces*, 2 vols. (New York: Putnam, 1920).
ISL	Emory Holloway and Vernolian Schwarz, eds., *I Sit and Look Out* (New York: Columbia University Press, 1932).
LG	Sculley Bradley and Harold W. Blodgett, eds., *Leaves of Grass*. Norton Critical Edition (New York: Norton, 1973).
LGV	Sculley Bradley, Harold W. Blodgett, Arthur Golden, William White, eds., *Leaves of Grass: A Textual Variorum of the Printed Poems*, 3 vols. (New York: New York University Press, 1980).
NF	Richard Maurice Bucke, ed., *Notes and Fragments Left by Walt Whitman* (London: Talbot, 1899).
NUPM	Edward F. Grier, ed., *Notebooks and Unpublished Prose Manuscripts*, 6 vols. (New York: New York University Press, 1984).

NYD	Emory Holloway and Ralph Adimari, eds., *New York Dissected* (New York: Rufus Rockwell Wilson, 1936).
PR	William White, "Walt Whitman: An Unknown Piece by 'Paumanok,' " in Vince Clemente and Graham Everett, eds., *Paumanok Rising* (Port Jefferson, NY: Street Press, 1981).
PW	Floyd Stovall, ed., *Prose Works, 1892,* 2 vols. (New York: New York University Press, 1963).
UPP	Emory Holloway, ed., *The Uncollected Poetry and Prose of Walt Whitman,* 2 vols. (1921; rpt. Gloucester: Peter Smith, 1972).
WM	Fredson Bowers, ed., *Whitman's Manuscripts: Leaves of Grass (1860)* (Chicago: University of Chicago Press, 1955).
WWC	Horace Traubel, *With Walt Whitman in Camden,* 7 vols. Vols. 1–3 (1906–14; rpt. New York: Rowman & Littlefield, 1961); Vol. 4, ed. Sculley Bradley (Philadelphia: University of Pennsylvania Press, 1953); Vol. 5, ed. Gertrude Traubel (Carbondale: University of Southern Illinois Press, 1964); Vol. 6, ed. Gertrude Traubel and William White (Carbondale: University of Southern Illinois Press, 1982); Vol. 7, ed. Jeanne Chapman and Robert MacIsaac (Carbondale: University of Southern Illinois Press, 1992). The notes for the last few years of Whitman's life remain unpublished and are in manuscript in the Whitman/Feinberg collection in the Library of Congress; quotations from this collection are abbreviated "*WWC* MS."
WWCW	Charles I. Glicksberg, ed., *Walt Whitman and the Civil War* (1933; rpt. New York: Barnes, 1963).

Introduction: "Wording the Future"

> To poets and literats—to every woman and man, today or any day, the
> conditions of the present, needs, dangers, prejudices, and the like, are
> the perfect conditions on which we are here, and the conditions for
> wording the future with undissuadable words. These states, receivers
> of the stamina of past ages and lands, initiate the outlines of repayment
> a thousand fold. They fetch the American great masters, waited for by
> old worlds and new, who accept evil as well as good, ignorance as well
> as erudition, black as soon as white, foreign-born materials as well as
> home-born, reject none, force discrepancies into range, surround the
> whole, concentrate them on present periods and places, . . . and show
> the true use of precedents. Always America will be agitated and turbu-
> lent. This day it is taking shape, not to be less so, but to be more so,
> stormily, capriciously, on native principles, with such vast proportions
> of parts! As for me, I love screaming, wrestling, boiling-hot days.
>
> Whitman, 1856 (*LG* 738)

For Whitman, it was all a question of turning cultural actions, as quickly
as possible, into language: he set out to absorb the "agitated and turbulent" conditions of his cultural present and to go about the work of
"wording the future with undissuadable words," rejecting nothing in the
culture and trying instead to "force discrepancies into range," to bring
the "boiling-hot days" to voice, and to do it all "on native principles."
Betsy Erkkila has noted that "if for Emerson the sources of language
were in nature, for Whitman the sources of language were in democratic
culture, which included—but was not limited to—natural facts. Language, Whitman argued, must express the multiplicity of habits, heri-
tages, and races that make up the American nationality" (85). With his
belief that language found its source in cultural acts and cultural facts,
not in some imagined "natural" realm, Whitman became one of the first

1

American cultural semioticians, reading cultural activities as a vast text of democracy, searching for ways these cultural actions could be turned into American words, into a rhetoric of democracy. *Leaves of Grass* is the record of that attempt, a text seeking to track in its verbal acts the cultural actions that were defining democracy. Whitman often defined his work in precisely such terms:

> Modern science and democracy seem'd to be throwing out their challenge to poetry to put them in its statements in contradistinction to the songs and myths of the past. . . . Whatever may have been the case in years gone by, the true use for the imaginative faculty of modern times is to give ultimate vivification to facts, to science, and to common lives, endowing them with the glows and glories and final illustriousness which belong to every real thing, and to real things only. (*LG* 564)

This book is an examination of Whitman's attempt to "give ultimate vivification" to cultural acts, to bring new words and new configurations of words into the American language so that the word "democracy" itself could finally claim a secure place in the dictionary, could earn a definition. "Democracy"—always Whitman's key word—was, he believed, an empty linguistic vessel waiting for the poet who could translate cultural actions into verbal texts that would eventually catalog a thick record of democratic actions, attitudes, tones, and accomplishments: "Without that ultimate vivification—which the poet or other artist alone can give—reality would seem incomplete, and science, democracy, and life itself, finally in vain" (*LG* 564). "We have frequently printed the word Democracy," Whitman wrote in *Democratic Vistas:*

> Yet I cannot too often repeat that it is a word the real gist of which still sleeps, quite unawaken'd, notwithstanding the resonance and the many angry tempests out of which its syllables have come, from pen or tongue. It is a great word, whose history, I suppose, remains unwritten, because that history has yet to be enacted. (*PW* 393)

I want to examine some major cultural activities that occurred during Whitman's life and to suggest how these actions helped him define democratic poetry and ultimately democracy itself. "We stand, live, move, in the huge flow of our age's materialism—in its spirituality" (*PW* 409), he said, and his easy slippage from materialism to spirituality is telling: he was looking for a language that would attune the material signs to spiritual meaning, join the things to vivified words.

I have been interested for many years in the the way Whitman's writings contain intensive and extensive reactions to important nineteenth-century cultural movements. I have been particularly interested in identifying major cultural movements that in some way began around the time Whitman became an adult, that developed during his adult life, and then culminated near the time of his death. Whitman offers a special kind of illumination for these particular cultural movements, for he makes them truly his own; he was always on the lookout for new art forms, new political formulations, new cultural diversions, anything that emerged fresh and first in America, that could be absorbed by the culture as original and could be developed as peculiarly "of these States." When he found these things, he latched onto them, examined them, probed them, tested and challenged them, to check their fitness for becoming part of what he called the "great American poem." He returned to them throughout his adult life, reviewing and assessing them, determining their applicability for his American art. Whitman was, after all, of the first generation of Americans who were born secure in the belief that the United States was indeed a *country;* he was fond of dating his poems according to the "years of these States," recording the originating year as 1776. Born around forty years after the revolution—some thirty years after the nation became a functioning governmental structure, and only a few years after the War of 1812 finally secured the nation's autonomy— and growing up in Jacksonian America, Whitman was among the first generation of American adults to think of themselves fully as *native* Americans. (During Whitman's early adult years, the phrase "native American" was itself a linguistic battleground as various groups, from American Indians to a fiercely reactionary anti-immigrant political party, claimed the right to call themselves by that name.)

The various cultural movements that began when Whitman was a young man seemed, then, to have an especially powerful defining impact on the emerging culture, and he was anxious to figure out just what cultural attributes each new event, each new activity, each new attitude, signified and to discover how the events could be transformed into language—not just as *subjects* for his poetry, but as generators of a new *kind* of language, a native diction and pacing and rhythm and form that emerged out of cultural actions. If his words were to ultimately vivify cultural actions, then cultural actions would first have to vivify his words. Various cultural movements would become not only something to speak *of,* but also a lexicon we would learn to speak *with.*

As these movements evolved over the course of his life, he traced the analogical relationships between the maturing of his culture and his own aging; he had an intense desire to understand his life in national terms, to determine the ways the arc of his own existence shadowed the arc of America's history. Thus, when he looked back on his own life, he saw it as an embodiment of the national drama—the decline of his own health becoming the private inhalation of the country's tortured history ("This late-years palsied old shorn and shell-fish condition of me is the indubitable outcome and growth, now near for 20 years along, of too over-zealous, over-continued bodily and emotional excitement and action through the times of 1862, '3, '4, and '5, visiting and waiting on wounded and sick army volunteers, both sides" [*LG* 538]). Whitman saw his work, then, as an enactment of the correspondence between his personal life and the nation's life, an inscription of the self as nationally *representative* person, "an attempt, from first to last, to put *a Person,* a human being (myself, in the latter half of the Nineteenth Century, in America,) freely, fully and truly on record" (*LG* 573–74). Whitman's purpose was, he said, "to express the whirls and rapid growth and intensity of the United States, the prevailing tendency and events of the Nineteenth Century, and largely the spirit of the whole current World, my time; for I feel that I have partaken of that spirit" (*LG* 750). He was keenly aware, in other words, that he himself was the ultimate cultural fact, a composite of tendencies, events, currents, and intensities; in putting himself on record, then, he would record his culture and become the native representative.

Whitman repeatedly underscored the ways he used late-nineteenth-century American cultural movements as the thread out of which he wove his poetic text: "Given the Nineteenth Century, with the United States, and what they furnish as area and points of view, 'Leaves of Grass' is, or seeks to be, simply a faithful and doubtless self-will'd record. . . . I would sing, and leave out or put in, quite solely with reference to America and to-day" (*LG* 563–64). His obsession was "the now ripening Nineteenth Century" (*LG* 564), and he was especially aware of the particular "rapid growths" that ripened as he did, that began when he began his project and culminated when his own work culminated:

> To absorb, and express in poetry, any thing of it—of its world—
> America—cities and States—the years, the events of our Nineteenth
> Century—the rapidity of movement—the violent contrasts, fluctua-
> tions of light and shade, of hope and fear—the entire revolution made
> by science in the poetic method—these great new underlying facts and
> new ideas rushing and spreading everywhere;—Truly a mighty age!
> (*LG* 740)

The following chapters explore some of the most resonant of those violent contrasts and fluctuations and great new underlying facts and ideas of late-nineteenth-century America—the "vast seething mass of *materials*" (*LG* 741)—that Whitman used to mold his new American poetics. He knew that his adult years had provided a remarkable number of defining cultural actions: "Out of that stretch of time, and especially out of the immediately preceding Twenty-Five Years, (1850–1875,) with all their rapid changes, innovations, and audacious movements—and bearing their own inevitable wilful birth-marks—my Poems too have found genesis" (*LG* 754).

Each of the following topics concerns a dramatic cultural change, one of the "rapid changes, innovations, and audacious movements" that took place during Whitman's lifetime and that affected and generated his poetic program:

• First come American dictionaries, a product of the burgeoning business of popular publishing and the emerging science of lexicography. During Whitman's life, one of the most widely publicized publishing controversies was the "war of the dictionaries" between Noah Webster's innovative *American Dictionary of the English Language* and Joseph Worcester's more conservative *Comprehensive Dictionary;* the various editions of Webster and Worcester fought for linguistic hegemony in nineteenth-century America, fought for the right to be, literally, the definitive authority for what the American language meant, what it contained, what it would sound like, where it came from, what shape it was going to take. As a poet trying to forge a truly American poetry out of a truly American language, Whitman had a personal stake in the outcome, and he followed the development of dictionaries carefully as he compiled a book of poems that can itself be read as something of a revolutionary dictionary. Dictionaries for Whitman were the conduit, the way the new whirling, rushing cultural actions could be "absorbed" so that they could then be "expressed in poetry." It was crucial for Whitman, then, that American dictionaries be open and alterable and expandable, active absorbers of change instead of prescriptive arbiters of traditional usage. As cultural developments like baseball, battles with Indians, and the evolution of photography took place, Whitman had faith that they would form their own lexicons and rush new words into the dictionary that was defining the United States by serving as a vast storehouse of potential native expression.

• The second topic comes from the arenas of athletics and popular culture: baseball became entrenched as the American national game during Whitman's adult lifetime. When he was a young man, the ancient Iroquois game called lacrosse was sometimes touted as the truly native game: it became, for a while, the national summer sport of Canada, and in 1881 it was popular enough to draw a large New York crowd as an American team played a Canadian team for the "Championship of America." Others argued for cricket as the perfect American game, since it was an English import, a traditional game that could naturally take root in American soil. But Whitman, like many others, looked for the hybrid, the stick-and-ball game that existed somewhere between the Indians' swift and chaotic stick-and-ball and the Englishmen's leisurely and formal version of stick-and-ball. Whitman looked for the popular sport that would correspond to America, would even become a metaphor for the culture, and he found it in baseball, a game that grew up in his city, an activity that during his lifetime was one of the vital "new ideas rushing and spreading everywhere," helping to knit a national identity as it was taken up in all regions of the developing country.

It has become a cliché to talk about how a society's particular sports reflect a myriad of its social attitudes—toward competition, toward domination, toward gender, toward time and space—but Whitman was among the first American writers to articulate the intimate relationship between a culture's play and its character. He was in his early twenties when baseball as we know it began to be played, and his adult life was framed by the emergence, development, and professionalization of the sport. He was keenly interested in its nature, its qualities, its fitness as the national pastime. He was immediately curious about its significance, its meaning, and what it told us about the developing country. He knew the question of a nation's sporting preference was vital, and he became our first writer to pronounce baseball the essentially American sport. The early development of baseball—its democratic movement away from a gentleman's game into a game for the working class, its increasing speed and difficulty, its continental expansion, even its role as amusement for Civil War troops—all pleased Whitman, but its later development into a game of specializations, pitching deceptions, and professional disputations disheartened him. His lifelong response to the game paralleled his response to America as his early ideals gave way to a disturbing sense that something somewhere had gone wrong: greed and specialized selfishness had crept into all aspects of society, and their appearance in baseball, the ritual national sport, underscored the pervasiveness of the problem.

• The third topic comes from the realms of history and anthropology: the volatile relationship of American Indians and the dominant white race. In William Swinton's *Rambles Among Words,* a kind of etymological guidebook that Whitman knew well and may even have helped write, we are reminded that Whitman's very name—arising "from some external or internal idiosyncrasy"—means "white man" (Swinton 222); the fact that the etymology is singled out in *Rambles* suggests that Whitman was keenly aware of it, too; perhaps its inclusion was something of a joke by Whitman's good friend Swinton. Whatever the case, Whitman *is* a "White Man," and his sometimes jingoistic American poetry has been heard by many as the battle hymn of manifest destiny, of the Indians' decimation. Certainly the history of the Indians during Whitman's lifetime offered one of the most remarkable of the "violent contrasts" that he came to see as essential characteristics of American culture. Whitman's attitudes toward Indians, however, were far more complex than anyone has yet indicated, and his explorations of America's native cultures had

generative results, especially in leading him to the discovery of an autochthonous language.

Whitman lived with a George Catlin painting of Osceola, the Seminole warrior, peering down at him, a painting the artist gave him. He
also studied other painters of Indians, like Alfred Jacob Miller and John
Mulvany. And he listened intently to philologists who studied the Indian
languages: seeking ways to experience the sensation of native languages
on his own tongue; seeking ways to preserve native geographical names
so that all Americans, in order to live in this land, would have to learn
to join native languages to English; seeking ways to embody native insights and words into his own absorptive national poetry. Whitman's life
was lived between two monumental historic events for American Indians: the Great Removal of the eastern tribes across the Mississippi, and
the death knell of Indian independence and resistance—the massacre at
Wounded Knee. His adult life spanned the sad and bloody years of the
decimation of native cultures, and Chapter 3 examines Whitman's complex and conflicting attitudes toward that history, as well as his surprising artistic uses of native materials. America's actions against the Indians
formed a part of our history that Whitman sometimes tried to ignore but
could never escape: what the nation was doing to Indians, Whitman
knew, threw into doubt the possibility that the country was becoming
the democracy that he envisioned.

• Finally, from the fields of art and technology comes photography,
which from its introduction in America in 1839 transformed the way
the society viewed the land, viewed the human face, viewed war; the
development of photography over the course of the century led to a radical redefinition of art (and of reality) and initiated a complex debate about
the relationship of art and technology. Photography was vital to what
Whitman called "the revolution made by science in the poetic method,"
and he stood at the center of such debates, quickly seeking to claim photography as part of the distinctive emerging American art. It was, in fact,
the emergence of a photographic way of seeing that allowed Whitman to
view the "events of the Nineteenth Century" as occurring with a radically new "rapidity of movement" in "fluctuations of light and shade";
the whole century seemed to have turned into a series of momentary
images captured on light-sensitive plates.

Photographic images have become such a pervasive part of our life
that it is difficult now for us to imagine a world not re-presented in
photographs, a world in which we have no pictures of ourselves as
younger creatures, no accurate external visual images of parents, friends,
former homes, the places we have visited. Such a world was one in
which "celebrity" as we think of the term was an alien concept, for visual

recognition of those we had never actually seen would have been rudimentary at best, based on drawings or verbal descriptions. It would be a world where our visual experience would seem massively constricted, limited to what we had directly encountered, what had been presented to us instead of re-presented: our experience of such a world would feel more grounded in what was around us, more abstract in relation to what existed outside our immediate field of vision; even the most "realistic" paintings came quickly to seem idealized and abstracted once photographs became common. Whitman grew up in such a world, as part of the last generation who would know a photographically unrepresented world.

The first daguerreotype arrived in America in 1839 when Whitman was twenty, and in the next couple of years the invention swept into American consciousness. By the early 1840s, lavish daguerreotype studios and galleries were commonplace in American cities, and the miraculous mirror of sun painting allowed for famous Americans to become sudden celebrities as their duplicated faces looked out on thousands of spectators all across the land. One of the most enthusiastic of those first observers was Whitman, who wrote fervently of the stunning effects that the first photographs of faces had on him. Within a couple of years of the advent of the art, Whitman had his own face photographed, and he never stopped during the course of his remaining fifty years. This evolving series of self-images is the subject of my final chapter: Whitman became one of the first humans to have the whole course of his adult life recorded in photographs, accurately tracking—for the first time in human history—the process of aging. By the end of that life, Whitman too was one of the celebrities that photography had produced, his own photo available for sale by famous photographers (who had themselves become celebrities) like Napoleon Sarony and Frederick Gutekunst.

During those fifty years of Whitman's adult life, photography grew from a fascinating oddity into a radically useful and omnivorous tool for recording reality and, in so doing, transformed the way humans saw the world. The last two chapters of this book investigate the wide-ranging interplay between photography, Whitman's life, and his democratic poetics. A couple of years before Whitman's death, the first Kodak camera—sold with film already installed—went on the market, and photography was on the brink of its popular explosion when it would become the tool and toy of virtually anyone who wanted it. It was becoming the first truly democratic art form, allowing everyone to make (or, as the language bent to deal with the apperception of the new art, "take") accurate images of whatever interested them. Whitman quickly realized the implications of the invention of photography: it promised, as Susan Sontag has noted, to turn the entire visible world into representations, and he absorbed its lessons into his own emerging poetry. Photography taught Whitman about a democratic field of seeing; it was an absorptive art that gained its effectiveness precisely because it did not discriminate but rather allowed, insisted on, every detail in order to create its overall impression.

Like many other advances in technology during the past two centuries, photography quickly became enmeshed with war. We now remember and visualize the Civil War in dark images of black and white and gray, because it was the first war to be photographed, the first war to have its carnage captured in permanent, unrelentingly detailed images. Whitman knew the two great photographers of the Civil War, Mathew Brady and Alexander Gardner (he was photographed in both of their studios), and their images were part of what taught Whitman to turn the war inside out, to center it on the hospitals rather than the battlefields, to focus on the lingering aftereffects instead of the momentary heroics. Camera technology in the early 1860s was such that photography best lent itself to recording the still battlefields after the action had ceased. There are very few "action" shots of the Civil War; instead, we are left with shots of proud troops in uniform before the battles and bloated corpses after the battles. Often the rows of neatly uniformed soldiers give way to images of neat rows of beds in government buildings converted to hospitals, each bed containing a war casualty. So also was Whitman's poetry more suited to dwelling on the effects, the remnants, of the war; his most memorable war writing, both in *Drum-Taps* and in *Specimen Days,* is about his visits to the hospitals, his lifting of the blankets from dead soldiers, his evocation of distant parents getting word of their son's death, his cataloging of the vast geographies of death that the war had left behind: "The Million Dead, Too, Summ'd Up." Since camera technology produced its images in black and white, casting a moonlit glow over our memory of the war, it is interesting to note, as M. Wynn Thomas has done, how Whitman's omnipresent imagery of the sun is replaced in his later *Drum-Taps* poems with lunar light, subduing and softening the brutal results that Whitman knew America had to absorb and transform into a new Union: "Look down fair moon and bathe this scene, / Pour softly down night's nimbus floods on faces ghastly, swollen, purple . . ." (*LG* 320); or, from another poem, "war and all its deeds of carnage must in time be utterly lost, / . . . the hands of the sisters Death and Night incessantly softly wash again, and ever again, this soil'd world" (*LG* 321). Like the photographic images that were forming America's memory of the war, Whitman's poems sought the light that could subdue bright contrasting colors, sought the bleak and still images of aftereffects.

I make no sweeping claims about the direct impact these cultural events had on Whitman's poetry; dictionaries and baseball and Indians and photography *do* appear in *Leaves of Grass,* but overall they may be more conspicuous by their absence than by their presence. Whitman was the poet of indirection, often announcing that his "works shall illustrate the divine law of indirections" (*LG* 386); he worked obliquely from his experiences to his poetry, seeking analogues rather than imitations. He came to realize that his poetry was a verbal embodiment of the culture not so much in its direct references as in more subtle ways: "I see now that I have unconsciously sought, by indirections at least as much as directions, to express the whirls and rapid growth and intensity of the United States, the prevailing tendency and events of the Nineteenth century" (*PW* 470). I hope, then, to demonstrate that Whitman was engaged in indirect but essential ways with these major American cultural transformations, and that he used a variety of cultural movements to help him define and clarify his own artistic purposes. If he did not often write about these particular cultural acts, he did regularly write on the basis of what he learned from them: the cultural acts became the generators of his poetic form rather than his poetic subjects.

These cultural activities finally come together in revealing ways: baseball was becoming the most familiar American sport at the same time the Indians were vanishing as viable cultures; photography developed just in time to record such comings and goings; and American dictionaries were first appearing at exactly this time, recording the new and realigned terms that allowed the culture to absorb and talk about these things. These seemingly disparate activities from different cultural arenas all simultaneously affected most Americans living during those years, and these disparate activities converged on Whitman, who found in each a native analogue to his poetry, and who wove such variety into the song of himself and the song of his nation. These were the American actions that he was turning into American words.

For Whitman, culture could be defined as the active building of vocabulary. The larger and richer the culture's lexicon, he believed, the broader and more accepting the culture itself. More than any other American poet, Whitman was concerned with the number of words available to him, concerned that too few words were a sign of overselectivity, a sign of dangerous refinement and exclusivity, a linguistic reflection of antidemocratic sentiments. What he loved about the English language was what he saw as its absorptiveness, its infinite expandability, its tendency to accept synonyms from other languages and adapt and align them into new shades of meaning, each word bringing a previously unvoiced aspect of experience into the language: "The English language befriends the grand American expression . . . . it is brawny enough and limber and full enough" (*LG* 727). He celebrated the way slang served as a liberating jester in the hallowed halls of proper usage: as English is derived from the "feudal institutes" of the Old World, Whitman said, it can be thought of as "some mighty potentate" into whose presence comes "slang, or indirection, an attempt of common humanity to escape from bald literalism, and express itself illimitably." He noted how "into the majestic audience-hall of the monarch ever enters a personage like one of Shakspere's clowns" and that jarring and disruptive presence is what "produces poets and poems" (*PW* 573).

It is no surprise, then, that Whitman was fascinated with the growth of American dictionaries and with the emerging science of etymology. From the first truly modern dictionary, Noah Webster's 1828 *American Dictionary of the English Language,* on through to the first volumes of what would come to be the *Oxford English Dictionary* appearing near the time of his death, Whitman would follow and measure the burgeoning growth of the language, as experience poured into more and more words. His fascination with photography, Indian affairs, baseball, and countless other cultural processes often centered on this concern with the language—with seeing the democratic attitude of expansive inclusiveness reflected in the particular brand of English that Americans were coming to express themselves in. The following chapters return again and again to words, to Whitman's fascination with how quickly, effectively, and expansively new cultural activity could be turned into language.

Some of Whitman's most idiosyncratic poetic diction—from "debris" to "Paumanok" to "crowds"—derives, as we will see, from his reactions to photography, Indians, and baseball. Indian words and names could tune English in a native American key; baseball phrases could enliven native American slang, which Whitman saw as the generative source of language growth; photography could offer not only a whole new technological vocabulary (words like "heliography," "actinism," "tintype," "collodian," and "negatives" were coined within a very few years), but also an entirely new system of visual signs embracing (potentially) all of visible reality. Whitman, then, saw such diverse cultural components as photography, Indians, and baseball all converging on his desire for a truly democratic dictionary, a "Real Dictionary" that would not discriminate against slang, vulgarisms, neologisms, regionalisms, and odd coinages, a dictionary that would not privilege traditional English formulations over native adaptations and immigrant borrowings and new technological lingo, a dictionary that would be as inclusive as his idealized America was. This book begins, then, by examining some of the cultural resonances of Whitman's remarkable lexicographical concerns: dictionary making, for Whitman, was an essential democratic activity.

1

Whitman and Dictionaries

Hurrah for positive science! long live exact demonstration!
Fetch stonecrop mixt with cedar and branches of lilac,
This is the lexicographer. . . .

Whitman, "Song of Myself" (*LG* 51)

In one of his most famous characterizations of *Leaves of Grass,* Whitman described his book as "only a language experiment." *Leaves,* he said, was

an attempt to give the spirit, the body, the man, new words, new potentialities of speech—an American, a cosmopolitan (the best of America is the best cosmopolitanism) range of self-expression. The new world, the new times, the new peoples, the new vista, need a tongue according—yes, what is more, will have such a tongue—will not be satisfied until it is evolved. (*AP* Foreword)

In essential ways for Whitman, not only *Leaves* but all of American culture became a language experiment. Whitman's fascination with such a wide range of American culture is grounded in what the various activities—sports, battles, technological changes—were doing to the language; he was interested in how they were giving the spirit and the body of America (and Americans themselves) new words, new ranges of self-expression. So much of Whitman's interaction with these cultural phenomena focuses on the language, on how the word "photography" and its myriad synonyms—an endless progeny of attempts to name the miraculous new phenomenon—were expanding and altering the American vocabulary, on how photographs themselves were becoming a new kind of language, visual signs representing aspects of reality that no previous system of signs had captured. His fascination with Indians focused on how to get them into our language, on how the use of native names for the places on this continent and how the appropriation of native words

12

were rooting American English in authentic ways to *this* continent and a
history of experience on this land. (Even American politics were becoming tinged with Indian-based words like "caucus" and "mugwump.")
Whitman approved of the way baseball expressions like "catching it on
the fly," "throwing him a curve," and "hitting a home run" were coming to be colorful metaphors in everyday American speech, blending
America's national sport into the distinctly American brand of speaking
and writing. All these roiling cultural activities were literally giving
voice to America.

Whitman was living during the first period when it was possible literally to watch and weigh the growth and expansion of the American language, to gauge the increasing distance between it and its British source.
When he was a teenager, the "war of the dictionaries" was just heating
up in the United States; it would last most of his life, as the works of
America's two pioneering lexicographers, Noah Webster and Joseph
Emerson Worcester, became fierce competitors in schools, homes, and
bookstores across the nation. Beginning in 1828 with Webster's monumental *American Dictionary of the English Language* and answered by
Worcester's 1830 *Comprehensive, Pronouncing and Explanatory Dictionary
of the English Language,* new and ever-larger dictionaries were issued by
the two rival camps; edition after edition of Webster's and Worcester's
regularly appeared in the 1840s, then the 1860s, then the 1870s. Whitman
closely tracked the battle, which was waged in newspaper attacks and
vitriolic pamphlets printed by the publishing houses responsible for each
dictionary. While most American authors endorsed the less brash
Worcester's (see Cmiel 86–87), Whitman owned and read editions of
both men's dictionaries and was pleased that the competition kept unsta-
ble the whole issue of "authority" in usage and pronunciation. It became
a true battle of words, as G. & C. Merriam, Webster's publishers, issued
charges of plagiarism against Worcester, who in turn made claims that
Webster wasn't all that original to begin with.

Noah Webster died three days before Whitman's twenty-fourth birthday; his "Blue-Backed Speller" (written to simplify the hopelessly complex and inconsistent spelling of English and to help him teach his new
system to his students) by then was already well on the way to annual
sales of over a million copies. (Whitman no doubt had used Webster's
American Spelling Book when he was a teacher on Long Island just a few
years before Webster's death.) In the *Spelling Book,* Webster had argued
for a declaration of American linguistic independence in words that
Whitman would echo many times: "For America in her infancy to adopt
the present maxims of the old world, would be to stamp the wrinkle of
decrepit age upon the bloom of youth, and to plant the seed of decay in
a vigorous constitution" (quoted in Burkett 152). Webster continually

enlivened the debate about what was happening to the English language as it took root in American soil; he was a reformer who saw the development of American English as a chance to rid the mother language of its difficult and inconsistent spellings and to make English grow, become more absorptive, while also becoming more native, a true American language.

I. "THE PROP REAL DICTIONARY"

Webster's first dictionary was published in 1806, and it proudly announced the addition of five thousand words "to the number found in the BEST ENGLISH COMPENDS." But that small dictionary was only the beginning for Webster. His dream was to compose a "Complete Dictionary of the English Language," with an emphasis on the new discoveries of etymology: "To deduce words from their primitive roots, and exhibit the affinity of the English Language, with various other Languages" (quoted in Burkett 140). By the time Whitman was born in 1819, Webster was still at work on the letter "F." But soon he devoted full time to his dictionary and managed to finish it in 1825. He proudly called it *An American Dictionary of the English Language,* and he claimed it added twenty thousand new words to those listed in other dictionaries, thus swelling his volume with a patriotic claim: the *American* version of English was more capacious than the British version. This dictionary appeared in 1828: two large volumes of nearly sixteen hundred total pages, with around seventy thousand words. A popular abridgement of the dictionary appeared in 1829, the work of Joseph Worcester himself, soon to leave Webster and become the main competitor; this popular "abridgement" contained over eighty thousand words, ten thousand more than the original! Just two years before his death, Webster completed a major revision of his dictionary, which he published in 1841; three years after he died, George and Charles Merriam published an edition of the *American Dictionary,* and the legacy of "Merriam–Webster" began.

Whitman was most familiar with the 1847 edition (revised by Webster's son-in-law, Chauncey Goodrich), the one that he depended on as he developed his notions of language and as he wrote the first poems of *Leaves of Grass* (see Warren 43n and Cmiel 85); it is in this version of the dictionary that we most clearly find the crucial definitions of words that would become keys for Whitman's poetic project. The 1859 edition, swelled by appendices, contained over 140,000 words. (Impressed by these word counts, Whitman would record on the flyleaf of his working copy of his 1860 edition of *Leaves of Grass* that his own book now had swollen to 183,500 words.) Meanwhile, Worcester followed each of

Webster's editions with an edition of his own dictionary, more conservative in spelling and pronunciation, more in line with British usage, dedicated to recording the heritage of the language instead of urging it to change. Though he owned editions of both dictionaries, Whitman of course was on Webster's side, looking for ways to tune English in an American key: "The English language befriends the grand American expression. . . . it is brawny enough and limber enough and full enough." Whitman believed that the American language, which would evolve as English became expressed in an American way, would become "the medium that shall well nigh express the inexpressible" (*LG* 727–28).

Whitman was an avid reader of dictionaries, which he realized were the compost heap of all English-language literature, the place where all the elements of literature, broken down, were preserved, as well as the place out of which all future literature would grow. The nation's unwritten poems lay dormant in that massive heap of words. Whitman's own poem "This Compost" played on the etymological identity of the word "compost" with "composition"; both words literally meant, as Whitman found in his 1847 edition of Webster's, "to place or set together." To compose was to put together in a new form; to compost was to take apart what was put together, to break down an old form so that it would furnish the parts, the elements, the nutriment, for a new form. Whitman's poem opens with the speaker's revulsion at all the "foul meat" that the countless "sour dead" have left on the earth, so that the earth itself is nothing but composted "carcasses," but it moves to a celebration of the new forms of life that grow out of the "endless successions of diseas'd corpses": "The summer growth is innocent and disdainful above all those strata of sour dead." (Life, Whitman realized, was like language: it always exists over and emerges out of dead layers.) "The grass of spring covers the prairies," the speaker observes, and the earth "gives such divine materials to men, and accepts such leavings from them at last" (*LG* 368–70). We hear Whitman's self-referential punning here, his own "leavings of grass," which are forms of words put together in order to be taken apart, composted again, reused to new purposes. His *Leaves,* like all literature, would be composted back into the elements of the words themselves, eternally available for new expression, new meaning; that is the process of life, Whitman suggests, and it is the process of reading and writing. The poem's title, after all, is self-referential: *this* compost, *this* composition, *this* poem, this formation of scattered material—myriad words, all of which had been used before and had lived in the writings of others—now are put together anew in order to enter the endless process of composting that will produce the literature of a nation. Whitman knows that "Life" is "the leavings of many deaths" (*LG* 87), and so are new poems the leavings (in the sense of "remains" *and* in the sense of "flowerings" or "fresh green growth") of many forgotten and outmoded poems.

The dictionary, then, became the ultimate linguistic compost heap, and every poet therefore always had a stake in the quality of the nation's dictionaries: in how complete they were, how tolerant of the nation's emerging characteristic slang, how open to native spellings, new usages, and regional variations of pronunciation. So Whitman not only read dictionaries; he even toyed with the idea of writing one himself, keeping lists of words, noting odd pronunciations, singling out foreign words that should be added to the American language because they expressed things that no English words yet did. He carefully studied and took notes on Webster's introductory essay that tracked the evolution and interrelationships of languages, and he argued with some of Webster's etymologies and pronunciations as he struggled to arrive at his own beliefs about language (*DBN* 713–18). He used the dictionary as he hoped readers would use his poems, as an arena for the "gymnast's struggle" that he believed the act of reading to be, a fertile dialectic between book and mind: "The reader is to do something for himself, . . . must himself or herself construct indeed the poem, argument, history, metaphysical essay—the text furnishing the hints, the clue, the start or frame-work" (*PW* 425). For Whitman, the dictionaries he read and responded to throughout his life were the ultimate example of texts that demanded reader response, texts that furnished the hints for endless poems to come. Dictionaries, for Whitman, challenged their readers to use the massive catalogs of words in new combinations.

The poet, Whitman said, "drinks up quickly all terms, all languages, all meanings" (*UPP* 2:84), and he believed that a true dictionary would become just as insatiable. Whitman had studied the early, rudimentary American dictionaries, and by 1856, he was keeping abreast of the latest Webster–Worcester developments, too; he realized there was still a lot of work to be done before America would have the true dictionary, the full compost of possibilities:

> *A Perfect English Dictionary has yet to be Written.*—Largeness of mind is more indispensable in lexicography than in any other science. To make a noble dictionary of the English speech is a work yet to be performed. Dr. Johnson did well; Sheridan, Walker, Perry, Ash, Bailey, Kenrick, Smart, and the rest, all assisted; Webster and Worcester have done well; and yet the dictionary, rising stately and complete, out of a full appreciation of the philosophy of language, and the unspeakable grandeur of the English dialect, has still to be made—and to be made by some coming American worthy the sublime work. The English language seems curiously to have flowed through the ages, especially toward America, for present use, and for centuries and centuries of future use; it is so

composed of all the varieties that preceded it, and so absorbs what is needed by it. (*NYD* 59)

Even words, the elements of the linguistic compost heap, are themselves a kind of compost, "composed of all the varieties that preceded" them. Later, Whitman would view the English language as "the accretion and growth of every dialect, race, and range of time, and . . . both the free and compacted composition of all." "Compacted composition": a culture uses words and fuses and adapts and abuses and blends and discards them, forming a continual compacting compost turning up ever-fresh compositions.

Etymology became a special fascination for Whitman, and his notes on Webster's introductory essay focus on this aspect of the lexicographer's enterprise. Etymology as a science grew up at the same time as geology and evolution; they were all conceptual systems that were taking hold and becoming dominant during Whitman's adult life. Emerson had been acutely aware of the analogous relation between etymology and geology and evolution when he called all words "fossil poems," and Whitman developed the analogy in his essay "Slang in America":

> The science of language has large and close analogies in geological science, with its ceaseless evolution, its fossils, and its numberless submerged layers and hidden strata, the infinite go-before of the present. (*PW* 577)

Just as in "This Compost" the "summer growth" emerged out of "all those strata of sour dead," so does the American language emerge out of the "submerged layers and hidden strata" of the dead languages, the linguistic "fossils." Words are organic growths, Whitman would insist again and again, and thus they leave fossils behind; they also struggle with each other for existence, dominance, common usage, in a kind of verbal survival of the fittest: "In the processes of word-formation, myriads die, but here and there the attempt attracts superior meanings, becomes valuable and indispensable, and lives forever" (*PW* 573). Just as in "This Compost" Whitman could celebrate the wondrous "chemistry" that turns the "infused fetor" into "sumptuous crops" (*LG* 369–70), in his writings about words he celebrates the composting chemical processes of language that decompose the old in order to recompose the new: slang words, the lifeblood of language for Whitman, are "the wholesome fermentation or eructation of those processes eternally active in language, by which froth and specks are thrown up, mostly to pass away; though occasionally to settle and permanently chrystallize" (*PW* 573). Language, Whitman concludes, "is more like some vast living body, or perennial body of bodies" (*PW* 577); it is the body unfolding out of other bodies, the process of birth and decay and rebirth, the process that allows Whitman to conclude in "Song of Myself":

> And as to you Corpse I think you are good manure, but that does not
> offend me,
> I smell the white roses sweet-scented and growing,
> I reach to the leafy lips, I reach to the polish'd breasts of melons.
>
> (*LG* 87)

With words as with people, there would always be a "procreant urge. . . . Always a knit of identity, always distinction, always a breed of life" (*LG* 31). The new dictionaries were, in Whitman's mind, an effort to keep up with the procreant urge, to record the distinction of each word as well as its knit of identity with all other words and with the whole past history of spoken and written thought. Dictionaries were for Whitman one more site for the working out of the democratic mystery wherein single separate individuals melded into a harmonious whole while never losing their distinct identities. (While each word in the dictionary had a unique meaning, that meaning could only be expressed by weaving the other words of the dictionary into a definition.)

Whitman, then, loved to get the latest edition of Webster's *American Dictionary* and feel its heft, boast of the new burgeoning growth in sheer quantity that each edition confirmed for the American language: the dictionary, like the country, was expanding, absorbing, creating, combining. We can imagine him exulting in the latest count of English words, today estimated at somewhere between 400,000 and 600,000, three or four times the number of French or Russian words. Just as he would count the words in *Leaves* and compare his total to that of the Bible, the *Iliad,* the *Aeneid,* the *Inferno,* and *Paradise Lost,* so Whitman loved counting the *grand* total, the full possibility, of what the language contained, and imagining how large the total might eventually be:

> In a little while, ~~here~~ in the United States, ~~this~~ the English language
> ~~by/fat/the/noblest/known~~, enriched ~~with/all/the~~ with contributions ~~x~~
> from all languages, old and new, will be spoken by ~~more/people/in/~~
> ~~American/than/any/other/one/language/any/where/else/is,/or/probably/~~
> ~~ever/was/spoken~~ a hundred millions of people:—~~now~~ perhaps a hundred thousand words ("seventy or eighty thousand words"—Noah
> Webster, of the English language). (*DBN* 732)

Whitman kept tabs in his notebooks as the new editions came out:

> Webster's Dictionary
>   Prefaces
> On English Language, from

70 to 80,000 words
Or rather, (same authority, about
100,000 words[)] (*DBN* 665)

Reading an article in the *Edinburgh Review* that claimed the English language consisted of 38,000 words, Whitman noted the magnitude of the error: "(100,000 words are said to be now in the repertoire) ?is not the no. greater than 38,000—yet the whole no[.] must be twice that" (*DBN* 679). He was anxious to examine the new editions of Webster; as late as June 1891, less than a year before his death, Whitman was exchanging a copy of his latest edition of *Leaves of Grass* for a copy of the latest edition of Webster's; he sent his "big book" (his *Complete Poems and Prose* [1888]) to G. & C. Merriam and Co. and happily recorded the receipt two days later of the "big International Dictionary" (*DBN* 595–96). He searched new editions of dictionaries to see if his own word coinages had been recorded and had thus gained the sanction of inclusion in the nation's wordlist: "When you get in town, somewhere within handling of a copy of the Century Dictionary," he said to Horace Traubel in 1891, "look up my word, see if it is there" (*WWC* 7:391–92). The word on this occasion was "Presidentiad," and it had not yet made the Century.

Both *Leaves* and the dictionary were growing simultaneously, each absorbing and cataloging the American experience in words, one putting the language into form, arranging the words to help form a nation, and the other dispersing the language back to its potential, arranging the words for easy access so that new forms of thought and expression could continue to emerge. When, in his working copy of the 1860 edition of *Leaves,* Whitman carefully tallied the number of words in his volume and compared the total to the number in the Bible, the *Aeneid,* and *Paradise Lost,* he was aiming to have *Leaves* surpass in verbal bulk all the classics, just as Webster out-worded his predecessors.

But even the giant-sized Webster's *International* no doubt left Whitman somewhat disappointed; his notion of what the "real" American dictionary eventually would be matched his democratic notions of America. The true American dictionary would have to be as democratic as his idealized nation, accepting and recognizing all words, regardless of status, impoliteness, crudity, regional or racial origin, or class: "The P̶r̶o̶p̶ Real Dictionary will give all words that exist in use, the bad words as well as any" (*DBN* 734–35). Whitman's self-correction here is telling— he began to write "Proper Dictionary" but then realized that there already *were* "proper" ones, ones that recorded the language that was considered "appropriate," ones that sanctioned usage. Instead, Whitman realized, we needed *real* dictionaries, ones that would record the vast whole of what is really there. The "true lexicographer," then, Whitman argues, "is not merely the 'harmless drudge' Johnson defines him to be, as any more than [a] general collection of words with their definitions and pronunciations achieve[s] the true Dictionary" (*NUPM* 1704). This true lexicographer would have to "love to go away from books, and walk amidst the strong coarse talk of men w̶h̶e̶r̶e̶/̶t̶h̶e̶r̶e̶/̶i̶s̶/̶w̶h̶o̶ as they give muscle and bone i̶n̶ to e̶v̶e̶r̶y̶/̶e̶a̶c̶h̶ every word they speak. . . . I say . . . the great Dictionary of the future must l̶o̶v̶e̶/̶t̶h̶e̶/̶s̶a̶m̶e̶/̶ and embody [in] it all those" (*DBN* 811).

The "Real Dictionary" would have to be, in some way, the all-inclusive record of the human imagination, history, and possibility: "The full history of Names would be the total of human, and all other history" (*NUPM* 1695). In "A Song of the Rolling Earth," Whitman would call on poets to write "the dictionaries of words that print cannot touch," that is, to reach voice out to the things of the earth that language has not yet named, that we have remained blind and deaf to because our language has not yet expressed them. So Whitman would continually remark on areas of life that needed to have new words brought to them; they are like the "dumb, beautiful ministers" at the end of "Crossing Brooklyn Ferry," the things of the world that have meaning, have something to tell us, want to minister to us, but cannot do so until our words express them and pull them into human consciousness and awareness. In his *American Primer,* Whitman notes that while there is "among the young men of these states . . . a wonderful tenacity of friendship, and a̶/̶m̶a̶n̶l̶i̶n̶e̶s̶s̶/̶o̶f̶ passionate fondness for their friends, . . . they yet have remarkably few words, t̶o̶ of names for the friendly sentiments . . . — they never give words to their most ardent friendships" (*DBN* 741). So Whitman seeks, through his coinage of "camerado" and his idiosyncratic use of "calamus," to begin the process of supplying the words that would bring the unspoken areas of human relationship into the lexicon and thus into the consciousness of the culture. The poet's job, Whitman argues, is not only to compost what is already contained in the dictionary into new imaginative forms, but to push beyond that and create new elements, new words, new combinations of words, in order to say what has not been said before: "There is that in me—I do not know what it is—but I know it is in me. / . . . I do not know it—it is without name— it is a word unsaid, / It is not in any dictionary, utterance, symbol" (*LG* 88). Always, for Whitman, silence is the realm of discovery, the place the true poet finds himself in again and again, working to bring "it" to speech, working to expand the American dictionary.

Like every other ideal, then—like America itself and like *Leaves* itself— the true American dictionary would only emerge by trial and error and growth and expansion, manifesting itself more completely in each successive incarnation, but it would never be complete until the entire uni-

verse was turned into words: thus the dictionary would remain a tantaliz-
ingly open book. Each edition of Webster, however, was still invaluable
despite its shortcomings, for it was a record of the current incomplete
state of the language, what had not yet entered the culture's awareness,
what the culture was officially ignoring, as well as what *had* become
spoken and thus known. And so while Whitman was looking for ways
to *expand* the dictionaries (his *American Primer* is a program for expanding
the lexicon), he was also finding creative ways to *use* these rapidly im-
proving linguistic tools, for they offered him words that no preceding
dictionaries had.

II. THE "ARRIERE-THREADS" OF WORDS

The new dictionaries also offered Whitman etymologies, a literal
reading of the "fossil poem" buried in each word. In one of his notebooks on language, Whitman records a simple definition for "etymology": "origin of words" (*DBN* 678). Etymologies became vital to him;
Webster's dictionaries had opened up the possibility that the ancestry of
words could be scientifically traced, had made the results of the new
science of etymology available to the masses. Many of Webster's etymologies now seem far-fetched, of course, based on his superficial knowledge of many of the languages through which he was tracing roots,
and colored by his literal belief in the Tower of Babel story. Whatever
their limitations, however, Whitman depended on Webster's word
origins, and he jotted down notes to remind himself of the importance
of a full awareness of the nature of the fossil forms of every word he
used:

> Trace adjectives to their roots—as tortuous cereal
> —Track adjectives *like* closely to their roots, and literal meanings
>   before using them.
>
> *Tracing words to origins*
> To get in the habit of tracing words to their root-meanings
> (*DBN* 725)

"Every principal word . . . in our language," noted Whitman, "is a condensed octavo volume, or many volumes" (*NUPM* 1699). At times he
felt an almost dizzying sense that etymologies performed the kind of
crossing of barriers of time and space that he attempted to achieve in
"Crossing Brooklyn Ferry," where he cajoles the reader into the realization that "distance avails not, and place avails not" (*LG* 162), that though
Whitman and we may never have shared the same time and place we
can still, through imaginative discourse, talk to and listen to each other,
overcome the impassable boundaries of different places in different

times: "what the preaching could not accomplish is accomplish'd, is it not?" (*LG* 164). Etymology opened up the same possibilities of time travel and space travel via language, for we cannot speak without mouthing the words of and giving voice to those who came before us:

> And what a pregnant & far-reaching fact that quite every sentence we articulate with our voices, and every type-line worked off from the printing presses here, to-day, 1881 by the Hudson, the Arkansas, the Tennessee or the Rio Grande, retains subtle, living, entirely unbroken chains of succession back through the Middle Ages, the Gothic and Osmanlic incursions, the Roman sway, Greece, Judah, India, Egypt the Aryan mists . . . with arriere-threads to all pre-history; and though but breaths and vibrations of the visible air more freely [firmly?] weld the inhabitants of New York Chicago, San Francisco and New Orleans to the vanished peoples retrospects of the past—to a hundred unknown nations—than could all the steel and iron of the globe. (*NUPM* 1684–85)

It was only toward the end of his life that Whitman would see the beginnings of the full flowering of scientific etymological research. Walter W. Skeat's *Concise Etymological Dictionary* appeared in 1882; William Dwight Whitney's six-volume *Century Dictionary,* the first work to go significantly beyond Webster's, was published during the three years before Whitman's death (1889–91); and the great project that would result in the *Oxford English Dictionary* began appearing in print in 1884 but would not reach its first stage of completion until 1928 with the appearance of the tenth and final volume of *New English Dictionary on Historical Principles.* Whitman followed newspaper accounts of this great lexicographic project as it got underway, and he saved a long article written on the publication of the first volume (Dressman 470). He realized in his final years—with the *NED* project underway, with the new Webster's *International* at his bedside, with Skeat's *Etymological Dictionary* paving the way for even more erudite studies of the lineage of words—that lexicography, a rudimentary science at best when he was a child, was now reaching its maturity. The notion of the Indo-European language itself developed during Whitman's lifetime, and he of course was attracted to the implications of unity and common origin that the reconstruction of this protolanguage indicated.

Modern readers of Whitman often overlook the widespread fascination with etymology in his time, and they tend to forget that he was using Webster's dictionaries with their often eccentric and incorrect etymologies, with their spirited and sometimes quirky definitions, which often have vanished from twentieth-century dictionaries, and with their biblical and Shakespearean examples of usage. We now read Whitman with the wrong wordbook, glossing his words with our definitions and with our current sense of the history of the language. It helps to return occasionally to the dictionaries that Whitman was using in order to understand more precisely what he had in mind with some of his more difficult and elusive concepts. Often we can hear in Whitman's use of certain words the same Shakespearean or biblical echoes that Webster has set up in his definitions: the frequent allusions to Shakespeare and the Bible in *Leaves* may derive as much from his study of Webster's as from his study of the direct sources.

We noted earlier Whitman's concern with the pockets of human experience that do not yet have words attached to them; Whitman noted the "remarkably few words" that Americans have "for the friendly sentiments," and he sought to fill in the silence by applying words like "calamus" and "camerado" to those relationships. It has often been noted that his choice of "Calamus" as the title of his cluster of poems of "fervid comradeship" relates to the nature and appearance of the calamus plant— its commonness, its tendency to grow away from the beaten track, at the sides of isolated ponds, its trait of (as Whitman described it) "presenting the biggest & hardiest kind of spears of grass" (*C* 1:347) with their phallic anthers. But Whitman, checking his 1847 Webster's ("see Webster's Large Dictionary—Calamus," he wrote to a friend who sought the meaning of Whitman's use of the image [*WWC* 3:229]), would also have been aware of other associations that "calamus" would engender in readers of his time: Webster traced the etymology of the word back to the Ethiopian and Arabic *kalaman,* which became *calamus scriptorius,* literally "a writing reed, or pen." Among the definitions that Webster offers are two that merit special notice: "A reed, used anciently as a pen to write on parchment or papyrus," and "in *antiquity,* a pipe or fistula, a wind instrument, made of a reed or oaten stalk."

In writing "Calamus," then, Whitman was composing another leaf of his grass, this one both an instrument to play his song on *and* an instrument with which to record that song on paper. In imagining "calamus" as a new sign for fervid democratic love among American males ("this boundless offering of sympathy—this universal democratic comradeship—this old, eternal, yet ever-new interchange of adhesiveness, so fitly emblematic of America . . . the beautiful and sane affection of man for man" [*LG* 751]), he employs and plays on the multiple meanings of the word. The word itself, newly signifying an aspect of life that had not before entered the written language (dealing literally with an "unspoken" or "unspeakable" subject, since it would not be until late in the century that words like "homosexual" would enter the lexicon), becomes Whitman's metaphorical pen, his reed pen allowing him to write what no one before him had, and the word also becomes the reed pipe on which he plays his new music, a music of intimate withdrawal and passionate commitment. The word is like a shepherd's reed, calling us along with Whitman to "paths untrodden . . . away from the clank of the world," to learn "to sing no songs to-day but those of manly attachment" (*LG* 112–13).

Whitman would also have been aware of the etymological suggestions in William Swinton's *Rambles Among Words,* a book that some scholars believe Whitman actually helped write. In *Rambles,* in the chapter entitled "Fossil Poetries," where many interesting and revealing etymologies are discussed, Swinton quotes Bacon's "account of the origin of the word 'CALAMITY' ":

> Another ill accident is drouth, at the spindling of the corn; which with us is rare, but in hotter countries common: insomuch as the word *calamitus,* was first derived from *calamus, when the corn coulde not get out of the stalke.*

Swinton goes on to call Bacon's etymology "at best dubious," but he nevertheless recognizes its "good degree of vraisemblance . . . for what *could,* in an agricultural community, be a greater 'calamity' than this?" (Swinton 68–69). We can imagine Whitman being very much attracted to this "fossil poetry," for he saw his own *Calamus,* his cluster of poems, as a political act ("The special meaning of the *Calamus* cluster . . . mainly resides in its Political significance"), as an attempt to name and bring into full cultural awareness a heretofore voiceless human relationship, one that would prompt "the United States of the future . . . to be most effectually welded together, intercalated, anneal'd into a Living Union" (*LG* 751). Whitman maintained that if the word took hold, flowered, if his *Leaves* became fully intercalated into the text of the society's values and thoughts, then a "Living Union" would be harvested; but if the poems were stillborn, if they were dismissed or cast away, then in his mind there would indeed be "calamity," for democracy would not grow where the calamus emotion was suppressed: the phallic calamus grass would be nothing but a congested parody of the procreant urge to create union, its seed unable to "get out of the stalke." The poet could offer up the new words, but the culture had to be the receptive and nurturant ground that would accept the linguistic seeds and allow them to grow into the familiar lexicon, that would transform the stunted calamus stalk into the hearty cornstalk. The nation's common usage would have to be the force that would intercalate these new linguistic offerings in the American dictionary.

III. "NEW LAW-FORCES OF LANGUAGE"

Webster was very much in favor of an American English that would evolve into a language distinct from and larger than the British

English it derived from, but Webster himself was no propagator of new words. As David Simpson, in his illuminating study of the politics of American English, has shown, Webster (like Whitman) looked to many new sources for American words—science and technology, politics, geography, Indian languages—but he himself coined only one new word ("demoralize") (see Simpson, 79–81). Whitman, on the other hand, through creative borrowings and adaptations from other languages and through original word formations created by bending grammatical rules, invented many new words and a whole new way of hearing English on the page (see Warren, 45–69), a written speech that worked to create oratorical effects, that put readers in a slangy linguistic swamp where they could experience a vocabulary in the process of formation. He was out to find what he called

> new law-forces of spoken and written language—not merely peda-gogue-forms, correct, regular, familiar with precedents, made for mat-ters of outside propriety, fine words, thoughts definitely told out—but a language fann'd by the breath of Nature, which leaps overhead, cares mostly for impetus and effects, and for what it plants and invigorates to grow. (*PW* 424)

For Whitman, English was loose and big, and in America it was becoming amoebic, flowing into and absorbing new physical and linguistic territories while shucking off constricting hierarchical rules and grammars. His poetry was dedicated to discovering a breathing, leaping form that welcomed that expansive spirit.

But there is another side to this open and expansive language: such a language cannot help but develop imperialistic ambitions. In 1806, Webster enthused, "In fifty years from this time, the *American-English* will be spoken by more people, than all the other dialects of the language, and in one hundred and thirty years, by more people than any other language on the globe" (quoted in Simpson 66). Whitman, as we have seen, often shared Webster's heady enthusiasm for the dominating future of this "brawny" language, and Simpson goes so far as to aver that the poet's "ideas about language" often "appear as expressions of a startling cultural megalomania," as when Whitman proposes that "names are the turning point of who shall be master" (231). In some of his more nation-alistic later writings, Whitman even termed his hoped-for language "im-perial": "America is become already a huge world of peoples . . . forty-four Nations curiously and irresistibly blent and aggregated in ONE NATION, with one imperial language" (*PW* 664).

Whitman's theories of language, then, resonate with his double-sided theories of America, democracy, and the self. Throughout Whit-man's work, there is always a danger of expansiveness slipping into imperialism, of an absorptive and welcoming self suddenly sounding like an appropriating and arrogating self, of a democracy that embraces diversity shading into one that flattens differences to a numbing sameness. Whitman, of course, was aware of this essential problem in defining largeness and union, whether of the self, the country, or the world. Language was one arena in which the problem was most acute: he wanted a dictionary that contained everything, a language large enough to express every distinction, but he wanted it all in one book—an American dictionary, where those distinctions could be expressed in words, tones, and rhythms familiar to him. He wanted the world's variety in an American wordbook.

Finding the balance between control and surrender, between union and fragmentation, between the one and the many, was not only his poetic problem, then, but also America's political challenge. Whitman was aware of the problem when he lifted the increasingly heavy American dictionary, tens of thousands of discrete word elements bound in one big volume. He was also aware of it when he worried about how the American Indians would become part of the evolving dominant culture that was destroying their way of life, and when he agonized over whether his individual photographic portraits suggested a single identity or a hopeless fragmentation of selves, and even when he thought about the American sport that highlighted individual skill while extolling the virtues of teamwork. Whitman's dream was of a common language, containing multitudes and embracing contradictions; his nightmare was that the evolving common language could be made to say such contradictory things that it would shatter back into its disparate parts. His hopes and fears applied equally, of course, to his language and to his nation.

2

Whitman and Baseball

Why do respectability and refinement and education and station present
   such deadening surfaces to me?
Even here in church, where they talk of communion and unity, the
   fashionable congregation is a mere chance collection of separate
   units.
For my part, I find more real religion at a base-ball match than in a Fifth
   Avenue church.

Ernest Crosby, "The Ball-Match"

I. "WALT WHITMAN STRUCK OUT, SINGING"

One of Whitman's most fervent early disciples was Ernest
Crosby, who in 1899 flattered the memory of his master by issuing a
book of poems written in something akin to Whitman's tone and style.
Crosby conceived it his duty to carry on what he saw as Whitman's
program to undermine institutional religion and to celebrate instead the
al fresco camaraderie of America's emerging sacred activities, lively baseball games instead of deadening church services. Crosby's poem goes on
to celebrate in a Whitman-like catalog the good fellowship of the baseball
crowd, the good-natured profanity and bantering and cheering, "the
prevailing note . . . of fellow-feeling, of common interest, of sympathy." "When I think of a ball-match," Crosby concludes, "St. Frigida's
seems to me like an ice-house" (93). He was aware of Whitman's own
similar feelings about religion and baseball, how Whitman groused about
religious groups that were trying to prevent any activity except
churchgoing from occurring on Sundays:

> Sunday—Sunday: we make it the dullest day in the week when it might
> be made the cheeriest. Will the people ever come to base ball . . . on
> Sunday? That would seem like clear weather after a rain. Why do you

27

suppose people are so narrow-minded in their interpretation of the Sunday? . . . It does seem as though the Puritan was responsible for our Sunday. (*WWC* 2:247)

But it wasn't only Whitman's disciples who noticed the poet's connection to the sport: it is probably significant that when a British writer like Virginia Woolf mentions Walt Whitman, the subject of baseball naturally pops up. In 1925 Woolf wrote that "the only American writer whom the English wholeheartedly admire is Walt Whitman" (113). He was, she said, "the real American undisguised," the true original who certainly did not imitate any figure in English literature; in Whitman, the "English tourist in American literature" would find no writer more "different from what he has at home." For Woolf, Whitman is the pure example of a writer who took "the first step in the process of being American—to be not English," "to dismiss the whole army of English words which have marched so long under the command of dead English generals" (116). And it is baseball, "a game which is not played in England" (123), that she finds to be the perfect American farm club for a new poetic language, a native activity with its own built-in localized slang and its own essential connections to American culture. It is a game, she says, "indigenous to the soil." Woolf points out that the English tradition is measured on a small scale; it assumes a small, familiar country, and "its centre is an old house with many rooms each crammed with objects and crowded with people who know each other intimately, whose manners, thoughts, and speech are ruled all the time . . . by the spirit of the past." "But in America," Woolf suggests, "there is baseball instead of society," and this peculiar national sport magically incorporates the vast space and uneven pace of "a new land, its tin cans, its prairies, its cornfields flung disorderly about like a mosaic of incongruous pieces waiting order at the artists' hands." Furthermore, the game generates its own language, a way of talking, a slang in America, and so "the Americans are doing what the Elizabethans did—they are coining new words," and "when words are being made, a literature will be made out of them" (126–27). It was in fact around the time that Woolf wrote this piece that baseball slang was finally working its way into official dictionaries: terms that Whitman knew, like "curveball" and "home run" and "base hit," and phrases like "to strike out," "to be shut out," "to play ball," had to wait for H. L. Mencken's monumental *American Language* (1919) before they would begin to enter the official lexicon. Mencken exulted in common American words that were incomprehensible to most Englishmen, and he celebrated the way baseball lingo had "entered the common speech of the country" (191), thus developing the implications of Whitman's and Woolf's belief that "American" was becoming its own tongue distinct from "English."

Woolf's analysis of American literature is incisive; she was not aware that Whitman had direct and long-standing associations with the game of baseball (she gets from Whitman to baseball by tracing out a tradition involving Sherwood Anderson, Sinclair Lewis, and Ring Lardner), but she intuitively senses the connection between the national poet and the national sport, a connection that was more direct and more fertile than she imagined. Other writers sensed the connection, too; John Dos Passos wrote an essay in college called "Art and Baseball," identifying Whitman as the model writer of precisely the kind of vitality that baseball represented (Clark 18–19), and Michael Gold, writing in the *New Masses* in 1928, noted how America's true poets learned from Whitman "to see America for the first time . . . to walk in their own strong American sun, to push and crowd with the American mobman at baseball games and picnics" (13), to come down off the pedestal in an act of linguistic and experiential democracy—poetry embracing the life of the great mass of people. And from the 1840s on, baseball became the emblem of that emerging American spirit. Baseball, Whitman said, is "America's game: has the snap, go, fling, of the American atmosphere—belongs as much to our institutions, fits into them as significantly, as our constitutions, laws . . ." (*WWC* 4:508). Whitman did indeed assimilate the lingo of baseball into his poetic vocabulary, appropriating its essentials as key metaphors, recognizing that a defining trait of American democracy was precisely the fact that we had "baseball instead of society."

Poets over the years, from Ernest Crosby to the present, have sensed how the game of baseball has related to Whitman. Jonathan Williams in the 1950s wrote a poem called "Fastball," "for WW, Hot for Honorary Installation at Cooperstown," a brief "Casey at the Bat," where the cosmic poet's bravado is punctured in solitary failure:

> not just folklore, or
>   a tall can of corn (or *Grass* on Cranberry Street)—
>
> to point at the wall and win
>   the whole ball of wax . . .
>
> yet
>   Walt Whitman
>
> struck out, singing: 'rambled
>   all around,
>   in & out the town, ram-
>   bled til the butchers
>   cut him down'
>
> hard from the heels, swung,
>   took a notion, had a hankering,

had good wood, but
came out—

a ripple
in the breeze

bingo!—

old solitary Whiff-Beard
(Williams 8)

Williams adjusts Whitman's boast—"Solitary, singing in the West, I
strike up for a New World"—into baseball jargon: "Walt Whitman /
struck out, singing." Ezra Pound had made a pact with Whitman who
"broke the new wood"; Williams transforms Pound's ambivalent image
of the "new wood" into the "good wood" of a baseball bat; Whitman
"swung, / took a notion, had a hankering, / had good wood, but / came
out— / a ripple / in the breeze / bingo!— / old solitary Whiff-Beard."
He had "good wood" (and good *would*—his intentions were grand); he
was the stuff of "folklore" who, like Babe Ruth indicating where he was
about to hit his home run, would "point at the wall and win / the whole
ball of wax"; he "struck out" to sing a New World, a new brotherhood
("stride on, Democracy! strike with vengeful stroke!" [*LG* 292]), but a
hundred years later, his "good wood" potential had dwindled to a pa-
thetic "ripple / in the breeze," and he just plain struck out. With its facile
puns quickly collapsing Whitman's vast purposes ("it came to me to
strike up the songs of the New World" [*LGV* 378]) into baseball slang
for failure, Williams's poem *is* what its title says—a "Fastball," leaving
Whitman standing at home plate, confused and unable to respond (like
the old sailor in Whitman's late poem, "Twenty Years," who set sail
when he "took some sudden, vehement notion"—just as Whitman in
Williams's poem "took a notion, had a hankering"—and now returns *"to
lay in port for good—to settle,"* wondering "What of the future?" [*LG*
531]).
    Williams modulates an old nursery rhyme by an incisive line break
that turns "rambled til the butchers cut him down" into the unexpected
"bled til the butchers cut him down." Whitman's initial open road optimism, his projected life of rambling ("The long brown path before me
leading wherever I choose" [*LG* 149]) in and out of the town, the poet
of the city as well as of the country, ran up against the bloody paths of
the Civil War, the bloodshed and butchery of which irretrievably dark-
ened Whitman's vision. Three strikes and Whitman's out, the old
"Whiff-Beard," but the fans sigh anyway, recalling his former greatness,
his "hankering" (he *was*, as he said, "hankering, gross, mystical, nude"
[*LG* 47]) after an ideal. After all, even the best hitters fail more than half

the time, and pointing to the spot where you plan to hit a home run is, like all prophecy, generally a risky business.

More recently, Stephen Bieler wrote "Poem to be Named Later," illustrated with a Whitman baseball card; the piece concerns an eight-poem trade about to take place between the "Sioux City Shakespeares" and the "Wichita Whitmans"; the Whitmans are anxious, of course, to get "some good defensive back-up poems / that could also hit with power. So / at the last moment they threw in an / undisclosed amount of rhyming / dictionaries and a poem to be named / later. You are now reading the poem / to be named later" (94). Bieler's poem underscores the Whitman–baseball association, a connection emphasized again in Mikhail Horowitz's wonderful *Big League Poets,* a book of American writers reincarnated as baseball players, where Whitman appears as Walt "Whitey" Whitman, "a vagabond outfielder (and switch-hitter as well)," author of *Leaves of Astroturf.* The connection has also been used as the deep structure of a popular 1988 movie, *Bull Durham,* where an attractive female English teacher named Annie Savoy chooses a minor-league baseball player each summer and initiates him sexually after tying him up all night and reading him *Leaves of Grass*—a book, she says, by Walt Whitman, who plays for the "Cosmic All-Stars." That movie ends with Annie's voice-over, reciting Whitman's words about the healing power of baseball, about its national significance. He really said these things, she testifies: "You could look it up."

II. "THE GAME OF BALL IS GLORIOUS"

What, then, was Whitman's actual connection to the game? How significant was baseball to his life and to his work? It is notable that baseball as we know it began when Whitman was a young man, and it began almost literally in his back yard. At the time, he was in robust health. Like all nineteenth-century writers who lived to be old men, Whitman has become set in our minds as an aged and infirm figure, as difficult as our own great-grandparents to envisage as a young athlete. We now tend to recall Whitman as America's good gray poet, to picture him as a paralyzed invalid with long white hair and beard who lived out his last years isolated in his small house in Camden, New Jersey. Even when he died in 1892, few people any longer associated this "batter'd, wreck'd old man" (*LG* 421) with the younger robust poet who sang songs of health, who claimed, "I am the teacher of athletes," and who boasted that "He that by me spreads a wider breast than my own proves the width of my own" (*LG* 84). We tend to forget that this was the poet who challenged American readers with what he called his "athletic books": "The process of reading is not a half sleep but in the highest sense a gymnast's struggle" (*PW* 424–25) requiring physical as well as intellectual training. Whitman's demands for American development were always as physical as they were mental: "Who would assume to teach here may well prepare himself body and mind, / He may well survey, ponder, arm, fortify, harden, make lithe himself" (*LG* 349). America would not fulfill its promise, Whitman argued, would not reach "ripeness and conclusion," until "there are plentiful athletic bards, inland and seaboard" (*LGV* 449). Certainly during the first four decades of Whitman's life, his friends and associates saw him as an "athletic bard," commenting frequently on his vitality and strength. Six feet tall and two hundred pounds, Whitman was an imposing figure in nineteenth-century New York as he sauntered the streets, walking for miles at a time. As a boy, he went fishing and speared eels, but his favorite child-hood sport was swimming, which he could rhapsodize over: "To be a daily swimmer during the warm season, to acquire that ease, muscle, lithness of physical action, so fostered by the free movements of the limbs in the water—who is not inspirited by the thought?" (*ISL* 102). (Because of his ability to float so easily, Whitman once called himself a "first-rate aquatic loafer" [*WWC* 2:21].)

So it is not surprising that in 1856, as he was developing his cosmic optimism and giving voice to his hopes for the limitlessness of the universe and of his own soul, he rested his vision all on a sports metaphor: "I do not doubt that the orbs and the systems of orbs play their swift sports through the air on purpose, and I shall one day be eligible to do as much as they, and more than they" (*LG* 447). The image is of the cosmos as a vast and endless ball game, the massive orbs in swift motion, pitched accurately and purposively by a transcendent deity. And Whitman's faith is that he has the potential in his own soul to be as divine a pitcher, knowing "that the hand of God is the promise of my own" (*LG* 33).

Ball games were more than an exalted metaphor for Whitman; they were an integral part of his day-to-day life. They seemed, in fact, repeatedly to mark important moments of his experience. In Boston in April 1860, for example, just after Whitman had had his famous stroll with Ralph Waldo Emerson when Emerson tried to convince him to tame his poetry by removing some of the more explicitly sexual poems, Whitman noted the emerging spring by writing of the reemergence of sports:

> Thursday, the grass begins to look green on the common, the buds on the elms are russet, the young fellows are playing football. Football! A noble and manly game—there they are in their shirt sleeves, running, crowding, tumbling together, quite an inspiring sight. (Furness 358)

As he rejected Emerson's advice to reduce the physicality of his poetry, Whitman turned to the inspiring sight of physical contact, Americans at play developing their bodies and character.

At various times over the years, Whitman would extol wrestling, track, quoits, sailing, and other sports, but there was only one sport he would return to throughout his life and that was baseball. Even when he was a virtual invalid in his final years, he still kept up with the sport, reading baseball reports in the newspapers; he often testified to his status as a baseball fan. In 1889, he told his young friend Horace Traubel, "I still find my interest in the game unabated: I suppose it's so with you, too: I can't forget the games we used to go to together: they are precious memories." He recalled his days playing ball and wistfully underscored the value of those times: "There may be more reasons some days for playing than for working." This particular reminiscence was prompted by Whitman's reading an unspecified "baseball story" in a newspaper in late February 1889 (*WWC* 4:223). That winter story was no doubt about baseball's first grand international tour, which was then in progress. Twenty years earlier, Whitman had been hard at work on a poem about international brotherhood and union: "Passage to India! . . . / Thou rondure of the world at last accomplish'd" (*LG* 414). Now, in the winter of 1888–89, American baseball had set out, quite literally, on its own passage to India, and Whitman clearly was fascinated with the possibilities.

Albert G. Spalding, later to become the sporting goods magnate, decided it was time to make a "Base Ball missionary effort" (4) to the world; his enthusiasm for baseball (like his alliteration) was unbounded:

> I claim that Base Ball owes its prestige as our National Game to the fact that as no other form of sport it is the exponent of American Courage, Confidence, Combativeness; American Dash, Discipline, Determination; American Energy, Eagerness, Enthusiasm; American Pluck, Persistency, Performance; American Spirit, Sagacity, Success; American Vim, Vigor, Virility. (6)

"Base Ball," concluded Spalding, "is a democratic game" (252). The game instilled what for Spalding were the distinctive American character values. Spalding's later life was dedicated to making sure that baseball would forever be perceived as pristinely American: conceived, developed, and originally played only in the United States. He helped create the Abner Doubleday–Cooperstown immaculate creation myth of baseball, and he fought the heresy of baseball's tainted conception (the repugnant notion that it had been fathered by the English children's game of "Rounders"). And he believed it was baseball's manifest destiny to export the American way of life to the rest of the earth. So as winter

descended on America in 1888, Spalding decided to pack up his successful Chicago White Stockings along with a team of National League all-
stars and accomplish the rondure of the world.

American baseball teams had once traveled to England in 1874, but
this tour would be the first that faced west from California's shores.
Starting from Chicago, the teams played their way across the continent
to San Francisco. Then they steamed on to Hawaii, where they arrived a
day late, and Sunday blue laws prevented their game from being held.
The teams had more success in New Zealand and Australia, where the
emulous shouts of thousands cheered them on and where Spalding announced to the players that they would indeed sail further: completely
around the world. They did play in Ceylon, but just missed completing
their true passage to India when they were warned that Calcutta was
unhealthy; prudently they bypassed that country and traveled on
through the Suez Canal. In Egypt, they used one of the Great Pyramids
as a backstop while playing a game in the desert. In Italy they attempted
to play in the Colosseum (with Caesar's monument as a backstop), but
the Italian government refused, despite Spalding's offer of five thousand
dollars. From there it was on to Paris and a game in the shadows of the
Eiffel Tower, then to England where the Prince of Wales politely
watched a game and then diplomatically responded: "I consider Base Ball
an excellent game; but Cricket a better one" (quoted in Spalding 263).
Arriving back in New York, the world travelers were greeted with a
Delmonico's dinner attended by such celebrities as Theodore Roosevelt
and Mark Twain, whose humorous speech contained a dark undercur-
rent as he hinted at organized baseball's uncomfortable growing com-
plicity with Gilded Age big business, calling the game "the outward and
visible expression of the drive and push and rush of the raging, tearing,
booming nineteenth century!" (Twain 145).

The baseball ambassadors, relaxed and triumphant and certainly un-
ruffled by Twain's cautionary note, now played their way across the
East back to Chicago, stopping off first in Philadelphia for a game and a
banquet. It was April, and across the Delaware River in Camden, Whitman had been following the story closely. On the day after the teams
steamed into New York harbor and were greeted by hundreds of well-
wishers, he discussed the tour with Horace Traubel: "Did you see the
baseball boys are home from their tour around the world? How I'd like
to meet them—talk with them: maybe ask them some questions!"
(*WWC* 4:508). This desire to talk with the athletes who, in America's
name, had saluted the world, was an appropriate reaction for Whitman.
His lifelong interest in baseball is significant, finally, because his adult
life coincides, geographically and temporally, with the development of
American baseball from its birth to its maturity. Whitman, growing up

with the sport, eventually came to see baseball as an essential metaphor for America.

Baseball as we know it was born in 1845 with the formation of the Knickerbocker Club in New York, where the first recognizable baseball rules were set down in writing, including a key new rule that prohibited throwing the ball at the runner in order to put him out. This change immediately allowed for the use of the hard, lively ball that altered the nature of the game drastically—speeding things up, increasing distances, requiring quicker reflexes, and promptly turning a children's game into a full-fledged sport.

On June 19, 1846, the Knickerbockers played the first game of baseball (under the new rules) at Elysian Fields in Hoboken. And only a month later, Whitman, young editor of the *Brooklyn Daily Eagle,* wrote an editorial entitled "Brooklyn Young Men—Athletic Exercises":

> In our sun-down perambulations, of late, through the outer parts of Brooklyn, we have observed several parties of youngsters playing "base," a certain game of ball. We wish such sights were more common among us. In the practice of athletic and manly sports the young men of nearly all our American cities are very deficient—perhaps more so than any other country that could be mentioned.

We can see, even this early on, why more than forty years later Whitman would be excited and proud about America's manly baseball players demonstrating to the world their athletic skills; for in this early editorial, Whitman exhorts the youth of the country to "enjoy life a little. . . . Let us go forth awhile, and get better air in our lungs. Let us leave our close rooms." Exercise was essential for success on the open road, and of all the forms of sport, Whitman from the start was most attracted to the young game of baseball: "The game of ball is glorious" (*GF* 207–209). As baseball was born, then, it immediately was bound up in Whitman's mind with qualities he would endorse his whole life: vigor, manliness, al fresco health.

Whitman followed his own advice; he was himself an avid player. As a young man, he often played ball with his brother, Thomas Jefferson Whitman (Berthold ix). Another brother, George Washington Whitman, recalled that Walt "was an old-fashioned ballplayer and entered into a game heartily enough" (Traubel 39). By "old-fashioned," George probably meant that Walt played "softball" or pre-Knickerbocker baseball, what was sometimes called "Town Ball" or "Boston Ball" (since, in Massachusetts, that form of the game remained more popular than the hardball version until after the Civil War). Whitman had plenty of opportunity to play some version of "Town Ball" with his students while he was teaching school on Long Island in the 1830s; one of his former students at Flushing, John Roe, recalled that there was "a fine ball ground" at the school and that the students often "played ball." (While Roe doesn't recall Whitman taking part in the games, he does remember him as "very quick, agile, supple in all his movements" [Roe 86].)

In any case, baseball teams multiplied and flourished in New York and Brooklyn after the Knickerbockers got things started. Within a decade Brooklyn had four outstanding clubs—the Excelsiors, Putnams, Eckfords, and Atlantics—and there were over twenty-five well-organized clubs in the New York City area; by 1860 there were well over a hundred. Indeed, this increasingly popular hardball version of the game came to be known as "New York baseball." It had begun as a gentlemen's game, but its demands proved to be democratic; the game insisted on conditioning and skill, not on social breeding. Strong working-class young men quickly became involved, sometimes as "ringers" secretly paid by the gentlemen in the club to improve their chances to win, the first hints of "professional" baseball. Then entire working-class clubs were started in the 1850s, many formed according to occupation—the firemen with their own club, the barkeepers with theirs. Harry Eckford of Brooklyn, a Scottish immigrant and shipbuilder, molded a young group of prosperous mechanics and shipwrights into the very first artisanal club and named them, of course, the Eckfords.

By the 1860s, the best teams were often made up of immigrants and working men. A typical early Brooklyn team, in fact, sounds like something Whitman would have celebrated; David Voigt, in *American Baseball*, describes the players:

> The pitcher was a former stonemason; the catcher, a postal employee; the infielders worked as compositor, machinist, shipping clerk, and compositor. Among the outfielders, two were without previous job experience and the other worked as a compositor. The team substitute once worked as a glass blower. (19)

The occupations listed on early team rosters often read like a Whitmanesque catalog of working-class America. As M. Wynn Thomas has recently demonstrated in *The Lunar Light of Whitman's Poetry*, Whitman's ideal America was a nostalgic dream of a Jacksonian artisanal culture cast into the future, and baseball rosters at this time were filled with players who were skilled craftsmen of one sort or another; the teams were emblems of highly individualized workmen united for a common cause. It is fitting that baseball developed in the mid-nineteenth century as a peculiar mixture of a middle-class and a working-class sport. Clerks and artisans dominated the teams, and the "skilled craftsmen represented in the baseball world," as Warren Goldstein notes, "came from trades that had so far escaped the complete industrialization and restructuring into 'sweated' workplaces characteristic of furniture, clothing, and shoe manufacturing in antebellum New York" (26). Baseball, then, was one cultural arena that affirmed for Whitman his anachronistic faith in an artisanal future. The national sport was born among a group of workers who were fast disappearing, and the game would evolve into a corporate enterprise as inexorably as the artisanal class would be transformed into a corporate work force. In the 1850s and 1860s, though, baseball thrived among the trades Whitman was most fond of and most involved in: printers, for example, had their own well-structured leagues and were known as "typographical base-ballers" (Goldstein, 26), and even the compositors on Whitman's *Brooklyn Daily Eagle* had their own ball club (Goldstein, 160n).

In the notebooks he kept during the 1850s, Whitman made long lists of young men he had met, affectionate catalogs of America's strong democratic workers; he described their jobs and characteristics (perhaps in preparation for one of his many never-completed projects: "*Cantos*— of my various Companions—each one . . . celebrated in a verse by himself" [*NUPM* 1358]), and he specifically identified many of the men as ball players: "Bill—(big, black round eyes, large coarse . . . Irish descent playing ball)." So it is not surprising that in "Song of Myself," after we have been through a catalog of carpenters, pilots, farmers, printers, machinists, paving men, canal boys, and conductors, we come upon (in the vast catalog of Section 33) an image of baseball. At this point in the poem, Whitman is "afoot with [his] vision," spanning the continent with his rolling catalog, when he records a refreshing group of manly pursuits:

> Upon the race-course, or enjoying picnics or jigs or a good game of
>   base-ball,
> At he-festivals, with blackguard gibes, ironical license, bull-dances,
>   drinking, laughter.
>
> (*LG* 63)

And in his vast, loving catalog of America working (the poem that would come to be entitled "A Song for Occupations"), Whitman included baseball in the list of activities that defined his wondrously variegated vision of democracy:

> The ladders and hanging ropes of the gymnasium, manly exercises,
>   the game of base-ball, running, leaping, pitching quoits.
>
> (*LGV* 46)

Whitman eventually removed this line when he altered the poem to emphasize occupations more than activities; he always remained ambivalent about baseball becoming an "occupation." The professionalization and specialization of the sport (which occurred largely in the 1870s and 1880s) cut against the grain of his ideal vision of a skilled society of individual artisans who used sport to keep themselves healthy for their crafts, not those who used sport to *replace* or displace their crafts.

But in 1855 when "Song of Myself" was first printed, baseball was still in its innocence and was clearly one of the distinctive and identifying elements of the American experience that Whitman found worth absorbing into the song of himself, even though the term "baseball" had not yet made its way into the dictionaries. By the time the 1847 Webster's was published, of course, the sport and the word barely existed; the closest Webster comes is in one definition of "ball"—"A well-known and familiar game"—which probably refers to rounders or some other protoversion of baseball. But the word and the sport gradually surfaced in the American vocabulary and the American experience in the late 1840s and 1850s; Russell Bartlett's 1859 *Dictionary of Americanisms* recorded the game of "base," and by Webster's 1864 edition, "baseball" merited its own limited but accurate entry: "A game of ball, so called from the bases or bounds (usually four in number) which designate the circuit which each player must make after striking the ball." *Leaves,* then, served Whitman as a "Real Dictionary," recording and absorbing words and concepts before the "proper" dictionaries granted them entry.

Whitman, of course, had already been using the word for years. Growing up and working in Brooklyn, working and living and walking in Manhattan, he found himself in the cradle of baseball while it was developing as a sport and as an institution. And as editor of several local newspapers, Whitman functioned as a roving local reporter and at times covered sports. He was one of our first baseball writers. Two of his stories, complete with box scores, are preserved, both 1858 articles he wrote while editing the *Brooklyn Daily Times.* The first article, in the June 11 *Times,* gives a detailed account of the Putnam–Excelsior game of the day before. Over the previous three seasons, the Puts had dominated the series between the two teams, but Whitman notes, "Both Clubs have recruited and increased their strength very much during the past year." The Excelsiors, in fact, had become the highly favored team, but in a stunning upset, the Puts, behind pitching that Whitman found "hard to beat," won 31–18. Whitman offers some consolation to the defeated Excelsiors by calling them "gentlemen both on and off the field" and by noting that they have "always reflected credit upon the manly and healthful game they practice." (Perhaps their very gentlemanliness was beginning to interfere with the physically rigorous demands of the game, as was the case with many upper-class teams that were losing to workingmen's clubs during this era; the development of baseball allows us to trace the decline of American gentility.) The game indicated to Whitman that the "season bids fair to be a very exciting one," and he tells us the big game would occur the very next week: "The Putnams play a match game next week with the Atlantic Club, the champions of Long Island, and if they *should* succeed in beating them, they will have great cause to congratulate themselves" (*Brooklyn Daily Times,* June 11, 1858). Clearly, Whitman was not about to miss *that* game, and his other preserved baseball article gives a careful account of the epic contest, one that certainly lived up to its billing: "The game played yesterday between the Atlantic and Putnam Clubs, on the grounds of the latter Club, was one of the finest and most exciting games we ever witnessed." We see in Whitman's enthusiastic description his fascination for and familiarity with the game. Despite all the anticipation, though, this was not to be the Puts' day; misfortune plagued the team: "The defeat was as much the result of accident as of superior playing." Whitman analyzes the effects of injuries on the hapless Putnam team (including two catchers who were disabled in the course of the game; protective equipment wouldn't make its appearance for another twenty years). He concludes, "The Atlantics, as usual, played splendidly, and maintained their reputation as the *Champion Club*" (*ISL* 106–107). We can imagine why Whitman would come to admire the Brooklyn Atlantics, a club composed of workingmen with outdoor jobs, and one that happened to spring into existence the same year *Leaves of Grass* did. These robust players dominated New York–area baseball for years and gave Brooklyn the reputation of having the best baseball in the country.

There is one other aspect of baseball behavior that would have appealed to Whitman during the late 1850s when he was writing his *Calamus* poems, and that is the sport's sanctioning of open expressions of male–male affection. Early baseball clubs were very close fraternities, sites of intense male bonding. Descriptions of early games often include mention of a physical and spiritual closeness among players, as in an 1860 description of players leaving the field, "many of them arm in arm with each other" (quoted in Goldstein 41). This tendency of players to express their camaraderie in physical terms would have struck Whitman, of course, as a healthy sign of the kind of intense friendship—he called it "fervid comradeship"—that he believed had to evolve in America to "offset . . . our materialistic and vulgar American democracy." Democracy, he argued, would be "incomplete, in vain, and incapable of perpetuating itself" without the "threads of manly friendship . . . carried to degrees hitherto unknown" that would rival "amative love" (*PW* 414–15n). Baseball remains in American culture one of the few public sites where men embrace, pat other males' rears, drape their arms around male teammates, without causing homophobic reactions. From the beginning, then, Whitman would have appreciated the possibilities for the game to produce the kind of comradeship that he believed would eventually lead to real democracy.

III. "IN AND OUT OF THE GAME"

When Whitman went to Washington, D.C., at the end of 1862 to look for his brother George, who had been reported wounded in the war, baseball had already preceded him. In 1859, Washington had formed its first two clubs, the Potomacs and the Nationals, both made up of government clerks. Their home field was literally the backyard of the White House. (Well-publicized games on the White House grounds during Andrew Johnson's administration helped legitimize baseball's claims to national significance [Gipe 81].) Whitman was not a member of either of these teams, but as a clerk himself (first in the Indian Bureau of the Department of the Interior, then in the Attorney General's office), he may well have joined in more informal games. His young companion Pete Doyle recalls Walt in the 1860s: "How different Walt was then in Washington from the Walt you knew in later years! . . . He was an athlete—great, great" (Bucke 23). Whether or not he played, though, he certainly watched. He wrote to John Burroughs in the summer of 1866 of his activities: "I am feeling hearty and in good spirits—go around more than usual—go to such doings as base-ball matches" (C 1:281). He must have felt some disappointment near the end of the 1866 season when several games were rained out: "We have had an awful rain storm of *five* days, raining with hardly any intermission. The water is way up on the base-ball grounds" (C 5:289). The previous summer, the Nationals had hosted a big intercity tournament, and Whitman was probably one of the six thousand fans there. All government clerks had been let off from work so they could cheer on the clerk-players of the Nationals, and even Andrew Johnson attended. Whitman wrote about the game to one of the soldiers he had nursed: "There was a big match played here yesterday between two baseball clubs, one from Philadelphia & the other a Washington club—& to-day another is to come off between a New York & the Philadelphia club I believe—thousands go to see them play" (C 1:266). The "New York" club Whitman refers to was actually the Brooklyn Atlantics, the same team he had reported on in the *Brooklyn Daily Times* a few years before. In fact, the three teams in the tournament, from Brooklyn, Washington, and Philadelphia, turned out to represent nicely the span of Whitman's life: Brooklyn, where he had lived his early life; Washington, where he now lived; and Philadelphia, across the river from where he would spend his final two decades. His life unfolded in the very fields that baseball came to occupy.

The Civil War, of course, had a tremendous impact on baseball. Some clubs suspended or reduced operations as their players entered service. But during the war, newspapers initiated a campaign to make baseball the recognized national sport; the newspaper Whitman had once edited, the *Brooklyn Daily Eagle,* began during the war to insist that baseball would become the "American game," and the paper campaigned against cricket ever gaining a foothold in American sport because it was "purely an English game," which could "never be much in vogue with Americans . . . who are for fast and not slow things" (quoted in Adelman 110). And in the war itself, baseball played an important role; it was during the Civil War, in fact, that it became the "National Game." The "New York" version of baseball caught on among Union soldiers; it was frequently played in camp, and after the war the soldiers took it home with them. Older versions of the sport gave way to New York baseball, which became firmly entrenched as the American game. During the war, it was already popular; a Christmas game in 1862 drew forty thousand soldiers as spectators. When Whitman visited the headquarters of the Army of the Potomac in 1864, he recorded in a notebook the scenes around camp, and it is clear how thoroughly baseball had become integrated into the daily routines of the soldiers: "Some of the men are cooking, others washing cleaning their clothes—others playing ball, smoking lazily, lounging about. . . . Near by are squads drilling" (*NUPM* 725). Teams from some Union regiments, passing through the capital, even played the Washington Nationals. And Whitman could only have admired his hero-president, Lincoln, all the more for Lincoln's own love of the game: he played baseball and watched it as well. Confederate troops played the game, too. Baseball was even played in prison camps, with Union prisoners sometimes taking on their Confederate guards. (In Herman Melville's *Battle-Pieces,* a key scene revolves around Union troops watching Confederate troops play baseball; the chasm that separates the two groups is real and wide, though there is a longing by Union troops to join in the game [128].) And Albert Spalding makes the startling claim that, during lulls in battles, Union and Confederate troops occasionally played each other. Spalding, in another of his alliterative flourishes, expresses awe over baseball's effect on the war:

> No human mind may measure the blessings conferred by the game of Base Ball on the soldiers of the Civil War. A National Game? Why, no country on the face of the earth ever had a form of sport with so dear a title to that distinction. Base Ball had been born in the brain of an American soldier [a reference to the myth that Abner Doubleday invented the game]. It received its baptism in bloody days of our Nation's direst danger. It had its early revolution when soldiers, North and South, were striving to forget their foes by cultivating, through this

grand game, fraternal friendship with comrades in arms. It had its best development at the time when Southern soldiers, disheartened by distressing defeat, were seeking the solace of something safe and sane; at a time when Northern soldiers, flushed with victory, were yet willing to turn from fighting with bombs and bullets to playing with bat and ball. It was a panacea for the pangs and humiliation to the vanquished on one side, and a sedative against the natural exuberance of the victors on the other. It healed the wounds of war, and was balm to stinging memories. (92–93)

Spalding goes on and on, finally envisioning the sport as a transcendent "beacon," lighting us all "to a future of perpetual peace" (95).

Bloated as these claims sound, they are in line with those made by many right after the Civil War, and at any rate they hardly outdo Whitman's own growing faith, following the war, in the significance of the game; some twenty years after the war, Whitman, praising Horace Traubel's love of the sport, saw the effects baseball had come to have:

> I like your interest in sports—ball, chiefest of all—base-ball particularly: base-ball is our game: the American game: I connect it with our national character. Sports take people out of doors, get them filled with oxygen—generate some of the brutal customs (so-called brutal customs) which, after all, tend to habituate people to a necessary physical stoicism. We are some ways a dyspeptic, nervous set: anything which will repair such losses may be regarded as a blessing to the race. (*WWC* 2:330)

As a repairer of physical losses, a blessing to the race, and a gauge of national character, baseball was one activity that helped Whitman bring together his persistent concerns with health, American originality, and preservation of the Union. Baseball was a force that affirmed America's "transcendental Union" (*LG* 457) and blessed the postwar fragile bonding; the sport was also one thing America could claim as its *own*; it was non-European, the *American* game, grown out of this soil. And it was a young man's game; Whitman loved the idea of a game that would join and bond the demobilized troops that he had come to love, would ease their transition back to civilian life by offering them more peaceful competition in uniforms of nonmilitary design.

Whitman was also aware that baseball would preserve the all-male enclaves that the military had provided, and the sport would thus furnish a cultural space in which Calamus affections could continue to develop; in this way, it would become an important part of preserving the positive values that the war had taught. Like the postwar pioneers in his poetry, who traded their weapons of war for implements of agriculture, who transformed their military marches into marches of progress, the postwar baseball players would become transformed troops, still uniformed and united in the purpose of victory, but in battles now turned bloodless and healthy, in battles that would strengthen rather than divide the Union. Baseball was in fact one way of effectively demobilizing the troops—turning guns into bats and transmuting sectional rivalries into healthy ritualized competition. Near the end of the war, one sports journalist noted that baseball uniforms had lost their distinctive qualities during the national strife, but that now there was "nothing to prevent a base-ball player's uniform from being as well known as that of a United States soldier" (quoted in Goldstein 109). The identification of the players with the soldiers was widespread, as was the faith that the learned actions of war could, through a unifying national sport, evolve into gestures of peace. Even the badly wounded could vicariously enter into the new national passion through the developing role of active spectator, for now baseball was emerging as an activity to be watched as much as to be participated in.

So, even as his own health declined, Whitman's interest in baseball never waned; as a spectator himself, he watched the sport become a reliable measure of American culture. Nationwide after the Civil War, baseball became increasingly popular and increasingly professional. The changes in baseball reflected more general changes in American society. The commercial spirit, the pressures of conformity, the loss of individual artisans in the mechanical specialization of large industries—all of these tendencies, which profoundly disturbed Whitman for the final twenty-five years of his life and caused him to question the future of America and to doubt the value of the massive sacrifice of life in the Civil War, took their toll on baseball as well. Like the rest of America in the decades following the war, baseball was incorporating; its artisan-players were becoming employees of large firms; the well-rounded skills of the pre-war players were not as much in demand as the more specialized skills of players who could fit themselves effectively into teams that functioned more and more like well-oiled machines. The National League, formed in the 1870s, developed in the age of the robber barons, and it shared their desire for monopoly; Douglas Noverr and Lawrence Ziewacz note that "no captain of industry directed his industry into a monopoly better than did these National League owners, who by the 1890s held a monopoly on the professional game, beating back challenge after challenge of rival leagues," and Albert Spalding's transformation from player to owner to sporting goods magnate—with monopolies on manufacturing everything from the baseballs used in major league games to the turnstiles the fans had to pass through to watch the games—made him baseball's Rockefeller (21). Christian Messenger notes how in these years the very nature of the sports hero changed from the pre–Civil War "individual in contest on the frontier with other men or with nature" to the modern sports hero "most clearly defined on a team to which he was subordinated—military, industrial, educational, societal": the sports hero himself had become "representative of the conflict between the individual and the modern organization" (Messenger 11–12; see also 90–92).

Baseball, then, reflected the most disturbing as well as the most idealistic elements of the culture. Its racist policies prohibiting teams with black players from joining the major baseball organizations mirrored the dominant cultural attitudes toward blacks in the postwar decades. Baseball even offered its own analogue for the Tammany Hall scandals in the form of a team called the Mutuals, a team that had been involved in baseball's first real scandal—a fixed game in 1865—and that had a notorious reputation for corruption and cheating: this team, fittingly, was bankrolled (out of city funds) by "Boss" Tweed himself, who served on its board of trustees. Gambling compromised the integrity of the game as well, and in 1867 *Harper's Weekly* noted, "So common has betting become at baseball matches that the most respectable clubs in the country indulge in it to a highly culpable degree." So many games have been "sold," *Harper's* said, "that the most respectable participants have been suspected of baseness" (quoted in Rader 112). It was enough to give a new meaning to the term "*base* ball."

Just after the war, however, Whitman was not so troubled by such ominous signs; he was still filled with enthusiasm for the brighter ways that baseball reflected the emerging American culture. Initially, then, he must have been cheered by the decision of his Washington team to follow the "resistless restless race" (*LG* 230) west in the postwar urge to claim and tame the rest of the continent. The Washington Nationals in 1867 headed in the direction of the frontier by sponsoring the first baseball trans-Allegheny tour; they played as far west as St. Louis. But out West, the Nationals ironically were responsible for forcing the creation of what became an emblem of the disturbing side of the emerging American spirit. Their resounding defeat of the Cincinnati team led to Harry Wright's founding the Cincinnati Red Stockings in 1869, the first all-professional, fully salaried team. For over a year Wright's team toured the country to restore Cincinnati's honor; they were undefeated from New York to San Francisco. Then in 1876, the National League was formed and modern-day baseball—where the players worked full time and performed for a paying public, for workers who ceased to be players and settled into the more passive role of spectator—was under way.

The emerging role of the spectator was one of the most significant developments in American sports during the last third of the nineteenth century. Whitman's well-known stance of being "Both in and out of the game" (*LG* 32) reflects the spectators' evolving sense of their duties and responsibilities. Allen Guttmann notes how a "historically unprece-

dented code of spectatorship" developed during the Victorian era, a code
that "was never perfectly institutionalized," but which nonetheless set
certain standards of expected behavior, including the acknowledgment
of outstanding play by opponents. The vast crowds, largely male, immigrant, and lower class that Whitman reported seeing at baseball games
were potential challenges to democracy: they could easily become vi-
cious mobs, ruled by violence and prejudice, so the code of spectatorship
served a civilizing function: "The spectators' passions were to be gov-
erned by strict rules of conduct analogous to the rules of the game (and
also analogous to the behavior of middle-class concert and theater audiences)" (Guttmann 88–89). As American sports developed specializations leading to the separation of professional athletes and paying spectators, most Americans who cared about baseball were involved in the
game as observers rather than as active players. As active observers, they
had to find ways to channel their passionate but necessarily passive
involvement into behavior that would allow the game to proceed fairly
but would still allow them to feel they were helping their team to victory; they had to figure out, in other words, how to maintain a stance of
being simultaneously both in and out of the game.

Whitman's poetry, of course, was precisely the poetry of the crowd;
his infamous "catalogs" became the poetic equivalent of a turnstile admitting a diverse group of individuals into one arena, where each detail
retained its uniqueness yet all worked together as they focused on one
action—a democratic diversity responding to the same sweep of energy.
The baseball crowd, then, one of the evolving common aspects of American experience in the late nineteenth century, came to be a gauge of the
democratic experience, a visible measure of the success of the attempt to
meld the individual and the "En-Masse." The baseball crowd came to be
the cultural icon for democracy; as the Boston Globe noted in 1883, "Every class, every station, every color and every nationality will be found
at a ball match" (quoted in Guttmann 112). But such democratic ideals
were undermined by the entrepreneurship of the growing baseball business; rising and differentiated ticket prices (the bleachers became the
cheap seats) led to an intensification rather than an obliteration of social
and economic distinction. In 1877, turnstiles were introduced at National
League baseball parks, just as Ladies' Days were becoming common:
these were the first signs of "crowd control," as baseball magnates attempted to diminish the potential problems of a lower-class male rowdi-
ness by diluting the crowd with a gender and a class that would provide
good behavioral examples.

It is crucial to remember that baseball was born in the city, not in the
country; Spalding worked hard to create the myth that the game was
born in rural upstate New York, but in fact it got its start in New York

City. The crowded infield represents the game's origins more exactly than the spacious outfields. From the start, then, baseball is associated with crowds and urban experience, with the hard lessons of coordinating individual skills into a team effort. That is one aspect of the game that Whitman particularly admired, both in the crowds that played and in the crowds that watched. His own poetry reflects his fascination with the new phenomenon of crowd psychology, of living an existence that is both swallowed up by crowd behavior and yet differentiated from the crowd it identifies with: we are all part of "the city's ceaseless crowd" (*LG* 389), and the nature of our identity forces us continually to assess our uneasy positioning between individual desire and social responsibility: "Just as any of you is one of a living crowd, I was one of a crowd" (*LG* 160), he tells us in "Crossing Brooklyn Ferry," and the tensed emphasis on *one* and *crowd* epitomizes Whitman's sense of American identity poised between the magnetic poles of self and society, finding itself in the balance of "pride" and "sympathy" (*LG* 716).

Crowds are everywhere in Whitman's work, and the word "crowd" becomes one of the characteristic marks of Whitman's diction. For him, the crowd is an image of democracy, a blending of individual differences into a heterogeneous unity. There is in his work a sense that the democratic "crowd" has its own personality apart from the individuals who make it up; like the baseball crowd in William Carlos Williams's "At the Ball Game," Whitman's crowds can be both venomous and generous, hateful and joyous, and their moods can shift quickly and unpredictably: "Hurrying with the modern crowd as eager and fickle as any, / Hot toward one I hate, ready in my madness to knife him" (*LG* 64). So it is crowd psychology that forces intolerance and antidemocratic discrimination, as seen in "Song of Myself" when the prostitute is mocked—"The crowd laugh at her blackguard oaths, the men jeer and wink to each other"—and the persona pauses to reprimand the mass facelessness of hatred: "Miserable! I do not laugh at your oaths nor jeer you" (*LG* 43). Whitman celebrates the individual issuing forth from the crowd, the self that can merge amicably with the crowd but also emerge from it in an unending systole and diastole of common and unique identity: "A call in the midst of the crowd, / My own voice, orotund sweeping and final" (*LG* 76).

But toward the end of his life, as crowd violence began to be a problem in baseball, as fans began taunting black players, Whitman saw that baseball was beginning to reflect some unsettling cultural changes. Not only the crowds, but the game itself seemed to be conforming to antidemocratic tendencies in the culture. One particular rule change symptomatic of the overall drift of the sport particularly bothered Whitman. Traubel records Whitman's concern in May 1889; Thomas Harned, a devoted friend, had come to see Walt after attending a baseball game, and Whitman jumped at the chance to talk about the state of the sport:

> Tell me, Tom—I want to ask you a question: in base-ball is it the rule that the fellow who pitches the ball aims to pitch it in such a way the batter cannot hit it? Gives it a twist—what not—so it slides off, or won't be struck fairly?

Harned affirmed that this indeed was the case, and Whitman's response indicates that he still followed the game even if he was now too debilitated to attend: "Eh? That's the modern rule then, is it? I thought something of the kind—I read the papers about it—it seemed to indicate that there" (*WWC* 5:145).

The rule that concerned Whitman has to do with the way the ball could be pitched. The original Knickerbocker rule forbade the *throwing* of the ball; instead, the ball had to be pitched underhand, smoothly, so that the batter could hit it. This rule had been refined over the years, first requiring that the hand not be raised above the hip, then requiring only that the hand pass below the hip as the ball was pitched, then only below the waist, then the shoulder (allowing for sidearm pitching). Originally, then, the pitcher's function was simply to put the ball in play by allowing the batter to hit it; one player usually pitched all the games. But as the skills of the players became more refined, the pitcher's role became more strategic. In 1884 the National League removed all restrictions on a pitcher's delivery, and by 1887 batters could no longer call for high or low pitches. The curveball, which occasionally had been accomplished underhand-style in the 1870s, now became a requisite skill. Whitman, however, was not impressed with this new skill and saw the rule change as endemic of the deception and lack of openness he saw creeping everywhere into America; we can hear echoes of the anger and despair of *Democratic Vistas* in his response to Harned, "denounc[ing] the custom roundly," as Traubel tells us:

> "The wolf, the snake, the cur, the sneak all seem entered into the modern sportsman—though I ought not to say that, for a snake is a snake because he is born so, and man the snake for other reasons, it may be said." And again he went over the catalogue—"I should call it everything that is damnable."

Harned is described as "amused" at Whitman's response, but Whitman seems in earnest. He has obviously had the matter on his mind for some time and has engaged in some lively debate about it: "I have made it a point to put the same question to several fellows lately. There certainly seems no doubt but that your version is right, for that is the version everyone gives me" (*WWC* 5:145). It's as if Whitman keeps hoping someone will "say it ain't so," will affirm for him that baseball remains the fair, open, and democratic game that he recalled it to be. Whitman already sensed the dangers that would come: the game becoming anti-democratic, the pampered pitcher rising above his teammates and playing only once every five days or so. (Indeed, it has come to pass that with the arm-mangling magic of screwballs, forkballs, knuckleballs, and hundred-mile-an-hour fastballs, pitching *is* now the predominant factor in the game.)

Despite his fears, though, Whitman persisted in holding on to an idyllic vision of the game: baseball as something essentially bound up with the best of America. Some of Whitman's last outdoor excursions were to watch the national sport, which he seemed to associate with Nature itself; for him, watching baseball was as natural and exhilarating as breathing the fresh air. Traubel notes how in the early 1890s Whitman "is taken out regularly in his chair, perhaps to the outskirts of the town, where he may scan the free sky, the shifting clouds, watch the boys at base-ball, or breathe in drowsily . . . the refreshing air" (142). Traubel recalls Whitman talking about one of his favorite topics in the last years—the idea of "free Sundays," with no blue law restrictions on activities (like the ones that prevented Spalding's international team from playing in Hawaii when they arrived on a Sunday): "W. believes in 'free Sundays.' The boys should have their ball or any frolic they choose" (*WWC* 2:52). Whitman here is entering into a raging controversy in the 1880s, as two baseball leagues, the American Association and the Union Association, directly challenged Sunday blue laws by scheduling games on the one day of the week that workingmen could easily attend (and by serving beer as well). Such actions led to widely publicized arrests of managers and players in Baltimore, Washington, and Cincinnati in the last two summers of Whitman's life and led to widespread denunciation of the sport by priests and preachers, one of whom sermonized that baseball was "a traveling contagion that should be quarantined for the public good" (Gipe 473). Whitman remained firmly in support of the baseball interests, though he never admitted the pecuniary interests the club owners had in challenging blue laws (Sunday games drew larger crowds); he argued instead on the basis of freedom from priestly and puritanical authority:

> Talking of Sunday agitation generally and Gloucester [New Jersey] baseball in particular W. said: "I believe in all that—in baseball, in picnics, in freedom: I believe in the jolly all-round time—with the parsons and the police eliminated. (*WWC* 1:267)

Whitman here gives early voice to what would become an American cliché: "baseball, picnics, and freedom" formed a commonplace nexus of

American values. (A *Time* article, written during the period of President
Reagan's greatest popularity, quoted a Democratic political analyst noting ruefully that "Ronald Reagan is a ball game and a picnic on a week-
end in July" [June 25, 1984, 14].) So it comes as no surprise to hear
Whitman express his despair in late autumn in the last years of his life as
he is taken outside in his wheelchair on a restricted Sunday and finds the
day hollow and cold as baseball has disappeared from the land:

> I was out in my chair yesterday—Warrie [Warren Fritzinger, Whit-
> man's nurse] took me and we went up towards the city hall. Generally,
> on weekdays, there are boys playing base ball—a fine air of activity,
> life, but yesterday everything was glum—neither boy nor ball to be
> seen. I thought then—told Warrie, too—how much better the play, the
> open air, the beautiful sky, the active movement, than restriction, Sab-
> bathism. (*WWC* 6:128–29)

Whitman, then, resisted the lingering power of the Puritan suspicion
about sport and the cultural perpetuation of the Puritan ban on Sunday
recreational activity. Like his disciple Ernest Crosby, he preferred the
ball games on Sunday over anything that organized religion had to offer;
he joined many writers who in the mid-nineteenth century came to "articulate the three major justifications of modern sport: to promote health,
to promote morality, and to instill character values" (Adelman 270).
Baseball, the American game with its American pace, had replaced the
church as the source of morality, value, and vitality, and the spirited
national debate in the 1880s and 1890s about Sunday baseball provided
Whitman one final opportunity to give voice to his desire to see a country in which "There will soon be no more priests" and where the crowds
will replace them: "A superior breed shall take their place. . . . the gangs
of kosmos and prophets en masse shall take their place" (*LG* 727).

IV. CATCHING MUCH ON THE FLY

When Whitman told Tom Harned in 1889 that he had been discussing baseball with "several fellows," he did not suggest who these
fellow baseball fans were, but one fascinating hint does exist. Several
times during 1888, Horace Traubel records visits from a Harry Wright,
always without comment (except once, when Whitman was irritated that
Wright had stayed too long), and in Whitman's daybook for 1885, Walt
records on January 25: "Sunday, visit from Harry Wright" (*DBN* 2:350;
WWC 3:100, 435; 4:137). As with Traubel's references, there is no further comment that might help identify this man, and he has in fact remained unidentified in Whitman scholarship. It's interesting, though,
that Traubel drops Wright's name as if he is someone the reader probably

would know. And there *was* one Harry Wright in the Camden area in the 1880s whose name would have needed no gloss; this was William Henry Wright—known to everyone as Harry—a fine ball player and, as we have seen, the founder of the first professional baseball team, the Cincinnati Red Stockings. After his playing days, he continued in baseball as a manager and finally as chief of the umpires for the National League. From 1884 to 1893 (Whitman bought his house on Mickle Street in Camden in 1884 and lived there until his death in 1892) he was the prominent manager of Philadelphia's best baseball team, the National League Athletics. He was one of the special guests at that Philadelphia dinner honoring the world-touring baseball players on their return to America in 1889; he talked to the players Whitman wanted so much to talk to himself. When we consider Whitman's fondness for, interest in, and belief in the game of baseball, it at least seems fitting that Harry Wright would have been among the well-known people who crossed the Delaware to visit Whitman on Mickle Street, especially on Sundays when the baseball diamonds were forced to be idle.

Whether or not he knew baseball's Harry Wright, though, there's no doubt that by the 1880s baseball had entered Whitman's very way of thinking. The democratic American game furnished him with figures of speech he seemed especially fond of, and his conversations with Traubel are peppered with baseball terms. So when he wanted to express admiration for a particularly effective passage written by William O'Connor, Whitman evoked baseball's supreme offensive achievement, the home run: "That's a home stroke. . . . O William: you can hit a thing like that off with absolute finality" (*WWC* 3:523). He referred to the success of his photographic portraits in baseball terms, nearly keeping a box score: "three out of four have been hits . . . first, the November Boughs picture, which I have always regarded as a hit" (*WWC* 4:394). He seemed attracted to baseball metaphors for their colorful, direct, and simple expressiveness. He even refers to his own writing techniques in terms of baseball, telling Traubel, for example, "That has mainly been my method: I have caught much on the fly: things as they come and go—on the spur of the moment" (*WWC* 3:149). And Traubel uses the same image to evoke some of his more fragmented conversations with Whitman: "Two or three things I caught from W. on the fly, as I busied about the room" (*WWC* 1:241). At the time of these conversations, "on the fly" was an important new baseball term, since the original Knickerbocker rules in 1845 allowed for an out if the ball was caught "on the first bound." Only gradually did this rule change; for years, teams would stipulate whether or not the games they played would be "on the fly" or "on the bound." If players chose to play on the fly, they had to be especially awake and alert, anticipating the unexpected. The controversy over the rule raged during the Civil War years, and the idea of catching the ball "on the bound" was increasingly derided as the "boy's rule," as the compromising rule that prevented the game from becoming as manly as cricket: "The key to the manliness of the fly catch," notes Warren Goldstein, "was that it made the game more difficult—it demanded more skill of the fielders" (49). So Whitman did not mean to imply, with the figure of speech, casualness about his poetic methods so much as alertness combined with an element of surprise: his method was to be awake for every opportunity that came his way, to take risks, to catch "much on the fly."

Once when discussing plans for an edition of his complete poetry and prose with Traubel, Whitman began to wonder about a new preface for the book. He wavered about whether or not one was needed. Finally he fell back on a baseball story to help him make up his mind: "My hesitations make me think of a story. The captain of a baseball nine was to be presented with a silver pitcher." Whitman goes on to tell how the captain and the club spokesman both prepared long speeches for the occasion, but when the presentation ceremony came, both men forgot them: "They flustered about, wondering what to do—then finally retreated to first causes, to their simple human nature—the spokesman exclaiming: 'Captain, here's the pitcher!' and the captain exclaiming: 'Is *that* the pitcher?' So the affair was a success after all, though not according to the rule set." Whitman of course admired this open honesty, this simple unadorned speech from the heart, displacing set rules and rehearsed elegance; his poetry, after all, had set out to do the same thing. Here, then, was the simple good humor and straightforwardness of the young American athlete, and Whitman decided to emulate this baseball player's way of speaking in his own writing:

> I guess I'll have to model my preface on that incident—and if the preface is half as successful as the incident I'll be satisfied. "Captain, here's the preface!" "Is *that* the preface?" We want to get the pitcher into the right hands—that's the whole object. (*WWC* 2:206–207)

Baseball for Whitman was the emblem and enactment of straightforwardness, and its pace and heritage made it the ideal athletic backdrop against which his poetry could be read. Even the baseball field itself was the manifestation for Whitman of how America should occupy the continent, joining with but not arrogating the natural landscape: "The desired thing was not an absolute cutting away but modification—nature not all wiped out, as if ashamed of" (*WWC* 3:528). Whitman dreamed of the United States reaching a communal culmination in the "Prairie States"

where the vast spaces would allow for huge populations without congestion, allow for human landscapes to merge with natural ones, where
neither man nor nature would "wipe out" the other:

> A newer garden of creation, no primal solitude,
> Dense, joyous, modern, populous millions, cities and farms,
> With iron interlaced, composite, tied, many in one.
>
> (*LG* 402)

The baseball field, long viewed as a microcosm of America with its congested infield arching around home and its vast and underpopulated out-
field expanding in an ever-widening arc beyond the congestion, was part
of Whitman's memory of his own childhood relation to America's
changing landscape:

> I remember—it is quite vivid—a spot off on Long Island, somewhere
> in the neighborhood of our old home—rough, uncultivated, uncared
> for—choked with underbrush—forbidding: people coming would
> avoid it—it was that kind of place: put to no practical uses, untouched.
> . . . I left the neighborhood—was away for years: wandering seeing:
> living: went back again: the whole face of it was changed: now a base
> ball ground, a park . . . yet it had required but little work to effect the
> transformation—simply clearing away the brush: now it is a perfect
> spot of its kind—a resort.

A wilderness had been transformed into a habitable place, a place of
American activity, yet in the process the natural had not been destroyed,
only enhanced. Whitman was quick to draw the lesson for his own poetry: "Carry the thought along: there is an art in such a situation—an art
of not doing too much" (*WWC* 3:527–28). It would be another way
Whitman's poetry and his country would imitate each other, transforming uncharted experience into form, but doing so gently, allowing
the experience itself to generate the form, learning, with words or plans
or tools, the "art of not doing too much," of nudging a baseball field out
of the brush.

V. "THE HURRAH GAME"

In recent years there has been a lot of serious talk about baseball.
Scholars have examined the sport as an analogue to American history or
as a way of understanding the American character; David Q. Voigt in
America Through Baseball, for example, investigates the sport in relation
to America's nationalism, sense of mission, racism, and the union ethic.
And George Grella, in his essay entitled "Baseball and the American
Dream," makes perhaps the broadest claim:

> Occupying a unique place in our national heritage, this most American
> of sports speaks as few other human activities can to our country's sense

of itself. . . . The game is as instructive, as beautiful, and as profound
as the most significant aspects of American culture. . . . Anyone who
does not understand the game cannot hope to understand the country.
(550)

Many of this country's best writers would seem to agree; Stephen Crane
was a first-rate ball player, and authors as diverse as Mark Twain, Frank
Norris, Marianne Moore, William Carlos Williams, James T. Farrell,
Ring Lardner, Zane Grey, Thomas Wolfe, F. Scott Fitzgerald, Ernest
Hemingway, Bernard Malamud, Wright Morris, Robert Coover, John
Updike, and Philip Roth all have used baseball as a major image at one
time or another. They are not alone: Anton Grobani's bibliography,
Guide to Baseball Literature, runs to three hundred pages and thousands of
entries. As Robert Frost said, "Some baseball is the fate of us all" (89).
It's important, then, to realize that Walt Whitman, our most essentially
American poet, was one of the first of our writers, perhaps *the* first, to
recognize the vital significance of baseball to America. Traubel once
called it "the hurrah game of the republic," and Whitman, in good humor, responded:

> That's beautiful: the hurrah game! well—it's our game: that's the chief
> fact in connection with it: America's game: has the snap, go, fling, of
> the American atmosphere—belongs as much to our institutions, fits
> into them as significantly, as our constitutions, laws: is just as important
> in the sum total of our historic life. (*WWC* 4:508)

No writer since has exceeded these extravagant and fervent claims for
the game. Clearly for Whitman, baseball was the sport that came to coin-
cide with the best aspects of the American character and eventually came
to absorb its worst aspects, too; like some cultural litmus paper, the
game absorbed events and attitudes, and it altered its appearance to reflect changes in the national environment. It was the sport that was precisely about Americans, and as such, it became for Whitman an analogue
for his poetry, which he hoped would be the literary equivalent of baseball—a cultural structure guided by a set of rules peculiarly American,
paced according to American needs and customs, available to all, somewhat incomprehensible to other cultures. Whitman's baseball credo
could only have been spoken by a man who grew up with the sport; saw
it develop from its slower, more sedate forms into a demanding game of
hardball with "snap and go"; saw the democratic demands of skill force
gentlemen to give way to the young roughs; saw the baseball team itself
become an image of America, accepting and absorbing men from all
walks of life, immigrants from all over the world, molding them into
one body, a union committed to a common purpose; saw the sport,
starting from Manhattan, spread westward and eventually be played

from coast to coast, affirming America's secure occupation of the continent; saw baseball, finally, become an athletic image of his soul, accomplishing the rondure of the world, spreading "America's game" and "the American atmosphere" to Australia, Asia, Africa, and Europe, then returning home in triumph and comradeship. Whitman had often prophesied the eventual completion of America's continental manifest destiny: "Long ere the second centennial arrives, there will be some forty to fifty great States, among them Canada and Cuba" (*PW* 413). The American bicentennial has long passed, and baseball even helped salvage this prophecy. Had he lived on into the twentieth century, Whitman would have seen American baseball first make the ultimate confirmation of manifest destiny by resettling the Brooklyn Dodgers and the New York Giants in Los Angeles and San Francisco, while it also reached south to Cuba for some of its finest players and then went north to absorb Canada, uniting Montreal, however improbably, into the *National* League and assimilating Toronto into the *American*.

All this was set in motion the year after Whitman's death when the Western League, progenitor of today's American League, was organized, and twentieth-century baseball was on its way. The sport had begun its acceleration into big business: the year before Whitman's death, the militant National Brotherhood of Baseball Players deserted the National League and began their own ill-fated league; it was the first bitter battle between management and players. The sport reflected a general cultural turmoil: the first actual brawls on the field had just begun; baseball's own Jim Crow laws formally excluded black players; the National League, burdened with debts and with a bloated twelve-team circuit, headed into an economic depression analogous to the wider national depression. What he had begun by celebrating as the natural union of good fellowship and team camaraderie (a team spirit so strong that it could help heal the divisions of the Civil War) had hardened over the years of his adult life into a corporate unity based on profit, greed, and control. As Whitman died, the country marked the end of what would come to be known as the Golden Era of baseball.

3

Whitman and American Indians

(Have I forgotten any part? any thing in the past?
Come to me whoever and whatever, till I give you recognition.)
Whitman, "With Antecedents" (*LG* 241)

Whitman was always on the lookout for cultural activities that signaled some emerging autochthonous form. If baseball was an enterprise that endorsed his hope for truly native patterns of shared experience, America's bloody encounters with the Indians undermined those hopes, for much of nineteenth-century American history had come to seem an outright attack on the aboriginal, an attempt to erase the autochthonous from our cultural memory. By the end of the century, it sometimes seemed that all that remained of the truly native was a parody.

A revealing icon of this parodic transformation appeared in baseball. In the 1890s, just a few years after Whitman's death, Lou "Chief" Sockalexis, a Penobscot Indian, actually played in the National League, the first native American to make it to the majors; though a talented hitter, runner, and fielder, he lasted only a couple of seasons, and his presence in the league prompted some of the first real crowd maliciousness. Every time the "Chief" would come to bat, fans would shout war whoops and yell threats. Sockalexis was ultimately suspended for drunkenness: only a few years after the Wounded Knee massacre, he was reduced to another cultural symbol of the stereotyped drunken Indian as he was ridiculed out of the national sport, which by National League edict had begun in the 1890s to be literally a white man's domain. (Black players were excluded from league play in 1889, and Sockalexis's presence in the league after that ban simply intensified the ambiguity of the red race's perceived position in relation to the white race—no longer seen as a cultural threat, Indians could be tolerated and ridiculed in the white man's game.) Like

55

the earlier endless Indian delegations to Washington, D.C., Sockalexis found himself in an alien uniform, playing an alien game, one he learned to play very well in a culture he adapted himself to skillfully. (He attended Holy Cross and Notre Dame.) Like those Indian delegations, and like the "civilized tribes" of the Southeast, he had played by all the rules, had taken on all the necessary beliefs and attitudes that should have merged him into the white man's culture, only to find that at best he would be incorporated into that culture as a token gesture and would eventually be betrayed by an ugly mass reaction that insisted on his difference.

There are two accounts of Sockalexis's postbaseball years: in one, he ends up a drunken beggar on the streets, a late casualty of the white man's traditional weapon against the Indian—whiskey; in the other (more reliable) account, he returns to the Penobscot reservation, works as a woodcutter, and dies in the woods at age forty-two. Either version of his demise turns his life into a symbolic tale of the commonly perceived plight of American Indians; they were corrupted by civilization if they tried to blend in, or they were doomed to be lonely hunters, unfit for civilized life and tragically destined to die in the disappearing forests. American Indians would never embrace baseball in any significant way, but American baseball would continue to use the Indian in coercive ways, naming its teams such things as the Mohicans (a nineteenth-century New York club); even today, the major leagues contain the Braves and the Indians, whose controversial club emblem—a grotesque, grinning, red-faced, feathered caricature of a native American—is a cartoonish nod back to Lou Sockalexis, who played his one year of major-league baseball in Cleveland. That emblem serves as a twentieth-century counterpart to the derisive war whoops that, a century ago, mocked the Indian in the white man's uniform.

I. "NATIVE STATES OF RUDENESS"

By the time Whitman was born in 1819, all the major battles between whites and Indians east of the Mississippi had been fought; Whitman grew up knowing this region as the secure United States. But during his adult years, a series of explosive battles west of the Mississippi occurred, from the Pueblo uprising in 1847 to the Grattan fight in 1854 and the Rains fight in 1855 (when *Leaves of Grass* first appeared), on through the countless battles and massacres of the 1860s and 1870s (when names like Birch Coulee, Canyon de Chelly, Rosebud, and Warbonnet Creek entered the American common vocabulary), culminating in the Wounded Knee massacre at the end of 1890, a little over a year before

Whitman's death. These were the troubling battles that America fought to take back what early explorers had dismissed as the great American Desert, the land west of the Mississippi that, it then seemed, only the Indians could ever want. Three days before Whitman's eleventh birthday, the Indian Removal Bill was passed by Congress, and Andrew Jackson, the former Indian fighter turned president, got what he wanted: the power to take away Indian lands east of the Mississippi by giving tribes western lands in exchange. The so-called civilized tribes of the Southeast, many of whom owned homes and farms, were moved out to what would become Oklahoma. The various skirmishes, court battles, and presidential orders that accompanied the removal continued over the next ten years, through Whitman's teenage years into his early adulthood, as the Choctaws, then the Creeks, then the Chickasaws, then—in the infamous "Trail of Tears" in 1838 and 1839, as Whitman turned twenty—the Cherokees; finally the Seminoles in 1842 surrendered and were marched west. By the time he had reached his majority, Whitman knew an America where the natives had been brutally separated and removed, an America where they had been promised western lands forever, and an America that was already hungry to make something out of the very lands it had just given up. His adult years, then, were framed by the Great Removal when he was twenty and the Wounded Knee massacre when he was seventy, and like many Americans who lived through this period, Whitman never stopped struggling with the insoluble "Indian problem." By 1890, he was comparing it to the Irish struggle for independence from Britain, where there were "two interests conflicting—strings pulling two ways—the one all Ireland, all for Irishman, who know nothing but Ireland—the other for the British Empire—that compact of vaster interests touching all parts of the globe":

> Indeed, it is our Indian question repeated—which has interests purely for the Indian, interests then of the whole body of states, leading to the largest results. In the meantime the poor aboriginals, so to call them, suffer, go down, are wiped out. (*WWC* 6:423)

The Indians, Whitman knew, had been abused and treated unjustly, but he also subscribed to the notion of progress and social evolution and believed that it was inevitable and ultimately valuable that America extend itself from sea to sea, in service of the "largest result" of the "whole body of the states." As always with Whitman, union was the overriding good; the only clear thing was the certainty that the Indians themselves would be "wiped out." So commonplace had the removal and betrayal of the Indians become during Whitman's life that by the time of the 1889 Oklahoma land rush—what Whitman called "the Oklahoma land grab"—which undid another sacred treaty with the Indians, he took little notice of it, dismissing it simply as a "funny affair altogether" (*WWC* 5:91).

When Whitman asks in the 1855 *Leaves* about "The friendly and flowing savage. . . . Who is he?" he embodies a key cultural question:

> The friendly and flowing savage. . . . Who is he?
> Is he waiting for civilization or past it and mastering it?
>
> Is he some southwesterner raised outdoors? Is he Canadian?
> Is he from the Mississippi country? or from Iowa, Oregon or
>   California? or from the mountains? or prairie life or bush-life? or
>   from the sea?
> . . .
>
> Behavior lawless as snow-flakes. . . . words simple as grass. . . .
>   uncombed head and laughter and naivete;
> Slowstepping feet and the common features, and the common modes
>   and emanations,
> They descend in new forms from the tips of his fingers,
> They are wafted with the odor of his body or breath. . . . they fly out
>   of the glance of his eyes.
>
>   (*LGV* 61)

If the "savage" is truly (as the roots of the word suggest) the sylvan occupant, the dweller in American woods and forests—with his simple words, lawless behavior, uncombed head, and common manner—then is he a white backwoodsman or a red native? Whitman's description could apply to either one, and his ambiguity underscores the cultural tension about who holds rightful possession of the American wilderness: "Is he waiting for civilization or past it and mastering it?" When Whitman asks about this emerging new American figure—"Is he from the Mississippi country? or from Iowa, Oregon, or California?"—he is asking a question that echoes much of the history of his own day, recalling perhaps Black Hawk's brave stand at Rock Island, Illinois, in 1832 as he refused to be moved across the Mississippi into the Iowa territory, or recalling perhaps the much more recent Whitman Mission murders in 1847, when his white namesakes were murdered in an episode that led to a decade of battles between white settlers and Indians in the Oregon country. Mississippi and Iowa in the 1830s and Oregon in the 1840s and 1850s were major stages on which the "Indian problem" was being most vividly acted out; the "savages" in Mississippi, Iowa, and Oregon were no longer "friendly," and as Whitman's emerging new white American savage came to replace the native savage, a half-century of unfriendly encounters would mark the transition: all that would be "flowing" would be blood. Whitman's haunting lines in "Song of Myself," then, capture the cultural ambivalence of a country that was at once destroying and honoring the "savage," that was denigrating "savagery" in the Indians while celebrating it in whites.

When Frederick Jackson Turner described the closing of the frontier in 1893, he created a memorable image of how the white frontiersman went through a process of deevolution back to the "savage," absorbing the natives' strength, cunning, energy, and independence, qualities that he would retain even as he once again regained his "civilized" status: that, in fact, is what made the distinctive American character, said Turner, a mixture of savage and civilized traits. Turner, who was a great admirer of and often quoted Whitman's Western poems to his university history classes, no doubt gathered some of his crucial insights from the poet. For Turner, as for Whitman, the individual who was uniquely American was a "friendly and flowing savage."

In Webster's 1847 *American Dictionary*, Whitman would have found the ambivalence about "savagery" embodied in the very definition: while Webster traced the etymology of the word to the Latin *silvicola*, "an inhabitant of a wood," he went on to offer a rambling description that embodied the very paradoxes that Whitman was working with in his "friendly and flowing savage":

> A human being in his native state of rudeness; one who is untaught, uncivilized, or without cultivation of mind or manners. The *savages* of America, when uncorrupted by the vices of civilized men, are remarkable for their hospitality to strangers, and for their truth, fidelity, and gratitude to their friends, but implacably cruel and revengeful toward their enemies. From this last trait of the savage character, the word came to signify, (2) A man of extreme, unfeeling, brutal cruelty; a barbarian.

Webster's definition underscores the association of sylvan existence with brutal behavior by offering the example of the American Indian (an example that, significantly, was removed by Chauncey Goodrich and Noah Porter when they revised the *American Dictionary* in 1864). American Indians, Webster posits, are models of virtue "when uncorrupted by the vices of civilized men," but they are "cruel and revengeful toward their enemies," and thus they are people of no feelings, of "brutal cruelty." This definitional slippage from innocent virtue to unbridled vice tracks the response of the culture toward its natives. Whitman and others would come to see the irony in taking the natives to task for their cruelty toward their enemies: Birch Coulee, Sand Creek, Rosebud, Wounded Knee, and countless other massacres during Whitman's adult life would demonstrate beyond doubt that Webster's second definition of "savage" applied at least as effectively to the white man as to the Indian.

While the savage, by this definition, can be very human, his gentle naive humanity is woven into a pattern that includes his dangerously uncivil behavior: he is hopelessly inconsistent and unpredictable, like a wild animal, by turns gentle and brutal. So, for Webster, "civilization" is "the state of being refined in manners from the grossness of savage life," and "savagism" is "the state of rude, uncivilized men"; each concept simply defines the other by opposition, and "savage" becomes precisely that behavior that "civilized" humans, by definition, do not engage in.

Roy Harvey Pearce used Webster's 1828 definitions of "savage," "savagism," and "civilization" (definitions that remained unchanged in the 1847 Webster's) as the epigraph for his *Savagism and Civilization,* a book that can be read as an extended meditation on the implications of how the American culture defined those words. For Pearce, Webster's definitions embodied the "American theorizing about the Indian" that led to the culture's belief in "the savage's essential inferiority, the final inferiority of even his savage virtues" (76, 95). While Pearce does not quote Webster's definitions of the adjectival form of "savage," that entry contains in many ways the most revealing meanings: Webster begins by tracing the etymology of the word to French, Armenian, Italian, Spanish, and Latin words meaning "a wood," then goes on to give a series of definitions that cumulatively sharpen the particular edge the word had gained in the American experience:

> 1. Pertaining to the forest; wild; remote from human residence and improvements; uncultivated; as, a *savage* wilderness. . . .
> 2. Wild; untamed; as *savage* beasts of prey.
> 3. Uncivilized; untaught; unpolished; rude; as, *savage* life; *savage* manners. . . .
> 4. Cruel; barbarous; fierce; ferocious; inhuman; brutal; as a *savage* spirit.

The series reads as if it is a developing set of circumstances moving inexorably to a particular condition—as if remoteness from "human residence and improvements" in an "uncultivated" place leads to "wild," "untamed" behavior because one has never been properly polished or taught the virtues of civilization, and this lack of polish, this rudeness, perversely blossoms as cruelty, barbarity, and brutality: remoteness from human residence, in other words, leads inevitably to inhumanity.

At times Whitman used "savage" very much in line with Webster's definitions: saluting the world, looking into "vapors exhaling from unexplored countries," he says he can "see the savage types, the bow and arrow, the poison'd splint" (*LG* 144). But most of the time when Whitman employs the word in his poetry, he does so in ways that undermine Webster's sure dichotomy between "savagery" and "civilization." We have already seen how Whitman's call for the "friendly and flowing savage" resonates with the culture's growing ambivalence about the loss of the "savage" side of life, the side of life that civilization seemed to repress. He uses the word continually as a kind of linguistic lure, to draw the "savage" close to him, to see the savage within himself; as he looks to the "Unnamed Lands" of the distant past, he sees how some of the people stand "naked and savage": "Afar they stand, yet near to me they stand" (*LG* 372). In "Song of Prudence," Whitman proposes that wisdom and moral virtue do not reside only or even necessarily with the refined and well-taught, and he collapses the "savage" into the full spectrum of human experience and action:

> Who has been wise receives interest,
> Savage, felon, President, judge, farmer, sailor, mechanic, literat,
>   young, old, it is the same.
>
> <div align="right">(<i>LG</i> 374)</div>

And while in the Platte Canyon, on his 1879 journey to the West, Whitman sensed the same wild "Spirit that form'd this scene" at work within his own soul: "I know thee, savage spirit—we have communed together" (*LG* 486). In the poem he chose as the conclusion to the body of *Leaves* ("So Long!"), Whitman offers a long series of announcements of what will eventually emerge in America; the poem culminates with the line: "I announce a race of splendid and savage old men" (*LG* 504): part of the emerging new Union would be a new "adhesiveness," and the "splendid and savage old men" will be a key part of the compact, vital and alive and challenging the notion that authority and power reside with the cultivated and the mannered. Whitman was aware that a civilization that repressed the savage or that pretended the savage did not exist within its boundaries was an artificial and self-blinding nation. So he would call his own poetry "my savage song" (*LG* 355) and would recognize "my wilful and savage soul's volition" (*LG* 119), always looking for ways to break down the barriers between savage and civilized, to achieve the wholeness that the culture seemed bent on dividing in half, to see within himself, a savage old man, rudeness and insolence and even brutality ("To taste the savage taste of blood—to be so devilish!" [*LG* 180]), for he knew that the real savagery was not external to civilization, but rather was buried at its heart:

> The devilish and the dark, the dying and diseas'd,
> The countless (nineteen-twentieths) low and evil, crude and savage.
>
> <div align="right">(<i>LG</i> 554)</div>

Through his subtle weaving of the word "savage" into the fabric of his poetry, then, Whitman created a text that embodied qualities of the Indian that the culture at large defined in negative ways, and then he shifted the meaning: the "savage" came to be not the brutal native out there, but the wild vitality within the soul. And it was the savage soul of white America, after all, that imposed the word and concept of savagism on the native peoples of this continent.

II. "CUSTER'S LAST RALLY"

In August 1881, Whitman sat for an hour in front of a massive new painting by John Mulvany entitled *Custer's Last Rally* and wrote a long meditation on it, which he published the next year in *Specimen Days;* he had never described any painting in such detail before. The giant (twenty by eleven feet) canvas was on a national tour, beginning a decade's travel that would make it one of the most familiar and popular paintings in nineteenth-century America. Whitman was transfixed by this haunting image that captured the history of the American West as it had been lived during his adult life; it was a summarizing emblem: "Altogether a western, autochthonic phase of America, the frontiers, culminating, typical, deadly, heroic to the uttermost." Whitman saw the painting as distinctively American, noting "an almost entire absence of the stock traits of European war pictures." But for all of its power and native artistry, the painting did not make for easy viewing: one needed, Whitman said, "good nerves to look at it." And seeing it only once would not suffice: "It needs to be seen many times—needs to be studied over and over again." Like the event it portrayed—the violent tableau of white man against Indian, of the new westward-flowing savage claiming nativity on this land against the original native savage (*this* was the "autochthonic phase of America," the violent seeking of sanction to the title "native")—this painting needed to be replicated to be understood, to settle into a pattern: "I could look on such a work at brief intervals all my life without tiring," Whitman notes, and of course he *had* looked in on such events (the endless battles between whites and Indians) at regular intervals from his childhood throughout his life. What made the painting "grim and sublime," "very tonic to me," with a bracing "ethic purpose below all" was the fact that it incorporated the repeated encounters of white and red and cast them in a condensed image onto a huge canvas in all their tangled ambiguity: the scene struck Whitman as "dreadful, yet with an attraction and beauty that will remain in my memory." The painting also struck Whitman as intensely realistic, with "no tricks": "It is all at first painfully real, overwhelming. . . . The physiognomy of the work is realistic and Western" (*PW* 275–76). But what was "real" in the artificial and highly composed image was not its physical accuracy (there were, of course, no white survivors to assess the accuracy of any image

Figure 1. John Mulvany, *Custer's Last Rally*. Kansas State Historical Society, Topeka.

of *that* battle), but its tensed ambivalence about the two groups it portrayed, an ambivalence that Whitman shared and struggled with his whole life.

The white men in the painting are a "great lot of muscular, tan-faced men," reminding Whitman of his own image of post–Civil War pioneers, those "tan-faced children" of "the youthful sinewy races" in his 1865 "Pioneers! O Pioneers!" In Whitman's poem, these pioneers are pursued by "those swarms upon our rear . . . ghostly millions frowning there behind us urging"; in this case swarms of white people from the past, urging the pioneers on to greater accomplishments, or swarms of the recent Civil War dead, urging the survivors on to deeds worthy of the sacrifices made for them (*LG* 229–30). In the painting, the pioneers face a different swarm: "swarms upon swarms of savage Sioux, in their war-bonnets, frantic . . . like a hurricane of demons." Wherever in art there are "swarms" of people, humans turned into undifferentiated vast force (a hurricane), there are individuals to stand up against and be defined by their difference from the swarm. In the painting, a number of individuals emerge in contradistinction to the swarm; the primary one, of course, is Custer himself, even given an uncharacteristic haircut (Mulvany had altered Custer's image at the last minute, shortening his "long yellow locks") to emphasize his civilized resistance: "Custer (his hair cut short) stands in the middle, with dilated eye and extended arm, aiming a huge cavalry pistol." Around him are individuated men—"death ahold of them, yet every man undaunted, not one losing his head"—singled out by the "every" and the "one," facing the swarm (*PW* 275–76).

But the ambiguities enter in when we examine Whitman's reactions to the Indians in Mulvany's painting, for they are of two types: on the one hand, savage, massed, and undifferentiated, as we have seen, but on the other hand, individual, large, heroic. In the background are the "swarms upon swarms of savage Sioux," but in the foreground are "two dead Indians, herculean, . . . very characteristic." For Whitman, Indians—when they were alive and in large groups—were worthy of extinction; isolated, alone, dead, or dying, they were noble and worthy of preservation. Other early commentators on the painting found these two dead Indians to have a "hideous countenance" and "features . . . horribly savage, even in death" (Taft 370). But Whitman sees no hideous savagery in the giant figures, only a kind of mythic largeness (*PW* 275–76).

In 1876, within days of the news of the Battle of Little Big Horn, Whitman had written a poem about Custer's last stand, a poem that has often been read as a jingoistic endorsement of Custer's bravery. It is instructive to compare Whitman's poetic visualization of the battle with Mulvany's painting that would so transfix him five years later. Whitman's Custer, with his "tawny flowing hair in battle," is clearly a different figure from Mulvany's shorn, controlled figure; he carries "a bright sword in [his] hand" rather than a "huge cavalry pistol" (many early romantic representations of the battle portrayed sabers as the main weapons [Taft 365, 367n, 382]), and unlike Mulvany's more realistic soldier, Whitman's Custer is portrayed as a hero straight out of romantic legend, is addressed as "thee," is in fact part of a historic chain of heroism, one who "Conti. es yet the old, old legend of our race." Whitman pictures the "little cir 'e" of men, "with their slaughter'd horses for breastworks," somet ing quite different from the "great lot" of men in Mulvany's painting (though Mulvany, too, portrays "The slaughter'd or half-slaughter'd horses, for breastworks," something that Whitman ironically finds a "peculiar feature" of the painting, even though it is one of the few things that Mulvany's portrayal shares with his [PW 276]). But in Whitman's poem, the Indians are virtually absent; the battle takes place in the lands of "the dusky Sioux," but the landscape is described only as "wild" and "lonesome" and silent, a "fatal environment" in which there is a mere mention of an "Indian ambuscade" but no real signs of actual Indians. The poem is finally more about Whitman's own "dark days," his reduced life in a reduced materialistic America, searching desperately for any signs of vital American ideas and ideals—"Lone, sulky, through the time's thick murk looking in vain for light, for hope"; the poet is looking west for a glimmer of a heroic democratic individual, some sort of reborn Civil War hero who could stir up the old fires of hope. Custer was the best that current events could offer. So, for Whitman, Custer ends up aptly described as "Desperate and glorious," and there is clearly some desperation on Whitman's part in having to cast up Custer as the model of American glory (LG 483–84).

The absence of the Indians in Whitman's poem tells us much about his conflicted and conflicting response to the American natives, for at first glance Indians seem absent not only in this poem but in all his poetry. Certainly we don't think of Whitman as a writer who dealt in depth with the problems of American Indians or devoted himself to telling their stories. But a more careful look at his work reveals a surprising frequency of Indian imagery. And that imagery reveals a tortured ambivalence about the role America's natives would play in the development of the country's character; it is an ambivalence so deep that by the time of Custer's last stand, the only way Whitman could deal with it was to leave the Indians out of the picture.

III. "WHITMAN THOUGHT THEY WERE HIS OWN"

In 1849, after Whitman had resigned as editor of the Brooklyn Freeman, a rival editor bid him a facetious farewell: Whitman, "hot-headed" and "full of egotism," is, said the editor, "what you call a civilized but not a polished *Aborigine*. And, by the way, it has been asserted by one of his brother Editors that he is a lineal descendent from some Indian tribe, with what truth we will not venture to say" (quoted in Rubin 223). There is no truth at all, of course: this sarcastic portrait of Whitman as the American primitive is the only recorded suggestion that Whitman actually had Indian blood in him. He did once point with pride, though, at the fact that one of the early Whitmans was "a great linguist, and sometimes acted in the courts as interpreter with the Indians" (*PW* 353), and there have even been several suggestions that Whitman was a spiritual compatriot of Indians. Maurice Mendelsohn has investigated what he calls a "kinship between Whitman's poetry and the folklore of . . . the Indians" and concludes that many of his poems "resemble American Indian folklore both in form and spirit" (25, 28). Norma Wilson claims that no "Ameropean" before Whitman had ever "approximated so closely the Native Americans' conception of the spiritual and commonplace as one"; she does not see Whitman's perspective as Native American but believes "that the important source and intention of his art were essentially the same as those of Native American writers," and she points out parallels between Whitman's thought and that of Lame Deer (14, 15). William Least Heat Moon, a contemporary Osage writer, endorses the resemblance and fuses Whitman's ways and native ways in his book *Blue Highways,* a record of his journey on what is left of the "open road" in America, driving his van named Ghost Dancing, carrying two guidebooks: Whitman's *Leaves of Grass* and John Neihardt's *Black Elk Speaks* (8). Joseph Bruchac, a contemporary American Indian poet, senses the kinship too; he finds "Whitman's spirit" in the works of recent Native American writers like Leslie Silko and claims that "Whitman's celebration of the earth and natural things, his precise namings, are very much like Native American song" ("Song of Myself" echoes, he says, the Navajo Night Chant) (Perlman 276).

The problem with finding "Whitman's spirit" in Native American works is that his spirit is many-sided and changeable. There is a Whitman spirit that is imperial and dominating, a spirit that can chant "we the virgin soil upheaving, / Pioneers! O Pioneers!," that can sing the song of the broadax, that can imagine the last redwoods gladly giving themselves up to the axes of "the superber race" (*LG* 230, 207). But there is also a Whitman spirit that absorbs and caresses, that catalogs and celebrates difference, that extols a self that embodies diversity: "Of every hue and caste am I, of every rank and religion, / . . . I resist any thing better than my own diversity" (*LG* 45). So, while we may agree with Bruchac that Whitman's spirit can be found in the works of recent American Indian writers, we need to be careful about clarifying just which Whitmanian spirit manifests itself where.

The dominating and imperialistic side of Whitman's spirit, in fact, has led some contemporary Native American writers to view Whitman in purely negative terms: Maurice Kenny, a Mohawk poet, mourns Whitman's "indifference" to the Indian and believes Whitman's heroes are the Custer-like scouts, frontiersmen, and Indian fighters: "Whitman, apparently, was a proponent of the *manifest destiny* bilge" (108), and he "closed his ears and shut his eyes to the Indians' death cries" (113). The contemporary American poet W. S. Merwin, who has long identified himself with American Indian causes, voices similar concerns: "It makes me extremely uneasy when [Whitman] talks about the American expansion and the feeling of manifest destiny in a voice of wonder. I keep thinking about the buffalo, about the Indians, and about the species that are being rendered extinct." The most extended condemnation of Whitman's attitude toward American Indians is Leadie M. Clark's 1955 study in which he charges that "Whitman might be construed as advocating genocide in the United States." In Clark's reading, Whitman believed "the Indians were not to be allowed to exist as an independent race of people," and "the Indian was marked as the man who must vanish": "The Indian was to be allowed no place in the developing society, and his contribution could only be the bequeathal of his past to the conquerors of his land" (68, 48, 51, 53, 56). There is some truth to Clark's portrayal of Whitman, of course, but it is an incomplete picture, a simplistic analysis of a highly complex mesh of attitudes.

Simon Ortiz, a poet from Acoma Pueblo, in his book-length poem *From Sand Creek,* records a growing ambivalence toward Whitman that helps illuminate Whitman's ambivalence about Indians. In a prose gloss to his poem, Ortiz inscribes his growing uncertainty: "When I was younger—and America was young too in the 19th century—Whitman was a poet I loved, and I grew older. And Whitman was dead" (80). Whitman remains for Ortiz a mystery, at once both the spiritual leader of America's destructive urgings of manifest destiny and the leader of the resistance to those destructive impulses, the poet of love and nature. In *From Sand Creek,* he raises the vexing question of how the poet would have reacted to the news of the Sand Creek massacre of Cheyennes in 1864 when the U.S. commanding officer ordered his troops to "kill and scalp all, big and little; nits make lice" (quoted in Drinnon 502); over a hundred Cheyenne and Arapaho women and children and twenty-eight men were slaughtered by more than seven hundred U.S. troops. Ortiz can imagine Whitman reacting with sorrow to America's bloody westering process, but he can also imagine him reacting with joy, and—the most troubling possibility of all—he can imagine him not reacting at all:

                    They wasted
            their sons and uncles
            as they came westward,
            sullenly insisting
            that perhaps, O Whitman,
            O Whitman, he was wrong
            and had mis-read the goal
            of mankind.
                        And Whitman
            who thought they were his own—
            did he sorrow?
            did he laugh?
            Did he, did he?
                                    (81)

We recall Whitman's response to the 1889 Oklahoma betrayal of the Indians, how he found it a "funny affair altogether." Ortiz sees the failure
of Americans to absorb the Indian, to manifest the friendly and flowing
savage, as leading to the construing of the Native American as alien and
other, as savage and primitive, as worthy of extermination. If the Whitman of 1855 articulated the dream of amalgamation, of absorption and
open embrace, by the time of the Sand Creek massacre this Whitman
and his dream had died:

            O Whitman
            spoke for them,
            of course,
                        but he died.
            That shed their sorrow
            and shame
            and cultured their anxiety.
            They spoke an eloquent arrogance
            by which they thought
            they would be freed.
                                    (81)

Once the sorrow and the shame were shed, once white anxiety was chan-
neled into cultural activity, Ortiz suggests, Native Americans became
mere hindrances to be wiped out. Sand Creek can be read as a symptom
of white America's cultured anxiety.

    The conflicting reactions of critics as well as of American Indian writ-
ers to Whitman's attitudes are understandable, for Whitman's association
with the American Indian is a deep and tangled one, and it has never
been more than superficially investigated. He had a lifelong fascination
with Indians, and he expressed that fascination in many forms, in many
moods, on a myriad of occasions. His attitudes toward the Indians—a

contradictory but characteristically American mix of disdain and admiration, of desires to absorb natives and find his antecedents in them fused with desires to distance himself from them—help to define a central problem in our culture's troubled relationship with its native people and let us see how Whitman was bound by the biases and preconceptions of his time, as well as how he occasionally and remarkably transcended them.

IV. THE TRAPPER AND THE RED GIRL

A fascination with Indians was, of course, not uncommon for a writer living during the years of the closing of the American frontier; Whitman was planning his own life work, *Leaves of Grass,* just as the ethnologist Henry Rowe Schoolcraft was issuing his massive study *History, Condition, and Prospects of the Indian Tribes of the United States* (1851–57) and just as the anthropologist Lewis Henry Morgan was publishing the first of his pioneering accounts of Indian tribes. *Leaves* appeared the same year as Longfellow's *Hiawatha,* a poem that cashed in on the national fascination with Indians; even Whitman liked *Hiawatha,* admiring its "Indian process of thought" (*NUPM* 5:1730). Whitman knew George Catlin, the painter of Indians and chronicler of tribal customs, and was a supporter of the movement to have the United States buy Catlin's gallery as the foundation for a national museum; as noted, his final years were presided over by a Catlin painting of the Seminole chief Osceola, given him by the artist, which hung on a wall in his Camden home (*NUPM* 241; Rubin 121; *WWC* 6:400). In Washington, he enjoyed visiting the Smithsonian to view John Mix Stanley's Indian paintings (*NUPM* 2:530). Whitman encountered actual Indians as a boy on Long Island and as a young editor in New Orleans (*PW* 606). He saw Indian troops who fought in the Civil War (*C* 212) and admired General Grant's military secretary, Colonel E. S. Parker, a Seneca Indian whose "squa mother," in a gesture Whitman approved of, refused to succumb to Anglo convention by choosing never to wear a bonnet (*NUPM* 347). Whitman was the only major American poet actually to work in the Indian Bureau of the Department of the Interior, and for the half-year he was there in 1865, he met several impressive Indian delegations and had "quite animated and significant conversations with them" (*PW* 579); on his western trip in the 1870s, he saw a "squad of Indians at Topeka" (*NUPM* 3:1039), and he visited a Chippewa settlement during a trip to Canada in 1880. Indians were a major part of Whitman's actual and imaginative life, and as he developed his distinctive American aesthetic, Indians became a crucial part of his ongoing poetic project. Setting out to absorb America, to open his lines democratically and indiscriminately to the world around him, Whitman was aware that American Indians would need to be part of the song of himself, but he also realized that his celebration of America's progressive expansion undermined any easy celebration of the natives that that expansion was displacing. In a manuscript notebook from the late 1850s, Whitman noted plans for a *"poem of the aborigines,"* one that would embody "every principal aboriginal trait, and name" (*NUPM* 1:275). He never wrote that poem, but, from the beginning, *Leaves of Grass* was more dedicated to that project than is generally recognized. (One early reviewer of *Leaves* actually noted the central importance of Whitman's concern with the Indian, though the insight was quickly lost; Whitman's style, said this reviewer, is "a fitting measure for the first distinctive American bard who speaks for our large scaled nature, for the red men who are gone, for our vigorous young population" [C.P.P., "Walt Whitman's New Volume," *Saturday Press* (June 23, 1860), 1:5]).

In his 1855 preface, as Whitman cataloged the ways "a bard is to be commensurate with a people," he noted, "To him enter the essences of real things and past and present events—of the enormous diversity of temperature and agriculture and mines—the tribes of red aborigines." The aborigines were to be an essential part of "the great psalm of the republic" (*LG* 711–12). In 1856, Whitman would portray this new American bard, "His spirit surrounding his country's spirit, unclosed to good and evil . . . / Surrounding just found shores, islands, tribes of red aborigines" (*LG* 344). And in "Pictures," the manuscript poem that anticipates the 1855 *Leaves of Grass,* Whitman catalogs the "many pictures" of his world, of his fantasies, and of history—the pictures that compose his imagination—and again Indians have their place: "A string of my Iroquois, aborigines—see you, where they march in single file, without noise, very cautious, through passages in the old woods" (*LG* 647). In his drafts for the poem, he celebrates the exotic domestic center of the Chippewas: "And here a tent and domestic utensils of the primitive Chippewa, the red-faced aborigines, / See you, the tann'd buffalo hides, the wooden dish, the drinking vessels of horn" (*LG* 649).

The first edition of *Leaves* (1855) contains twelve poems; five of them explicitly embody Indians. In his catalog of human faces (in the poem later entitled "Faces"), Whitman demonstrates that all people "show their descent from the Master himself": "I except not one . . . red white or black, all are deific. . . ." (He affirms this antidiscriminatory stance in "I Sing the Body Electric": "Examine these limbs, red, black, or white, they are cunning in tendon and nerve" [*LG* 126, 98].) And in the 1855 poem that would become "To Think of Time," Whitman again makes an effort, somewhat strained with double negatives, not to exclude the Indians from those he "shall go with," those who are part of the universal soul: "The common people of Europe are not nothing . . . the American aborigines are not nothing, / A Zambo or a foreheadless Crowfoot or a Camanche is not nothing" (*LGV* 106). "I see not merely that you are polite or whitefaced," says Whitman in the poem that would later become "A Song for Occupations," as he looks to absorb life beyond the genteel surface: "Iroquois eating the warflesh—fishtearer in his lair of rocks and sand . . . Esquimaux in the dark cold snowhouse" (*LGV* 86). In the poem later titled "The Sleepers," Whitman records a haunting dream/memory of a "red squaw" who visits his mother for an afternoon and then disappears forever (*LGV* 115–16). And in "Song of Myself," the Indian enters the long catalog of America in Section 15, where, surrounded by the "Wolverine" setting his trap on a creek near the Huron and a "connoisseur peer[ing] along the exhibition gallery," appears "The squaw wrapt in her yellow-hemm'd cloth . . . offering moccasins and bead-bags for sale" (*LG* 42). In other catalogs in "Song of Myself," Indians add essential ingredients: as Whitman absorbs Jehovah, Kronos, Zeus, Brahma, Buddha, and other deities into his universal religion, he places "Manito," the nature god of the Algonquian Indians, in his "portfolio," and as he encloses "worship ancient and modern and all between ancient and modern," dancing in "phallic processions," "minding the Koran," he also walks "the teokallis, spotted with gore from the stone and knife, beating the serpent-skin drum," thus admitting Aztec sacrifice worship into his all-absorbing faith.

The one extended image of the Indian in "Song of Myself" is the well-known passage in which Whitman imagines himself (with the help of an Alfred Jacob Miller painting) "far in the wilds and mountains" (*LGV* 11):

> I saw the marriage of the trapper in the open air in the far-west. . . .
> the bride was a red girl,
> Her father and his friends sat near by crosslegged and dumbly
> smoking. . . . they had moccasins to their feet and large thick
> blankets hanging from their shoulders;
> On a bank lounged the trapper. . . . he was dressed mostly in skins.
> . . . his luxuriant beard and curls protected his neck,
> One hand rested on his rifle. . . . the other hand held firmly the wrist
> of the red girl,
> She had long eyelashes. . . . her head was bare. . . . her coarse straight
> locks descended upon her voluptuous limbs and reached to her
> feet.

Here, this marriage on the frontier between the East and the West, the civilized and the savage, anticipates the birth of Whitman's new American character, emerging from the encounter of Europe and the New World, the refined civilization of the past penetrating the raw topography of the future: it is Whitman's first attempt to resolve the paradox of celebrating both the American Indian and the expansion of the United States. As he so often does, Whitman resolves irreconcilable opposites by marrying them, by constructing a unity that is large enough to embody both; the marriage of the Indian girl and the white man suggests that America cannot achieve fulfillment without absorbing the native it displaces, and that the native cannot achieve a fullness of meaning until absorbed into the expanding and inevitable creation of the white man. Thus, as we have seen, Whitman's suggestion of "The friendly and flowing savage" (*LG* 73) is cast in such a way that it portrays a person who is simultaneously both Whitman himself and a stereotypical Indian. As his early rival editor said, Whitman was a "civilized but not a polished *Aborigine*," straddling the frontier, looking for a formless form, trying to make himself the issue of the marriage of the trapper and the red girl, looking to join what he saw as the dumb natural eloquence of the Indian to the vocalized expression of the English language.

For Whitman, the Indian was synonymous with authenticity, a raw and unmediated experience of this land, the natural embodiment and expression of the topography. As such, the Indians' images, attitudes, words, all would become crucial elements in Whitman's poetry. Whitman once criticized Emerson's work because it was, he said, "always a *make,* never an unconscious *growth."* Emerson's writings were like "the porcelain figure" of the "Indian hunter"—"a very choice statuette too— appropriate for the rosewood or marble bracket of parlor or library." But, Whitman added, "The least suspicion of such actual . . . Indian, or of Nature carrying out itself would put all those good people to instant terror and flight" (*PW* 515–16). Whitman was out to smash the statuette, to haul the actual Indian into his poetry, to make words that didn't cushion experience but *became* experience.

V. "POISON-TIPPED ARROWS"

Whitman's fascination with the Indian extends long before the beginning of *Leaves of Grass.* One of his earliest poems, in fact, is about an Indian. "The Inca's Daughter," a newspaper verse written when Whitman was twenty, tells the story, in conventional ballad rhyme and meter, of a "captive Indian maiden" preferring death over living "ingloriously" as "the white lord's slave." She stabs herself with a poisoned arrow and gives the Spaniards a lesson in pride:

> "Now, paleface see! the Indian girl
>   Can teach thee how to bravely die:
> Hail! spirits of my kindred slain,
>   A sister ghost is nigh!"
>   (*EPF* 6–7)

Whitman is a long way yet from any marriage of the Indian and white man, any resolution of racial and experiential opposites.

Two years later, in 1842, he published a temperance novel, *Franklin Evans,* and chapter 2 is an Indian tale, later reprinted separately as a story, "The Death of Wind-Foot." It is a revenge tale about a chief named "The Unrelenting" whose only living son, Wind-Foot, is killed by a Kansi after the Unrelenting had killed the Kansi's father to avenge his older son's death: the cycle of death and grief is unbreakable. There is a "poison-tipped arrow" in this story, too, and the bathos is just as deadly as in "The Inca's Daughter." But Whitman's method of framing this tale in *Franklin Evans* anticipates a deepening of his concern for the Indian. A group of characters are on the journey from Long Island to New York City, and one of the journeyers tells the tale; he is a Whitman-like figure, a "sportsman" with a "fondness for prying into the olden history of this, his native island; a sort of antiquarian taste for the stories and incidents connected with the early settlers, and with the several tribes of Indians who lived in it before the whites came." He sounds, in fact, much like the Whitman of 1861, who would himself write a long series of articles called "Brooklyniana," in which he would indulge in exactly this antiquarian taste, telling of the first settlers and aboriginal inhabitants of Long Island. The sportsman of the novel dwells "with much eloquence upon the treatment the hapless red men had received from those who, after dispossessing them of land and home, now occupied their territory, and were still crowding them from the face of their old hunting-grounds," again sounding much like Whitman, who in an 1850 newspaper piece wrote:

> Alas! that was a bad day for the red man—that day, nearly two centuries and a half ago, when the Half-moon sailed up these waters, with the first civilized visitors . . . to the island of Manhattan, and its long brother nearby. Poets have sucked all the juice so completely, however, out of this sort of reflection that I may as well forebear,—though to tell the truth, I feel powerfully like adding to the heap. (*PR* 34)

Later, in "Brooklyniana," Whitman, touring Montauk, would take pride in the fact that

> the long peninsula contains many thousands [of] acres, lying comparatively waste. And it makes one think better of humanity when he doth discover such a fact as I did in my travels, that the valuable tract of land is kept thus unseized and unsold by the town of Easthampton, principally because the few remaining Indians hold in it a usufructuary interest, or right of enjoying and using it. (*UPP* 2:316–17).

The sportsman goes on to point to rum as "the greatest curse ever introduced" among the Indians: "A whole people—the inhabitants of a mighty continent—are crushed by it, and debased into a condition lower than the beasts of the field." The Indians "drink this fatal poison"—rum is the vengeful poisoned arrow that the white man uses to murder the Indian—and find themselves "deprived not only of their lands and what property they hitherto owned, but of everything that made them noble and grand as a nation!" The listeners on the journey are literally, though only temporarily, sobered by this horrifying tale: "We could not but feel the justice of his remarks" (*EPF* 133). The temperance moral is clear: like the endless revenge cycle of the warring Indian tribes, the poison of rum will come back to destroy the white man who used it as a weapon to destroy the Indian.

Whitman wrote another Indian tale in the 1840s, called *Arrow-Tip,* later revised as *The Half-Breed: A Tale of the Western Frontier.* This novella is set on "one of the upper branches of the Mississippi" in a new settlement that only recently had been "a tangled forest, roamed by the savage in pursuit of game." If Whitman's idealized "friendly and flowing savage" in "Song of Myself" was the unifying and noble offspring of "the marriage of the trapper" and "a red girl," the main character of this story is the fragmented, dark other side of such Indian–white coupling: here the half-breed is Boddo, a deformed and deceitful amalgam of the worst qualities of both races, a "monstrous abortion." Boddo's father is a white hunter-adventurer who repents of his "wild and wayward course of life" and becomes a monk; Boddo's mother is presented to us only as an "Indian girl." Arrow-Tip and his brother, the Deer, are purebred Indians, and so they, of course, are noble and doomed. Boddo lies and tricks his way into having Arrow-Tip hanged for a murder that never took place, and the Deer vanishes into the sunset: "Many hundred miles distant, an Indian leader, the remnant of his family, led his tribe still farther into the west, to grounds where they never would be annoyed, in their generation at least, by the presence of the white intruders" (*EPF* 272, 291).

VI. "UNLIMN'D THEY DISAPPEAR"

We can see that, to this point, most of Whitman's attitudes toward the Indian finally amount to little more than a melange of savagist stereotypes—what Roy Harvey Pearce and others have defined as savagism, a cultural construct that portrays Indians as generally of a lower order than white Americans, as childlike hunters, innocents whose every encounter with civilization corrupted them. Indians, in the savagist view, were incapable of adaptation and improvement, bound to arcane traditions, and superstitious and lazy. Alone, solitary, they could be admirable noble vestiges, like the Inca's daughter or Arrow-Tip; but as tribes, in groups, they were dangerous, cunning, cruel, like the Unrelenting's tribe in perpetual combat with the Kansi tribe, or, as Whitman said in 1850, like "the aboriginals of Long Island"—a "tolerably war-like people . . . frequently involved in disputes and hostilities, accompanied by all the savage cruelty known to be practiced among them toward enemies" (*PR* 33). Given all of these qualities, Indians were doomed to extinction, doomed to evaporate before the inexorable progress of civilization, to which they could never accommodate themselves. White Americans might be saddened or moved by this inevitable loss, but they would acquiesce to it nonetheless. (It was a widespread attitude in nineteenth-century American culture and one that Whitman could well have picked up in cleverly articulated form from Frances Wright, whose works he studied and admired.) Frederick Jackson Turner, in his influential frontier thesis, endorsed the idea that it was "the universal disposition of Americans to emigrate to the Western wilderness, in order to enlarge their dominion over inanimate nature," and felt that the Indians were devalued by being identified with that "inanimate nature," victims of "an expansive power . . . inherent" in Americans, so that "long before the pioneer farmer appeared on the scene, primitive Indian life had passed away" (Turner 36). In Turner's scheme, Indians were not decimated as America manifested itself on the continent, but rather they magically "evolved" into the hunter or trapper, who in turn evolved into the rancher, who evolved into the farmer, who evolved into the townsman, who evolved into the city-dweller. Whitman was fond of portraying a similar almost instant evolution among the "war-like" Long Island Indians once they were absorbed into the white man's ways: "That the Indians of Long Island . . . have the germs of a good intellectual development in them, has been proved through the cases of several native children, brought up in white families and educated thoroughly" (*PR* 32). But for Whitman such cases were always the exception; late in his life, he would still be recalling the failure of Indians to be "informed" by white institutions of education; he recalls his conversations with early authorities on Indian life:

> When I was a young man, these men were interested with others in educating Indians. They reasoned: we will select samples out of the tribes, put them in the schools, colleges,—inform them—use them to our ways—then send them forth among their people, to enlighten, to reform them. And so they persevered—sent out many men in this way—with the usual result: one out of a dozen would come to a little something, the others almost totally relapse. (*WWC* 6:56)

The easy assumptions here—that "our ways" are superior, that "inform[ing]" the Indians will lead to their "reform[ing]" other Indians— are instructive, for the concept of "form" is for Whitman the key: if white ways can be injected into the natives so that they are formed into "us" from within—"inform[ed]"—then they will be "use[d]" to our ways just as we "use them" to endorse our ways. Then, fully "inform[ed]," they will be ready for the larger effort of "reform[ing]" their people, "us[ing]" them all to our ways. But the effort at in-formation and re-formation failed, ended in collapse and "relapse": the native material was too rigidly formed to old ways, could not be reformed even when informed of the new and superior ways. The superior natives become, then, by definition, those rare few who re-form themselves into us, who leap evolutionary generations in their desire to be used by our ways. So Whitman celebrated Indians who had in effect evolved into white men, like the Reverend Samuel Occum, "the glory of the Indian nation," who, after he became a Presbyterian minister, "taught . . . the little red children" and left descendents who carried on the evolutionary disappearance act as they "intermarried with the whites." Another "very pious" Indian preacher was Paul Cuffee, whom Whitman admired because he "labored earnestly to restrain his countrymen from their vices and degrading habits," one of which was no doubt the rum curse; even the good Reverend Occum "had one failing . . . being a little too much addicted to drinking." For Whitman, even the most advanced Indians still had vestigial vice trailing from them as a result of their lower evolutionary status (*PR* 32–33). Such thinking allowed the destruction of the Indians to be disguised behind an evolutionary model that saw them as somehow absorbea in us, thus absolving us of guilt.

This absorption of the Indians into the American as Indians themselves vanished from the land was a crucial concern of Whitman's. He sang of an America that was to be a "Union holding all, fusing, absorbing . . ." (*LG* 203). We have seen that he set out to assure that his song absorbed the Indians, fused them into the unifying song of himself and his country. We have also seen that he saw the Indians as inevitably vanishing— the Deer leading his people endlessly westward until there was no more West and they vanished. It is consequently not surprising that the most extended poems that Whitman wrote about Indians were of them dying. From his very early "Inca's Daughter" to his very late "Red Jacket (from Aloft)" (1884) and "Osceola" (1890), the focus was on noble death. Red Jacket, the great Iroquois leader, is pictured as "a towering human form" aloft in the clouds, watching bemused, "a half-ironical smile curving [his] phantom lips," as the puny people who displaced him and his people erect a monument to him (*LG* 519–20). And Osceola, a Seminole chief, is pictured "When his hour for death had come" as a prisoner of U.S. troops at Fort Moultrie; he puts on war paint, puts "the scalp-knife carefully in his belt," then smiles and sinks "faintly low to the floor (tightly grasping the tomahawk handle)," dying as stoically as the Inca's daughter. This poem was written, Whitman said, "almost word for word out of conversations I had with Catlin: Catlin, the great Indian man." Whitman, we have noted, lived his final years—what he called "the Indian Summer of my life" (*NUPM* 1092, 1109)—in Camden with a Catlin lithograph of Osceola hanging on his wall (*WWC* 6:400). (It is as if Whitman sensed that the demise of the Indians was analogous to his own physical decline, with his latter years truly an Indian summer—a final, brief flourish before disappearance.) The chief was a lingering presence in Whitman's life, and the final line of his poem for Osceola is quiet, parenthetical: "(And here a line in memory of his name and death.)" With the poem about Osceola, Whitman seems to be making a late acknowledgment of white betrayal of Indians, incorporating at the end of *Leaves* an oblique recognition of white racism, even while he would elsewhere ascribe Osceola's virtue to his "dash" of white blood: "Osceola was like a great many of the niggers—like Douglass—in being of mixed blood, having a dash of white, not pure Indian" (*WWC* 6:400). Osceola, a brave leader during the so-called Second Seminole War (the First Seminole War was that in which Andrew Jackson had made his reputation fighting Seminoles, Creeks, and runaway slaves in what he called "this savage and negro War" [Drinnon, 106]), led the Seminole resistance using remarkably modern guerrilla tactics; he was captured finally only by an act of treachery, when U.S. troops promised to meet him under a flag of truce and then incarcerated him—his wife was sold as a slave and he died in prison. Whitman's note to his poem ignores these facts, focusing instead on how the U.S. physicians and officers "made every allowance and kindness possible" for the chief, but then again Whitman claims to have heard the story firsthand from "one of the return'd U.S. Marines from Fort Moultrie, S.C.," where Osceola was imprisoned (*LG* 550–51). What does come through in Whitman's poem is a sense of honor betrayed and a quiet gesture toward righting the wrong by offering "a line" in *Leaves* to the Indian's bravery.

To give Indians a *line* in the song of America seemed to be Whitman's continual motivation, to absorb them into the American song before they vanished forever, to preserve them in English words. So Whitman's most successful late poem about Indians, "Yonnondio" (1887), dwells on this desire:

> A song, a poem of itself—the word itself a dirge,
> Amid the wilds, the rocks, the storm and wintry night,
> To me such misty, strange tableaux the syllables calling up;
> Yonnondio—I see, far in the west or north, a limitless ravine, with
> plains and mountains dark,

I see swarms of stalwart chieftains, medicine-men, and warriors,
As flitting by like clouds of ghosts, they pass and are gone in the
    twilight,
(Race of the woods, the landscapes free, and the falls!
No picture, poem, statement, passing them to the future:)
Yonnondio! Yonnondio!—unlimn'd they disappear;
To-day gives place, and fades—the cities, farms, factories fade;
A muffled sonorous sound, a wailing word is borne through the air
    for a moment,
Then blank and gone and still, and utterly lost.

(LG 524)

Whitman includes a note, telling us that the title is an "Iroquois term," the sense of which is "lament for the aborigines" (*LG* 524), though he reveals through his uncertainty about the meaning of the word just how distant he really was from any true understanding of native languages. In 1888, talking to Horace Traubel, he recounted his problems with the word:

> Yonnondio: you notice that name? They printed it in The Critic first, and the Critic fellows objected to it that my use of the word was not correct, not justified. You remember, see . . . I make it mean *lament* and so forth: they say, no, that is not it: Yonnondio signifies governor—was an Indian name given to the French governors sent over to this continent in colonial times. No doubt there's considerable to warrant their argument, but . . . I had already committed myself to my own meaning—written the poem: so here it stands, for right or wrong.

Whitman goes on to tell Traubel that he picked up his meaning of the word from "an old man—a wise, reticent old man—much learned in Injun tongues, lore—in Injun habits and the history of them so far as known," and he concludes that finally the argument would be "inconclusive" anyway and would remain "always as wide open at the end as at the start" (*WWC* 2:269). The word was one more sign of the unbridgeable differences between the cultures, of the essential mystery of Indians to the white man.

But what Whitman insisted on was not so much the meaning of the word as the way in which the word itself functioned as a poem, calling up the vanished wilderness and its inhabitants, reversing Turner's progressive frontier evolution as "cities, farms, factories fade" and "stalwart chieftains" appear in their place. And what Whitman laments here is not so much the loss of the Indians as the fact that there is "No picture, poem, statement, passing them to the future"—no mechanism by which they are absorbed into America: "*unlimn'd* they disappear." If only they were limned, drawn, portrayed in words, illuminated in the poet's manuscript: thus, this poem gives them words, includes them in *Leaves of Grass,* utters them as part of the American poem. Otherwise they are "blank and gone and still, and utterly lost" (*LG* 524). Without the act of absorbing them, giving them a *line,* the page that should contain them is blank, the words that should evoke them still, unuttered, "utterly lost." In the 1880s, echoing his expressed desire of thirty years earlier to write a long *"poem of the aborigines"* complete with "every principal aboriginal trait, and name," Whitman laid out plans to write a poem of "some length to be called *Yonnondio"* and vowed to do research: "get Indian acct's & books" (*NUPM* 1211); he may have been inspired by William Howe Cuyler Hosmer's lengthy and popular narrative poem called *Yonnondio, or Warriors of the Genesee.* Allen Ginsberg has gone so far as to see Whitman's brief "Yonnondio" as a remarkably deep and compact prophecy ("It's an odd little political poem at the end, warning us of Black Mesa, of the Four Corners, of the civilization's destruction of the land and the original natives there" [Perlman 251]), but clearly the poem is far less than Whitman had originally conceived. Whitman's vast plans diminished, and what began as a major project ended up imitating in its compact final form the reduced but still powerful presence of Native Americans in Whitman's overall vision. They indeed ended up limned, given only a few lines in the vast poem of *Leaves of Grass.*

But it was a line, an utterance, nevertheless, and to give the Indian voice in *Leaves* was vital. As early as 1846, Whitman had announced this concern in an editorial in the *Brooklyn Daily Eagle;* he lamented that people would flock to lectures about ancient Egypt, while programs dealing with "Indian life and past history"—the "graphic and authentic narrative of aboriginal matters"—would draw "a baker's dozen only." Whitman expresses a desire to find "some itinerant author," who, "willing to travel through wood and forest, over prairie and swamp, . . . in short, amid any and every part of what is now the margin of our cultivated American territory," could "gather up the stories of the settlers, and the remnants of Indian legends which abound among them." Then, Whitman says, we would have "the true and legitimate romance of this continent." The Indians were disappearing, utterance of them lost:

> Have we no memories of a race, the like of which never was seen on any other part of the earth—whose existence was freedom—whose language sonorous beauty? Far, far in the darkness of times past, we may turn our fancy—and bring up the spectres of the Brown Men, with their stately forms, and their flashing eyes, and their calm demeanor— and say, Are *these* not the proper subjects for the bard or the novelist? Who can produce better? (*GF* 2:136–37)

And the need for the American bard to capture the native American was urgent, for the Indian stock was weakening quickly:

In the course of events, it is but reasonable to suppose that not many seasons will recede, before every tangible representative of true Indian character will have passed from sight. Indeed it is almost so now. The weakened, degraded, and effeminate beings who prowl our frontier towns, make the name of their forefathers synonymous with disgrace. (*GF* 2:138–39)

This would often be the attitude Whitman took when he actually saw Indians: in 1880, visiting the Chippewa reservation in Canada, he found "nothing at all of aboriginal life or personality" (*DBN* 617). And when, around the same time, Whitman wrote his autobiographical reminiscences, he gauged the accelerating disappearance of the native; he recalls seeing "the few remaining Indians, or half-breeds" on Montauk as a young man, "but now I believe [they are] altogether extinct" (*PW* 11). The quick native vanishing act seemed to be going on all around Whitman; his notes on his 1877 journey to the New Jersey Pine Barrens record the loss: "60 years ago the Indians were quite plenty (a fragment of the Delaware tribe used to come round & work among the farmers . . .)." Whitman fondly records that "there used to be an old Indian called Joe" who "used to work around"; Joe still had a few descendants scattered about, but Whitman's incessant past tense undermines any notion of a real remaining native presence: "They were good basket makers" (*NUPM* 991).

VII. "ALL ABORIGINAL NAMES SOUND GOOD"

So what could the bard do to absorb the Indian before it was too late? "We may love the traditions of the hapless Indians—and cherish their names—and bestow those names on rivers, lakes, or States, more enduring than towering monuments of brass" (*GF* 2:138). Here Whitman announces a lifelong passion: absorbing into the muscular and malleable English language the exotic rich words of the Native Americans. He was part of a revival of interest in native names, a movement in the 1840s to absorb Indian words into the language by restoring their names to the geography of the land. Webster himself was a part of the group urging native names (though he argued that they needed to be "accommodated to a civilized people" by having pronunciation "softened" and spelling normalized [quoted in Simpson, 211]). The popular poet Lydia Sigourney had summed up the argument for the preservative effect of Indian names in a poem written in the early 1840s: "Ye say, they have all passed away, / That noble race and brave, / . . . That mid the forest where they roamed / There rings no hunter's shout; / But their name is on your waters, / Ye may not wash it out" (258).

Whitman's own notions of the power of native languages may have been prompted by his study of the chapter "Language" of Emerson's "Nature" (1836), an essay that influenced much of Whitman's work. In that essay, Emerson observed:

> Because of this radical correspondence between visible things and human thoughts, savages, who have only what is necessary, converse in figures. As we go back in history, language becomes more picturesque, until in its infancy, when it is all poetry; or all spiritual facts are represented by natural symbols. (199)

But Whitman's admiration of native words went beyond Emerson's love of their symbolic power; for Whitman there was a physical power as well. He loved the feel of their words in his mouth—"Yonnondio" was a "song, a poem of itself . . . a dirge." And part of Whitman's campaign was to realign the English tongue, tune it American, by absorbing the Indian nomenclature, the native names for this land, "Making its rivers, lakes, bays, embouchure in him, / Mississippi with yearly freshets and changing chutes . . ." (*LG* 344). Whitman's friend Richard Maurice Bucke once called "those lines of Indian names . . . one of the choice bits" in *Leaves of Grass,* and Whitman agreed (*WWC* 4:324). In his *American Primer* from the 1850s, Whitman explained,

> What name a city has—What name a State, river, sea, mountain, wood, prairie, has—is no indifferent matter.—All aboriginal names sound good. I was asking for something savage and luxuriant, and behold here are the aboriginal names. I see how they are being preserved. They are honest words—they give the true length, breadth, depth. They all fit. Mississippi!—the word winds with chutes—it rolls a stream three thousand miles long. Ohio, Connecticut, Ottawa, Monongehela, all fit. *Names* are magic.—One word can pour such a flood through the soul. (*AP* 19–20)

The sportsman who tells the Wind-Foot story in *Franklin Evans* introduces it by pointing out a lake and calling it by "a long and unpronounceable word, which he said was the Indian name for it" (*EPF* 133). Those long and unpronounceable words needed to enter into English, Whitman felt, to replace European name-impositions, to come to sound familiar, *American:*

> *Names of cities, islands, rivers, new settlements, &c.* These should/must assimilate in sentiment and in sound, to something organic in the place, or identical with it.—It is far better to call a new inhabited island by the native word, than by its first discoverer, or to call it New anything.— Aboriginal names always tell finely. . . . All classic names are objectionable. How much better Ohio, Oregon, Missouri, Milwaukee &c. Iowa than New York, Ithaca, Naples, &c. (*DBN* 705)

Whitman's belief was that *"All lies folded in names,"* and he knew that "real names never come . . . easily" (*AP* 33), so it would be necessary to undo the hasty European naming of this continent: "California is sown thick with the names of all the little and big saints. Chase them away and substitute aboriginal names" (*AP* 29–30). He expressed disappointment when the state of Washington was admitted bearing a non-Indian name, preferring "Tacoma! how fine that would have been for one of the new States!" (*WWC* 4:324). He was attracted to the proposition in the late 1880s to rename West Virginia "Kanawtha" (though he felt Virginia had "its own old long reasons for being what it is," and he could see already the imposed names taking on their own tradition) (*WWC* 4:324). He praised the name "Dakota," finding it the "right" name for the territory where "the proud & vengeful Dakota warriors had lived," and he argued that, in a similar fashion, " 'Chippewa' is the best name for the new n. w. Territory" (*NUPM* 5:1672, 1707). He admired the Indian names of towns he passed through or near on his Western trip in 1879: "Tonga-hocksa . . . Eagle Trail after a chief" (*NUPM* 3:1040). He felt relief that Indian names had "saved" many American rivers with their "Majestic & musical names—Monongahela, Alabama," but he advised, "some one should authoritatively re-name the mountains," even if it would take "an act of Congress" (*NUPM* 5:1672). Whitman's necessary American alignment of names was not a project that would deal only with *places:* "In These States, there must be new Names for all the Months of the year—They must be characteristic of America— . . . What is the name January to us?" (*DBN* 3:700–701).

Late in his life, Whitman lost hope that Indian names would become as widespread as he had hoped or that they would replace European-imposed names, but he never gave up his fervid desire to have American topography keyed to the names native to it. Occasionally Whitman reso-lutely resisted the classically imposed names because they were so foreign to the continent; Horace Traubel records in 1889 a moment when Whitman

> tried to name one of the Western rivers—a Greek name—but it "failed" him. He laughed—"It was a terrible one." I put in—"Named by the drunken pedagogue who gave names to the New York towns?" He laughed—"Probably a relative: you mean the Ithaca, Utica, Troy man?"

Whitman went on to lament city names like "Memphis," "a fearful name—with no smack of the soil whatever—yet hundreds, thousands, like it!" "The great Indian names," mourned Whitman, " 'lost like so many opportunities!' " (*WWC* 5:358).

Whitman came to think of his poetry, his own new speech tuned to conversational rhythms, away from European conventions, as aboriginal. His early notes on oratory show that he derived his characteristic emphasis on the first person, his disarming familiarity with his readers, from Indian models: "Why not mention myself by name, Walt Whitman . . . aboriginal fashion?—as in the speech of Logan [Tah-gah-jute, a Cayuga chief]? or that of Boh'ongahelas [Delaware Indian chief]?" (*NUPM* 2233). Indian names, he said, "are totally genuine—we could say of them what [Richard W.] Gilder said of my poetry—that they stand specifically alone—are not to be imitated—not to be manufactured" (*WWC* 5:488). He enjoyed sitting with friends and reciting Indian place names; "No one," he said, "has better reason for believing [in the beauty of Indian names] than I" (*WWC* 5:487). Whitman claimed he "often threatened . . . to make a collection" of Indian names—perhaps as part of his often-projected but never-realized "poem of the aborigines"; for "nothing in all language, ancient or modern" was "so significant—so individual—so of a class—as these names" (*WWC* 5:488). While Whitman says that he never actually did make such lists, some of his early notebooks do contain catalogs of Indian words (see *DBN* 670, 726); he at least initiated the project. He even toyed once with the idea of writing a play "embodying character of strength savage wildness   Indian" (*DBN* 822).

The word "Indian" itself demonstrated to Whitman the problem of European naming, of losing verbal touch with the native land. Indians were the native people of the land for whom English had only awkward terms, dispossessing names. "Indian" was a European-imposed word, meaningful only from the perspective of European history, misrepresenting, grossly misnaming, even displacing the natives of a land that the original European explorers could not see for what it was and thus named for what it wasn't. "Of course the word 'Indian' does not apply to the American aborigines," Whitman chastised in a notebook; "An Indian is a man or woman of the southern and eastern half of Asia. It confuses and vexes language to have such synonyms with contra-meanings" (*DBN* 3:709). This practice of "calling the American aborigines *Indians,*" he said, is a lesson in how "names or terms get helplessly misapplied & wrench'd from their meanings," clouding the language by allowing "a great mistake [to be] perpetuated in a word," so that even if "the mistake is rectified . . . the word remains" (*NUPM* 5:1664). Whitman, then, generally avoided the term, preferring "aborigines," with its root emphasis on "origin"; his own emerging sensitivity to the issue can be traced in his manuscripts, in which he often crosses out "Indian" in favor of "aborigine" (*NUPM* 275). The word "aborigine" actually has no clear etymology, only dim origins; it relates to "original," suggesting people that were there *ab origine,* from the beginning. But Whitman, given his fascination with etymologies, no doubt knew that there were problems with this word too—it probably derives from a botched Latin echo of the native name of some now-forgotten European tribe, the word itself doing what Western cultures seem so proficient at doing to cultures they label primitive: misnaming them, burying them in a misnomer and preserving them in wrong words so that they always seem, both topographically and linguistically, out of place. In *Rambles Among Words,* the book that Whitman may well have coauthored with the linguist William Swinton, we find a long discussion about how words of abuse and misrepresentation evolve, how the word "barbarians," for example, may be nothing but "a general imitation of a (to the Greeks) foreign tongue," thus revealing much more about the Greeks and their "infinite contempt" for "foreign nations" than about the people the word referred to. We must remember, *Rambles* tells us, that many words that appear to have "some inherent virtue and valor of their own" are in fact "poverty-stricken and impotent" (Swinton 126). Clearly "Indians" was such a word for Whitman, while "aboriginal" at least retained a satisfying echo of "original."

In the 1847 Webster's, "Indian" is defined as a "general name of any native of the Indies; as, an East *Indian* or a West *Indian*. It is particularly applied to any native of the American continent." The adjectival form of the word, said Webster, had to do with "pertaining to either of the Indies, . . . or to the aborigines of America." In this definition, Webster seems to agree with Whitman that "aborigine" is the accurate word for American natives; he defines "aborigine" as a "word not regularly formed, but [one] that has become generally prevalent" for referring to the "first inhabitants of a country," and an "aboriginal" according to Webster is any "original inhabitant," as the "Indians in America." "Native," on the other hand, is not associated by Webster with Indians (except for the one moment when he uses it in his definition of "Indian"); it is a word reserved for "one born in any place" who becomes "a native of that place, whether country, city, or town." Clearly "country, city, or town" suggests a "civilized" person. By definition, then, an Indian who had been exiled from the United States would never become a "native American." By 1864, Webster's dictionary had added to the definition of "Indian" an acknowledgment of the inaccuracy of the word: "One of the aboriginal inhabitants of America;—so called originally from the idea, on the part of Columbus and the early navigators, of the identity of America with India." Succeeding dictionaries would continue to note the error, but it wouldn't be until a century later that a general uneasiness with the word would bring about attempts at new coinages ("Amerindian," "Native Americans").

These aboriginal inhabitants, Whitman knew, formed the origin of human contact with this land; the words, legends, rituals, and stories that evolved out of their long contact with this land were therefore vital for Euro-Americans to absorb, to learn, if they were to make the land their own. But Whitman, like Webster, would never grant the Indians the word "natives." That was a word he reserved for what "real" Americans would come to be when they fully and democratically absorbed the world around them: "As for native American individuality, though certain to come . . . it has not yet appear'd" (*LG* 571; see *NUPM* 1588). In 1860 Whitman entitled his group of poems that celebrated an emerging distinctive American character *Chants Democratic and Native American*. He wanted to "promulge Native American models" so that "foreign models" would be reduced to "the second class" (*NUPM* 1588). Whitman's concern with the term "Native American" seemed calculated to wrest the name away from those who were tainting it—it was the name of a vehemently antiimmigrant, anti-Catholic, and generally antiabsorptive political party, better known as the Know-Nothings, that flourished from the 1840s until about 1860. Whitman sought to associate the quality of being native American with the qualities of absorption and democratic inclusiveness; in this sense, Indians could at best *become* a part of the native Americans, but were themselves *pre*-Americans, native to the land but not native to the country that in Whitman's view brought that land to life.

But the Indians' nativity on the land was for Whitman a vital quality. Probing his native ground for authentic origins, Whitman made an attempt to rename his own locales with aboriginal accents, calling Long Island "Paumanok" and referring to New York City as "Mannahatta." He admired the accurate name of Jamaica—a town he lived and taught in—which derived, he believed, from the Yeniachah Indians (*NUPM* 456). He insisted on the accuracy and vitality of such names, affirming that he got "Mannahatta" from two of the country's best philologists ("knowers of Indian tongues"): "How this word clung and clung!" (*WWC* 5:470). In the 1850s, he lashed out against the absurdity of naming his great democratic city after "the meanest and feeblest tyrant that ever press'd the English throne, the Duke of York, duly James the Second—the burner of women and torturer of men, for the least freedom in thought or words." Whitman was rankled that "every time the hitherto name of this city is written with the pen or spoken with the mouth it celebrates that man." "Mannahatta," then, was a far superior name for "the grandest freest and most beautiful city of the world" (*NUPM* 407–408). In 1878, Whitman records his exhilaration at seeing New York for the first time from the top of a skyscraper—"Up, up, up, in the elevator some eight nine or ten stories, to the top of the tall tower" where his "thoughts of the beauty and amplitude of these bay & river surroundings [are] confirmed" and where his conviction of "a fitter name" was "also confirmed": "*Mannahatta*—'the place around which there are hurried and joyous waters continually'—(that's the sense of the old aboriginal word)" (*NUPM* 1010–11). And late in his life, he was still explaining how "the Indians use the word to indicate a plot of ground, an island, about which the waters flow—keep up a devil of a swirl. . . . To me it is all meaning and music!" (*WWC* 5:470). In his 1860 poem "Mannahatta," he recorded his initial joy at finding the word:

> I was asking for something specific and perfect for my city,
> Whereupon lo! upsprang the aboriginal name.
>
> Now I see what there is in a name, a word, liquid, sane, unruly,
>   musical, self-sufficient,
> I see that the word of my city is that word from of old,
> Because I see that word nested in nests of water-bays, superb.

(LG 474)

And in an 1888 poem, he was still praising the "fit and noble name": "Choice aboriginal name, with marvellous beauty, meaning" (*LG* 507). Near the end of his life, even when his friend Dr. Daniel G. Brinton, a well-known anthropologist, tried to correct Whitman about the meaning of "Mannahatta" (Brinton had been told by Indians that the word meant "the place where bows are bought"), Whitman clung to his original notion: "That seems to me improbable: according to the definition I got of it, it meant some center point about which the waters whirl and storm with great vehemence . . . a point of land surrounded by rushing, tempestuous, demonic waters: it is so I have used it—and shall continue" (*WWC* 6:56). Whitman's turbulent definition was vital to him, for it allowed him to connect his place, his city, with his view of the self as a still point in the ceaseless whirl of experience:

> Trippers and askers surround me,
> . . . Battles, the horrors of fratricidal war, the fever of doubtful news,
>   the fitful events;
> These come to me days and nights and go from me again,
> But they are not the Me myself.
> Apart from the pulling and hauling stands what I am.

(LG 32)

Like Mannahatta, Whitman would be the native quiet center, formed by but apart from the unstoppable wash of life that crashed on his shores.

Magical, too, was the name of Paumanok, where Whitman started from. He often signed his early poems and newspaper essays with the pen name "Paumanok," thus associating himself with the native view of his home ground. In his "Brooklyniana" articles, he argued for the new/ old name for his island:

We have heard it suggested, (and we think the idea worth serious consideration), that the original name of this island ought on many accounts to be resumed, and made the legal and customary name again. That original name was PAUMANOK, the sense of which is . . . "the island with its breast long drawn out, and laid against the sea." This is a beautiful and appropriate signification, as the word itself is a pleasant one to the ear. (*UPP* 2:274)

Again, the native definition of place essentially characterized the position of the poet *of* that place; Whitman, like Paumanok, would stretch out on the ground, lean and loaf at his ease, absorbing the sea that surrounded him. Whitman referred to the restoration of the name as "poetic justice" for the vanished Delaware tribes: "Now that they have all forever departed, it seems as if their shades deserve at least the poor recompense of the compliment connected in preserving the old name by which they themselves designated and knew this territory" (*UPP* 2:275). The contemporary poet James Schevill, in his poem called "A Changing Inventory for Walt Whitman," turns such comments by Whitman—his love of the word "Paumanok" and its Indian associations—into a biting irony:

> *Once Paumanok,* what is it about your name, your thing, Walt?
>   we know Long Island and its commuter-luxuries,
>   Paumanok has a wistful Indian tone of memory . . .
>   We killed most of them good, Walt, the Redskins,
>   why should a commuter long for a Redskin?
>
> (30)

But if today we can see the dark and hypocritical underside to Whitman's affectionate use of the Indian word for his home place, for Whitman himself the utterance still seemed to work magic.

In "By Blue Ontario's Shore," Whitman refers to his poetry as a "savage song"; the title of that poem, situating Whitman's ruminations beside a lake that carries its Iroquois name, is another instance of his love of native place-names. During Whitman's adult life, of course, the new states entering the Union often carried native names, as did an increasing number of the rivers, lakes, mountains, and other named features within the landscapes of those states. So Whitman's hopes that Indian words and names would enter into the American dictionary were slowly realized. *Rambles Among Words* in 1859 had celebrated the fact that there was "scarce a tongue on the planet which the all-absorbing Saxon genius has not laid under contribution to enrich the exchequer of its conquering speech" (Swinton 279), and it goes on to list words that have entered the lexicon from "aboriginal American dialects," words like "tobacco," "wigwam," "Yankee," and "potato." As early as 1800, when Samuel

Johnson, Jr., and John Elliott published their *Selected, Pronouncing and Accented Dictionary* (the rudimentary forerunner of Webster's work), American lexicographers had seen the potential for identifying the emerging American language through inclusion of Americanisms, including Indian-based words; Johnson and Elliott included such things as "tomahawk" and "wampum" (Friend 12). Webster increased the number of Americanisms and included several dozen words of Indian origin; Whitman used a good many of these words in *Leaves:* in fact, it is almost as if Whitman scoured the 1847 Webster's to find the native words that had already worked their way into the language, then included them in *Leaves* so that his book would have a noticeably strong native American accent. Whitman's Indian-based lexicon includes "hickory," "moccasin," "opossum," "pecan," "moose," "persimmon," "poke-weed," "powwow," "quahaug," "raccoon," "sachem," "squaw," and "wigwam"; all of these words were available to him in the 1847 Webster's, identified there as "derived from the natives." But the overall impact of native languages on English would remain modest, far less than Whitman imagined and hoped for; today's dictionaries do not carry noticeably more Indian-based words than did the dictionaries of Whitman's time.

VIII. "SEE, IN ARRIERE, THE WIGWAM"

It was on Paumanok that Whitman first saw Indians, learned of their aboriginal money (quahog shells, among other things) and way of life, even saw "the cave of an old Indian hermit" who "must have been a pretty fair counterpart of Chingachgook" (*UPP* 2:316). In "The Sleepers," he tells what may be a true story of an Indian woman visiting the "old homestead" of the Whitmans on Paumanok and spending a day with his mother: "Her step was free and elastic. . . . her voice sounded exquisitely as she spoke." Whitman's mother is delighted and amazed at the woman's beauty, "her tallborne face and full and pliant limbs." We feel the mother's love of this native woman, and we feel Whitman's own desire for her as he recreates her in words: "The more she looked upon her she loved her." When the squaw leaves in the afternoon, the sense of loss is palpable:

> O my mother was loth to have her go away,
> All the week she thought of her. . . . she watched for her many a month,
> She remembered her many a winter and many a summer,
> But the red squaw never came nor was heard of there again.
>
> (*LGV* 116)

It is a cultural loss seen through the filter of a family memory; this squaw with her natural beauty vanishes from the real world and evanesces into a legend, enacting the imminent disappearance of an entire race. Whitman's sensitive portrayal of a maternal love for the "red squaw" stands as a quiet and uncharacteristic counterpoint to the violent decimation of the native race that America's cultural fathers would be engaging in during the very years this poem kept appearing in edition after edition of *Leaves* (1855–92).

Generally, then, by Whitman's time, the noble Indians seemed few, and his usual encounters with the natives were far different from his dream/memory of the beautiful squaw's visit; the real Indians around him did not lift his spirits, even seemed anathema to poetry: "Several specimens of men, women and children whom I saw were quite enough to take the poetry out of one's aboriginal ideas. They are degraded, shiftless, and intemperate—very much after the lowest classes of blacks" (*UPP* 313).

This racist side of Whitman's attitude coexisted with his admiration for the Indian; the paradox seems more pronounced for us today certainly than it did in the nineteenth century. The degradation that he found in modern-day Indians seemed to justify their "elimination" in the name of evolution and progress: "The nigger, like the Injun, will be eliminated: it is the law of races, history, what-not: always so far inexorable—always to be. Someone proves that a superior grade of rats comes and then all the minor rats are cleared out." (When Horace Traubel hears Whitman say this, he tells the poet, "That sounds like Darwin," and Whitman replies, "Does it? It sounds like me, too" [*WWC* 2:283].) In moods like this, Whitman felt that "amalgamation" of the races was not possible, would result only in human debilitation, in monsters like Boddo, his demented half-breed character. Thus, the Indians often appeared in his catalogs of the "Encircling . . . American Soul," but only in "arriere," in the back of the parade of progress and evolution. "After all," wrote Whitman in the 1850s, "are not the Rocky Mountain and California aborigines quite as bestial a type of humanity as any?" (*NUPM*, 1976). To such "backward races," Whitman would offer only the comfort that "I do not say one word against you away back there where you stand, / (You will come forward in due time to my side.)" (*LG* 148). But by the time these backward races came forward to him, they would have been, of course, magically transformed into whites as they themselves disappeared. So as the American soul lunged into the future, it would absorb but leave behind the vanishing native: "In arriere the peace-talk with the Iroquois the aborigines, the calumet, the pipe of good-will, arbitration, and indorsement, . . . / The drama of the scalp dance" (*LG* 174).

That terrifying drama was an all too realistic one for Whitman, and late Indian uprisings prompted his most sweeping condemnation of the aborigines. For a while he dismissed them all as regressive savages and found the idea of the noble savage nothing but sentimental rubbish. After hearing Jane Grey Swisshelm's account in 1863 of the 1862 Sioux uprising, Whitman wrote:

> It was enough to harrow one's soul. The poetical Indian is all lollypop. The real reds of our northern frontiers, of the present day, have propensities, monstrous and treacherous, that make them unfit to be left in white neighborhood. The details of their murders, mutilations, last fall in Minnesota and the violations of women and children, make as bloody and heart-rending an episode as there is in American history. (*NUPM* 565)

As people from myriad countries came to the shores of America to forge a new amalgam of identities, then these "real reds" had to make way, fade out: "See, in my poems immigrants continually coming and landing, / See, in arriere, the wigwam, the trail, the hunter's hut . . . and the backwoods village" (*LG* 27). As the frontier vanishes, transformed into civilization, the Indians disappear with it. It is this attitude that leads Leadie Clark to conclude that, for Whitman, "that the Indian was disappearing was regrettable but right, for it was a circumstance that could not be prevented. The Indian was to be allowed no place in the developing society." Clark avers that "Whitman generally excluded the Indian from his catalogs because he could find no place for the only truly native American man" (56–57).

But this is only part of the story. Whitman, as we have seen, did not exclude the Indian from the catalog of his writings; quite the opposite. While he was usually disappointed in current manifestations of the Indian, such was not always the case. Even at the time of his most sweeping condemnation of the Indians, Whitman was working his way beyond the easy route of simplistic stereotyping. Watching an army brigade on drill near the end of 1862, Whitman records in a notebook that "the drill closed with a spirited charge, the men shouting like wild Indians." Then, as if he suddenly realized the absurdity of this easy characterization, he corrects himself. He crosses out "Indians" and writes in "Comanches," at least narrowing the scope of his abuse and pulling back from outrageous generalizations. But then he goes even further: "This is an error," he writes to himself, and goes on to observe that while the men "do cry loudly," this does not reflect on the behavior of Comanches so much as it reflects on the behavior of any warriors of whatever color entering battle: "Our troops generally go in with loud cries" (*NUPM* 515). A few months later he jotted down his admiration of the First Kansas Colored Volunteers: "a fine reg't," with several companies "of Indian breed." This regiment was sent West to fight in the Indian territory, and now

```
        Checked out item summary for
             Arredondo, Edward L.
              10-16-2014 7:53PM

BARCODE: 31299004121845
LOCATION: em100
TITLE: Walt Whitman's native representat
DUE DATE: 10-30-2014

 ARCODE: 31299006669312
 OCATION: em100
 ITLE: Journeys on Old Long Island : tra
 UE DATE: 10-22-2014

BARCODE: 31299006403548
LOCATION: em100
TITLE: The Montaukett Indians of eastern
DUE DATE: 10-22-2014
```

East Meadow Public Library

1886 Front Street · East Meadow, NY 11554
516.794.2570 · 516.794.2949 (TTY)
www.eastmeadow.info

Whitman admires what at other times he condemned: "They fight like demons, use the knife, scalp the dead, &c. They are real warriors in every respect, nothing to take them back" (*NUPM* 637). In the 1860s, then, Whitman is clearly struggling (as were many Euro-Americans) with his attitudes toward the Indians, attitudes that had developed an uneasy mixture of fear and respect, horror and fascination.

In 1865, while working at the Indian Bureau at a job that he initially seemed most pleased with for its light work load, he actually encountered Indians, and they began to break through his biases, overwhelm him with the force of their personality and strength, restore some of the "poetry" to his aboriginal ideas. At times for Whitman, these "aborigines, left by time and events upon our hands" were "strange and impressive," but they were also quite human (*NUPM* 2:785). Once he told a delegation of "these Natural Kings" that "we are all really the same men and brethern together, at last, however different our places, and dress and language" (*NUPM* 2:881). But the Indians' response, an "approving chorus of guttural 'Ugh's,' " serves to undercut Whitman's affirmation of oneness and sameness. Years earlier, Whitman had noticed "one peculiarity about the Indians, under all circumstances—they are hard to be on thee-and-thou terms with." He was confused, in effect, by their refusal to be backslapping, embracing American camerados: "They will not readily talk and tell all about themselves, and where they came from, and where they are going to, to a stranger. All my attempts to 'draw them out' in this way have been met with a cool indifference" (*PR* 32–33). In fact, Whitman usually was more struck by Indians' difference from, rather than their similarity to, white Americans, but occasionally that difference made them seem superior:

> There is something about these aboriginal Americans, in their highest characteristic representations, essential traits, and the ensemble of their physique and physiognomy—something very remote, very lofty, arousing comparisons with our own civilized ideals—something that our literature, portrait painting, etc., have never caught, and that will almost certainly never be transmitted to the future, even as a reminiscence. No biographer, no historian, no artist, has grasp'd it—perhaps could not grasp it. It is so different, so far outside our standards of eminent humanity. (*PW* 2:579)

Here again is Whitman's obsession with trying to capture the Indian in words, to absorb Indians into "our" art in order to transmit them to the future. These Indians he saw in front of him could not be dismissed as mere primitives, savages: "I should not apply the word savage (at any rate, in the usual sense) as a leading word in the description of those great aboriginal specimens." Indeed, by contrast, *white Americans* at times seemed the diminished race, the evolutionary falling off from a finer form: "There were moments, as I look'd at them or studied them, when our own exemplification of personality, dignity, heroic representation anyhow (as in the conventions of society, or even in the accepted poems and plays,) seem'd sickly, puny, inferior" (*PW* 2:579). These Indians were "real American Red Men," their "savage and hardy Nature" standing in proud contrast to "the cities of the pale face" (*NUPM* 2:881).

This revelation of American society's "inferior" status is not a usual one for Whitman, but it does play into the complex of his attitudes toward the Indians. In order to reach this realization, Whitman carefully frames his statement: he is looking at "specimens" of the aborigine, and he is "certainly" seeing "many of the best"; they are "the most wonderful proofs of what nature can produce," but unlike the "degraded, shiftless and intemperate" vestigial specimens of Indians and half-breeds he had seen on Paumanok, these "aboriginal visitors" represent the other end of Darwinian law—"the survival of the fittest, no doubt—all the frailer samples dropt, sorted out by death" (*PW* 2:577). As the fit survivors of a race they are "indeed *chiefs*, in heroic massiveness, imperturbability, muscle, and that last and highest beauty consisting of strength— the full exploration and fruitage of human identity." These Indians were the culmination not of " 'culture' and artificial civilization," but of *nature,* "tallying our race, as it were, with grand, vital, gnarl'd, enduring trees, . . . humanity holding its own with the best of said trees . . . and outdoing them" (*PW* 2:577). These Indians were indeed model representatives of Whitman's "friendly and flowing savage" with "Behavior lawless as snow-flakes, words simple as grass" (*LG* 73). They were the hearty embodiments of a rugged life lived in consonance with nature, not a life artificially constructed in false and modest recoil from the "fleshy sensual, eating, drinking and breeding" (*LG* 552) that constitutes life in this world, that constitutes the life Whitman celebrated in his poetry, the life that America would have to embrace, Whitman believed, in order to fully realize its democratic potential.

IX. "LEAVING SUCH TO THE STATES THEY MELT"

So, for Whitman, depending on his moods and motivations, Indians could be the debris of evolutionary progress, the primitive versions of American selves that were left far behind, in "arriere," on the road to what the culture became, or they could be the advance guard, the model fit survivors, embodying qualities that Americans had to move *toward.* In either case, though, the Indians were doomed to extinction; if they were degraded and primitive, they would die out by the Darwinian law of the survival of the fittest; if they were themselves the fittest, they would die a noble and poignant death in the name of civilization—they were simply too good, too pure, to exist in the still unperfected present. Whitman sometimes contorts to make it all work: in the Indian Bureau, the heroic people he saw, he noted, were generally old; the best specimens were "the old or elderly chiefs, and the wise men." It's as if the Indian tribes had been thinned out, winnowed down to these few fit, heroic, and ancient samples, blazing forth in one final moment of greatness and leaving only degenerate and unfit heirs, who would soon of necessity disappear. Their fate clearly was now out of their own hands, these "five hundred? thousand . . . American aborigines, left by time & events upon our hands" (*NUPM* 786).

It might help here to recall Whitman's description of John Mulvany's painting of Custer's Last Stand, in which Whitman perceived that the Indians were of two types: on the one hand, savage, massed, and undifferentiated; on the other, individual, large, heroic. In the background are "swarms upon swarms of savage Sioux, in their war-bonnets, frantic, . . . like a hurricane of demons"; but in the foreground are "two dead Indians, herculean, . . . very characteristic." As usual for Whitman, alive and in large groups, Indians were worthy of extinction; isolated, alone, dead or dying, they were noble and worthy of preservation.

It was the heroic and noble side of the natives, their healthy attachment to American landscape, that Whitman believed he could absorb into the American consciousness via native words, stories, sounds. As the natives died out, the bard had to lead the way in ensuring that, in departing, they left us their words embodying their wisdom, buried deep in the sounds that they attached to this continent over thousands of years. So, in "Starting from Paumanok," a poem of origins, Whitman pauses "a moment . . . for America," celebrating the present and future. (This section of the poem was a late insertion; originally Whitman had conceived of the section as a separate poem, entitled "Aborigines," and as such it may represent another of his failed attempts to compose a long poem about native Americans [see *WM* lii–liii, 30–31].)

> And for the past I pronounce what the air holds of the red aborigines.
> The red aborigines,
> Leaving natural breaths, sounds of rain and winds, calls as of birds and
>   animals in the woods, syllabled to us for names,
> Okonee, Koosa, Ottawa, Monongahela, Sauk, Natchez,
>   Chattahoochee, Kaqueta, Oronoco,
> Wabash, Miami, Saginaw, Chippewa, Oshkosh, Walla-Walla,
> Leaving such to the States they melt, they depart, charging the water
>   and the land with names.
>
> (*LG* 26)

The Indians "melt" into their words, which flow into American language, nomenclature, and poems; thus the Indians are "leaving" (it's the central pun of *Leaves of Grass*)—leaving in three ways: as they "depart," vanish, *leave;* as they put forth leaf in us, *leaving* in a new spring cycle of birth; and as they are absorbed in our language and our works, charging our *leaves,* our pages, as we absorb their words that are literally their breaths, the sounds in which they breathed out their inspiration of this land. It was an old dream of Whitman's, expressed first in an 1856 article he wrote for *Life Illustrated,* in which he noted that "of all that nations help to build, nothing endures but their language, when it is real and worthy." The Indians have been left to their words and live there:

> There are, doubtless, now in use every hour along the banks of the Hudson, the St. Lawrence, the Sacramento, and the Colorado . . . words but little modified, or not modified at all, from the same use and sound and meaning they had twenty thousand years ago, in empires whose names have long been rubbed out from the memories of the earth. . . . The American aborigines, of whom a few more years shall see the last physical expiration, will live in the names of Nantucket, Montauk, Omaha, Natchez, Sauk, Walla-Walla, Chattahoochee, Anahuac, Mexico, Nicaragua, Peru, Orinoco, Ohio, Saginaw, and the like. (*NYD* 58)

The poet's job was to fight to preserve these names, for he came to discover that the words do not always persist on their own.

X. "THE PALIMPSEST ON WHICH EVERY PAGE IS WRITTEN"

And so Whitman embarked on a life-long poetic archaeological expedition; in 1888, he was still concerned with digging up and preserving America's autochthonous past: "I think now is the time for archaeology to be exploited here anyhow—especially American archaeology." He was stung by British poet Monckton Milnes's remark that "your people don't think enough of themselves . . . they do not realize that they not only have a present but a past, the traces of which are rapidly slipping away from them" (*WWC* 1:128–29). In early notebooks, Whitman had sketched out his poetics of archaeology: he believed there "were busy, populous and powerful nations" on the American continent thousands of years ago, but "no one can now tell the names of those nations." There is a "total vacuity of our letters about them, their places blank upon the map, not a mark nor a figure that is demonstrably so." Whitman was haunted by the sense of loss, by the absence of words for these original inhabitants:

> The Ruins in North America—the copper mines of Lake Superior which have been worked many centuries since—probably more than a thousand years ago, perhaps two or three thousand—the mounds in the

valley of the Mississippi—the vast ruins of Central America, Mexico and South America—grand temple walls &c., now overgrown with old trees—all prove beyond cavil the existence, ages since, in the Western World, of powerful, populous and probably civilized nations, whose names, histories, and even traditions had been lost long before the discovery of Columbus and Vespuccius. (*NF* 76–77)

The vanishing Indians, then, were the last vestiges of Atlantis-like "civilized nations" that had long since disappeared beneath the wilderness growth of America. (Such a belief was commonplace in the mid-1800s; William Cullen Bryant's "The Prairie" is built on the conceit that the aboriginal native race on this continent was noble but was displaced by the ignoble red man.) There is always, Whitman said, "the palimpsest on which every page is written" (*BG* 21), and he recommended that we should keep that in mind in reading *Leaves*. He called the United States the "greatest poem" (*LG* 709), but it was a poem written over other texts, scratched over a palimpsest of past cultures. Part of his purpose was to illuminate the subtexts, the dim lower layers of the palimpsest, those "Nations ten thousand years before these States, and many times ten thousand years before these States," those nations of which "Not a mark, not a record remains—and yet all remains." His faith was that those "billions of men" lived on in some "unseen world," but that the way they really lived on was by our poets giving them voice, reaching back, imagining them into our present and giving them room (a line) there: "Afar they stand, yet near to me they stand" (*LG* 372). For Whitman, nothing vanished, but rather all was absorbed in the widening and voracious American soul, which expands without discarding, carves out the future while giving voice to the past. So the broadax, tool of the American frontier, also "Served the mound-raiser on the Mississippi, served those whose relics remain in Central America" (*LG* 191). Americans are joined in mystical and yet palpable ways to their aboriginal past, which stands at the center of what they have become.

In 1883, Whitman still did not feel that his poetic archaeology had had the necessary effect on the country: "We Americans have yet to really learn our own antecedents, and sort them, to unify them" (*PW* 2:552). We need something to "counterbalance" (*PW* 2:553) the notion that the United States was fashioned on European models. One place to search for the necessary native antecedents, Whitman affirmed, was in "American ethnology":

> As to our aboriginal or Indian population—the Aztec in the South, and many a tribe in the North and West—I know it seems to be agreed that they must gradually dwindle as time rolls on, and in a few generations more leave only a reminiscence, a blank. But I am not at all clear about that. As America from its many far-back sources and current supplies,

develops, adapts, entwines, faithfully identifies its own—are we to see it cheerfully accepting and using all the contributions of foreign lands from the whole outside globe—and then rejecting the only ones distinctively its own—the autochthonic ones? (*PW* 2:553–54)

Whitman often argued for the value of these autochthonic sources, associating Indian song and poetry with the "florid, rich, first phases of poetry" that produced the Greek and Hebrew epics (*NUPM* 1555), and in notes for "Song of Myself," he searches for a primitive authenticity— "Something that presents the sentiment of the Druid walking in the woods . . . of the Indian pow-wow . . . of the Sacramental supper . . . of the Grecian religious rites" (*NUPM* 1312). He even saw the native singers as models for the new American poet to emulate; Whitman speaks with some envy of the "audiences for the singers and poets of those rude races, . . . [that] made the bards who spoke to them sacred and beloved" (*NUPM* 1559).

XI. WELDING THE PRESENT TO THE PAST

Whitman, starting from Paumanok, wandering Mannahatta, chanting the Indian names, looking for the aboriginal words, seeking the "friendly and flowing savage," did his best to begin to accept aboriginal sources for the American character. He tried to trace out "arriere-threads to all pre-history" and demonstrate how those seemingly fragile threads are actually stronger than "steel and iron" and "weld the inhabitants of New York, Chicago, San Francisco and New Orleans to the vanished peoples retrospects of the past—to a hundred unknown nations" (*NUPM* 5:1684). It would be up to "Poets to Come" to "prove and define" what Whitman began. We can see William Carlos Williams's *In the American Grain* as one attempt to "justify" Whitman with an imaginative history that guides us back to the native and the land as the ground of our being, that allows us to trace our genealogy in such a way that our origins root us "Here, not there" (74). And Gary Snyder's *Turtle Island,* with its resurrection of "the old/new name for the continent, based on many creation myths of the people who have been living here for millennia," is an intensification of Whitman's poetic archaeology: "The 'U.S.A.' and its states and countries are arbitrary and inaccurate impositions on what is really here." In an essay echoing Whitman in many ways, appropriately called "Passage to More Than India," Snyder puts forth the idea of "White Indians," of white Americans who absorb the legends, rituals, chants, and "old ways" of the Indians and live by them, becoming "literally hunters and gatherers, playfully studying the old techniques of acorn flour, seaweed-gathering, yucca-fiber, rabbit snaring and bow hunting."

When the haunting memory of the American Indian eventually is so fully absorbed in the American mind that it can "claim the next generation as its own," then "citizens of the USA will at last begin to be Americans, truly at home on the continent, in love with their land" (Snyder 1969, 110–12). Snyder sees the fulfillment of Whitman's democratic vistas in a growing reemergence of Indians and Indian ways: "When [Whitman] says there should be more democracy, I go along with that. We all see what more democracy means, too. It means that the Navajo should get their own nation, that Rosebud and Pine Ridge maybe should be a separate nation, that the Indians of Puget Sound should have fishing rights" (Snyder 1980, 74).

Absorption of the Indian words, tales, rituals into the English language and the subsequent creation of "White Indians" has its negative side, too, of course. The dilemma of many Indian writers and visionaries has been whether they should allow their tribe's tales and visions to be absorbed into and conquered by the white man's language. The poet and translator W. S. Merwin, speaking of the translations of indigenous American works, notes the hopeless and sad irony of how "our knowledge of these words out of the past of the America in which we were born and learned to speak depends (entirely, in most cases) on their representations in languages brought from Europe by the same conquest that overran the American natives." And Merwin, too, sees the double-edged nature of this linguistic conquering of native cultures:

> One thing that troubles us in their presence is the growing certainty that what has been lost was rightfully ours, a part of ourselves not only in so far as we are Americans—but in so far as we are a people—or people—at all.

He notes:

> We are drawn with a peculiar insistence by these works to the recognition that what of America has been lost to us was ours like our own forgotten dreams, and that it had something to impart to us about ourselves, which we may now have to grope for in nameless bewilderment, before we can truly awaken. (Merwin 277–78)

It is the American dilemma: as the old ways of various tribes die out, is it better to have the visions die with the tribes, or to twist them into translations, freeze ever-changing oral tales into a single written form in the language of those who destroyed the cultures that produced the tales? There are no easy answers. Black Elk tells the story of his vision, through an interpreter, to John G. Neihardt, who tells it in English. Black Elk knows that his vision, handed over to the white man's culture, has lost its power and purity, but his hope is that nevertheless it might alter the white man's mind-set, make him see, even if only indistinctly, a possibility for a different and better relationship to the natural world. So he takes the risk. Whitman's plan to absorb the Indian via his poetry was similarly double-edged: his project admitted the inevitable loss of Indian cultures, but it simultaneously argued for the significance of those cultures and for the necessity of preserving them—as a warning, lesson, inspiration—at the heart of our memories, deep in the lines of authentic American poems.

4

Whitman and Photography

Greatness is simply development.
Whitman (*DBN* 770)

The development of the technology of portable photography coincided with the demise of open Indian lands. Part of the reason that the fading of native cultures is rendered so powerfully in the American imagination is that photographs (like those of Edward Curtis) began recording Indians in their own landscapes just as those lands were dwindling into reservations. But before the camera could easily be taken out to Indian lands, Indians had come to places where the camera was. Whitman's favorite photographer, Alexander Gardner, devoted a good part of his career to photographing the lands that had so recently belonged to the Indians and to photographing the Indians who came to Washington to try desperately to negotiate some final access to the land they had been told they would have access to forever.

Gardner was a Scotsman who came to the United States originally to take part in a utopian community scheme and who instead joined Mathew Brady's photographic enterprise, then in 1863 set out on his own to photograph the Civil War and later to follow the Union Pacific railroad as it built its way across the West. A great fan of *Leaves of Grass,* Gardner offered some of the first accurate images of the post–Civil War American West, grounding Whitman's imaginative Western flights in the black-and-white visual facts of immense space. Just as photography taught us to remember the Civil War in a particular way, so did Gardner's photos of the West come to represent for many Americans the fact of the open lands of the future: countless Americans traveled West via the photos (and engravings done from them) that Gardner made as he carted his equipment and a cramped darkroom by horse-drawn wagon across the plains. His Western scenes show a vast emptiness, a rudimentary settling by westering whites, an absence of Indians. But back in Washington, Gardner encountered huge delegations of Indians arriving to talk with the Great White Father about maintaining some claim to this continent; Gardner photographed many of these delegations, preserving those haunting moments when native chiefs in hybrid dress gathered on the Capitol steps to meet the white men, uniformed in their bureaucratic gray. We have seen how Whitman, then working in the Indian Bureau, met some of these very delegations and wrote of his encounters. Gardner's photos and Whitman's words make a revealing pair, for both record the fading but still palpable grandeur of America's native race as it confronted a whiteness as foreign and vast and imposing as the Capitol building itself. Gardner's images—of Civil War bloated dead, of vast unpopulated western space, of Indians in Washington facing the inevitability of a European occupation of the continent—served as visual challenges for Whitman, American facts that he worked to turn into American words.

I. "LETTING NATURE HAVE ITS WAY"

There are many technological developments that we could examine in relation to their impact on poetry and poetics in America, but perhaps none is more illuminating than the advent and development of photography, the merging of sight and chemistry, of eye and machine, of organism and mechanism, that became the peculiarly appropriate American instrument of seeing. No culture was more in love with science and technology than America was, and the camera was the perfect emblem of the joining of the human senses to chemistry and physics via a machine. Whitman was of the first generation to experience the representation of the world in photographic images; his poetry emerged at precisely the time photography was literally taking hold of the American imagination. Whitman's poetics, of course, were in large part built on his attempt to meld the mechanical and the spiritual, to discover and sing the deeper meanings of science ("Hurrah for positive science!" [LG 51]) by delineating, for example, the ways such technological achievements as the Suez Canal, the Transcontinental Railroad, and the Transatlantic Cable joined humankind in a tighter knit of brotherhood; from the beginning, Whitman argued that "Exact science and its practical movements are no checks on the greatest poet but always his encouragement and support," that in fact the scientists were "the lawgivers of poets" (LG 718). For Whitman, a viable poetry could not retreat to the past, could not cling desperately to a pretechnological vocabulary and worldview, could not cower before the materialistic onslaught of the nineteenth century, but rather would have to embrace progress, invention, and technology as well as trace their deeper implications: the "true use for the imaginative faculty of modern times," he said, "is to give ultimate vivification to facts, to science" (*LG* 564), and he sought "plentiful crops of words . . . arising out of the general establishment and use of new inventions," including the telegraph, the sewing machine, the newspaper press, and "the daguerreotype" (*DBN* 710).

Photography, then, came to be one of the key tests for Whitman's theories; it was clearly a scientific invention, emerging directly out of exciting developments in chemistry and physics, but it also clearly had an immediate impact on art, since it seemed to render more quickly and more accurately the same images of reality that painters trained so long and worked so hard to achieve. There was, in fact, a great deal of controversy at the birth of photography about just what the invention would mean to art; the camera initially emerged, after all, out of the desire of painters to have an accurate aid for delineating reality. (The original camera obscura had been used by painters like Canaletto and Vermeer to record details of scenes they were painting.) But as the technology developed, its product soon rivaled the accuracy and even beauty of the paintings it supposedly was in the service of. Some observers went so far as to prophesy the death of painted art; other artists would eventually praise photography for releasing painting from the tyranny of the object. Late in his life, Whitman was still intrigued by the controversy:

> I find I like the photographs better than the oils—they are perhaps mechanical, but they are honest. The artists add and deduct: the artists fool with nature—reform it, revise it, to make it fit their preconceived notion of what it should be. (*WWC* 1:131)

He liked the idea that technology had arrived at a point where it seemed almost to have gained a soul, a sensibility; he remarked how most ordinary painters were "beaten out completely" by a good photograph, and he believed the vast majority of competent painted portraits "would be entitled to be set aside" by competent photographs of the same subjects: "I say so knowing that photography involves a mechanism—is, as some might say it, without soul, spirit: think how much chemicals have to do with it all!" (*WWC* 4:124). Some might say it had no soul, but Whitman knew it had chemistry, and for him, that was close enough.

Chemical properties, after all, were hardly a negative quality for the poet who could celebrate the wonderfully renewing properties of an endlessly composting world, who could exclaim, "What chemistry!" as he observed how the earth "grows such sweet things out of such corruptions" (*LG* 369). Whitman was, after all, the poet of transmutation, and photography was another wonderful example of magical science, of chemistry turning the ordinary into the beautiful ("chemistry" is simply our modern word for alchemy), turning the fleeting into the permanent. As Whitman lovingly examined a photograph of a friend, an image that emerged through physical and chemical processes from a soulless machine, he admiringly traced its simple, unelaborated honesty:

> See these lines—how faithful they are, how undoubtedly true! perhaps a little too chemically definitive now and then: so full, so adequate, yet so damned simple, too. . . . The photograph has this advantage; it lets nature have its way: the botheration with the painters is that they don't want to let nature have its way: they want to make nature let them have their way. (*WWC* 4:124–25)

This is the key to Whitman's unwavering devotion to photography; precisely because it mechanically reproduced what the sun illuminated, it was for him a more honest re-presentation of reality than the paintings of most artists, who let their various biases, discriminations, and blindnesses alter the world that was before their eyes. As such, photography was the harbinger of a new democratic art, an art that would not exclude on the basis of preconceived notions of what was vital, of what was worth painting.

As we might expect, Whitman quickly realized the implications of photography for his own art. The twentieth-century photographer Walker Evans saw the role of photographer as, both literally and figuratively, the "seer" of the culture: the artist always on the alert for the significant fleeting impression, the odd angle, the charged passing moment. The camera taught us to see beauty where we had not before sought it out, to see significance in the overlooked detail. So Whitman, in his 1855 preface, defined the emerging American poet as an embodied imagination on the lookout for whatever had before been judged to be trivial or insignificant; like the absorptive camera, "The greatest poet hardly knows pettiness or triviality. If he breathes into any thing that was before thought small it dilates with the grandeur and life of the universe. He is a seer" (*LG* 713). It is fitting, then, that one of the earliest reviews of *Leaves of Grass* should have used photography to define Whitman's radically new aesthetics: "The great poet is he who performs the office of the camera to the world, merely reflecting what he sees—art is mere reproduction" (quoted in Rubin 382). Whitman, of course, would reject the notion of poetry as "mere reproduction"; he knew that the camera represented the *marriage* of the human and the technological, the imaginative and the mechanical; he knew that the photograph was not self-generated, that the photographer in his selectivity, framing, and alertness joined with the remarkable mechanical attributes of the camera to create the new art. Photography put limits on, checked, subjectivity but did not obliterate it. Discussing Alexander Gardner, the photographer he most admired, Whitman identified his genius in his ability to go "beyond his craft" for he "saw farther than his camera—saw more" (*WWC* 3:346). So also, for Whitman, would poetry do more than merely reproduce reality; like the photographer, the poet must accurately work with the materials of the world, but must do so for the purpose of revealing the significance and unrecognized beauty of those materials; the poet's job, as Whitman outlined it in the 1855 preface, is to capture the world in the most illuminating way: "folks expect of the poet to indicate more than the beauty and dignity which always attach to dumb real objects. . . . They expect him to indicate the path between reality and their souls" (*LG* 714). Thus, in one of his own reviews of *Leaves*, Whitman used the image of photography to suggest the marriage of the objective and the subjective, the external and internal, reality and the soul: "The contents of the book form a daguerreotype of [the poet's] inner being" (*Brooklyn Daily Eagle*, September 15, 1855).

Whitman's poetry, though, would continue to be attacked by others for its photographic qualities; H. M. Alden, the editor of *Harper's*, argued in 1880 that "while Whitman is moved by thought, (often grand and elevating,) he does not give the intellectual satisfaction warranted by the thought, but a moving panorama of pictures. He not only puts aside his 'singing robes,' but his 'thinking cap' also, and resorts to the stereopticon" (quoted in Scholnick 244). So, well into the 1860s, Whitman had to continue to argue with the implications that his poetry was simply a reductive "camera to the world"; in *Democratic Vistas*, Whitman would "hail with joy" the "demand for facts, even the business materialism of the current age," would endorse the idea that poetry was an activity of "absorbing materials" and including "the shows and forms presented by Nature," but he argued that the poet must go beyond such facts and forms to "project them, their analogies, by curious removes, indirections, in literature and art": "No useless attempt to repeat the material creation, by daguerreotyping the exact likeness by mortal mental means." Rejecting the purely mechanical role of camera, Whitman celebrates instead the true poet's "image-making faculty," which is always "coping with material creation, and rivaling, almost triumphing over it." The poet, Whitman demands, must begin with facts, absorb them, but must make sure they are framed in such a way that they "tend to ideas," for only then will he be able to "endow [the material creation] with an identity" (*PW* 418–19).

The poet, in other words, does "photograph" the world around him, but he catalogs it in the service of collecting the real materials out of which a perfected democracy will be constructed. Whitman's ideal visions are not composed of ethereal materials, but rather out of the actual stuff of this world; Whitman was devoted to the real, in other words, for its potentiality more than its actuality. Photographs helped teach Whitman, though, to see how all the actual stuff of the world was crucial to its wholeness. So in the early 1870s, Whitman would characterize his major work in terms of photography: "In these *Leaves* everything is literally photographed. Nothing is poetized, no divergence, not a step, not an inch, nothing for beauty's sake, no euphemism, no rhyme" (*CW* 6:21). He knew that such stark photographic truth "gives offence to many good people," but that an "awful adherence to the truth" was the only way to approach the wholeness of life that was "secretly precious to the soul" (*CW* 6:22). Over his adult years, Whitman had an increasingly high regard for photographers, for the way their eyes and their spirits turned a photograph into a convincing image of identity, for the way they made the actual things of the present suggest ideals and possibilities, for the way they made the overlooked or discarded details of the world glow with a newfound beauty, a redefined and unconventional kind of beauty that many would persist in seeing only as ugliness.

Whitman thus began to conceive of the way the mind gathered the real world (and stored it for later use) as a kind of mental photography; reality was "real" only insofar as it was impressed like a photograph on the memory:

> As in every show & every concrete object & every experience of life the serious question is, What does it stamp—what will it leave daguerreotyped for the future for weal or woe—upon the mind? These physical realities, we call the world are doubtless only essentially real in the impressions they leave & perpetuate upon the rational mind—the immortal soul. (*NUPM* 2214)

And for all his resistance to seeing his poetry as mere verbal photography, Whitman settled upon—as the very image of *Leaves of Grass*—the most popular type of photograph in late-nineteenth-century America: "I look upon 'Leaves of Grass,' now finish'd to the end of its opportunities and powers, as my definitive *carte visite* to the coming generations of the New World, if I may assume to say so" (*LG* 562). The *carte de visite* was a small photo mounted on a calling card, and in the 1850s it became the first truly mass-produced photographic product, making self-images available cheaply and conveniently to the masses. So Whitman conceives of *Leaves* as his photographic calling card: always filled with photographs of himself and engravings of photos, the book was in fact just that, "an attempt," he said, "from first to last, to put *a Person,* a human being (myself, in the latter half of the Nineteenth Century, in America), freely, fully and truly on record" (*LG* 573–74) and to make that represented self available inexpensively to a democratic readership.

II. "LATENT WITH UNSEEN EXISTENCES"

From the 1840s on, as first daguerreotypes and then photographs entered human consciousness and redefined the way we see the world, words began to alter their relationship with reality too. Photographs were voracious and endless; they were quick and absorptive; they were relentlessly focused on both the present moment and the real. They were bound to a first-person perspective, and the perspective itself defined what was seen and how it was to be viewed. They were democratic in their seeing; the first photographs stunned people with their clutter—every detail of a scene insisted on equal emphasis, and nothing was ignored. Nothing was left out because it was considered irrelevant or unaesthetic or inessential. The lens and the light-sensitive field were radically democratic; they absorbed what the light revealed. If we want to capture the whole, photographs seemed to argue, we must not miss *anything;* every detail contributes to the fullness. A camera and film would not discriminate, not prefer one aspect over another; only photographers could do that, and even then photographers would end up surprised at what the camera had found that they had not seen. Photographs in the mid-1800s were often called "sun-paintings"—Whitman called early photographers "Priests of the Sun" (Rubin 283)—for it was as if the sun itself had done the detail work, bringing to our attention what we had not noticed before. To be as democratic and as inclusive as the sun was, for Whitman, the goal of the new American poet: "He judges not as the judge judges but as the sun falling around a helpless thing" (*LG* 713).

Susan Sontag discusses how "photography first comes into its own as an extension of the eye of the middle-class *flaneur*," how the photographer "is an armed version of the solitary walker reconnoitering, stalking, cruising the urban inferno, the voyeuristic stroller who discovers the city as a landscape of voluptuous extremes" (55). "The *flaneur*," Sontag says, "is not attracted to the city's official realities but to its dark seamy corners, its neglected populations" (55–56). Whitman, of course, as a newspaper reporter in the 1840s, identified himself as a *flaneur,* described how he "sauntered forth to have a stroll down Broadway to the Battery," and in the 1850s his identity as a poet would emerge as exactly that of the voyeuristic stroller, looking into bedrooms, dreams, operating rooms, wandering alone to the city dead house to confront the corpse of a dead prostitute on the abandoned sidewalk, always absorbing the extremes, celebrating the neglected, casting words into the dark corners of existence—the solitary walker. It is fitting that Whitman entitled his 1862 series of articles for the New York *Leader* "City Photographs," for there he offers brief sun paintings of the city's neglected populations, as he roams among the surgery patients in the Broadway Hospital, the country boys in the Bowery hotels, and the immigrants and workingmen in their beer halls (*WWCW* 15–62).

When Sontag calls photography a "promiscuous form of seeing" (129), she means that there is no limit to the areas of reality that photography will record; it is voracious, transcends all attempts to guide its development or limit its realm; it wants nothing less than to turn all of reality into images. As such, photography is closely allied with Whitman's democratic poetics, a promiscuous poetics that was out to break down all walls between "art" and "reality," to open the poem to all words, to all that words could re-present, the verbal record of everything the senses contacted during the soul's transit through the world. For Whitman, taboos were nothing but signals of resistant pockets of reality that had not yet been shown by the poet to fit into the ecstatic fullness and wholeness of life; they needed only to be translated into art to be seen as embraceable and finally as necessary components of a truly democratic art.

In an early notebook, Whitman works out a cosmology based on the poet's attraction to such hidden and forbidden beauty:

> I think ten million supple-wristed gods are always hiding beauty in the world—burying it every where in every thing—and most of all in spots that men and women do not think of and never look—as Death and Poverty and Wickedness.—Cache! and Cache again! all over the earth, and in the heavens that swathe the earth, and in the waters of the sea.— They do their jobs well; those journeymen divine. Only from the Poet they can hide nothing and would not if they could.—I reckon he is Boss of those gods; and the work they do is done for him; and all they have concealed, they have concealed for his sake. (*DBN* 770).

For Whitman, the poet would follow, or lead, the photographer into the areas of life that had been off-limits to art, places where beauty was not believed to lie. Then, performing the democratic feat of translating death, poverty, and wickedness into life, worth, and goodness, the poet would open America's eyes to hidden beauty. "I do not doubt but the majesty & beauty of the world are latent in any iota of the world . . . I do not doubt there is far more in trivialities, insects, vulgar persons, slaves, dwarfs, weeds, rejected refuse, than I have supposed" (quoted in Sontag 29). "You objects that call from diffusion my meanings and give them shape!" exults Whitman in "Song of the Open Road," celebrating everything that can be brought to light, "You light that wraps me and all things in delicate equable showers! / . . . I believe you are latent with unseen existences, you are so dear to me" (*LG* 150).

Reality for Whitman became something like a photograph being developed: beauty is "latent" in the "rejected refuse" of the world; discarded objects and vulgar experiences need only impress themselves, through the lens of the eye, on the poet's sensitized imagination, and then, slowly, the image will develop, beautiful in its detail, radiant in its newfound significance, released from its degraded position in old hierarchical value systems. In the early 1840s, William Henry Fox Talbot discovered the first process of chemical development of photographs and was startled by the effect produced as the initial exposure of light on the sensitized plate left no visible image: "The impression is latent and invisible, and its existence would not be suspected by any one who was not forewarned of it by previous experiment." As he describes the ensuing process of development, Talbot's tone of scientific detachment gives way to mystery and enthusiasm: "It is a highly curious and beautiful phenomenon to see the spontaneous commencement of the picture, first tracing out the stronger outlines, and then gradually filling up all the numerous and complicated details" (Newhall 116). Talbot's early description of photographic development sounds like an analysis of Whitman's poetic technique, where an impression of what is before the eyes is absorbed onto a sensitized field, offering up first broad outlines, then filling in the outlines with vast detail. Webster's 1847 definition of "daguerreotype" captures the same melding of science and magic; after a lengthy technical description of the process, the definition concludes by describing how the exposed copper sheet is "exposed to the vapor of mercury; then heated to 167 degrees Fahrenheit, and the images appear as by enchantment." (By 1864, the enchantment had vanished from the definition of "daguerreotype," which became simply a cause–effect relationship of a chemical reaction "producing an image.")

When we consider Whitman's fascination with the "curious mystery of the eyesight," with latency, with development, with spontaneity and its resultant "Pictures," with the working of the "flaunt of the sun" on reality, we become aware of just how much his poetic vocabulary shares with the evolving vocabulary of photography. When he says that "Greatness is simply development," we can begin to feel a double edge to the word, an edge that is present in many of his statements: "If nothing lay more develop'd the quahaug in its callous shell were enough" (*LG* 57); or

> I chant the chant of dilation or pride,
> We have had ducking and deprecating about enough,
> I show that size is only development.
>   (*LG* 49)

To allow the latent beauties, the hidden significances, to emerge—that is the lesson of photography, of development, and it is the faith of Whitman's poems. "Development" means literally to unfold, and the process of unfolding for Whitman is the central physical mystery: all life is "unfolded out of the folds of the woman," and all development *is* an unfolding. Whitman would often talk about "infolding" or "enfolding" experience into his poems—"You can do nothing and be nothing but that I will infold you" (*LG* 74)—so that the poems would work on the reader like a chemically sensitized photographic plate, containing latent meaning, waiting for the reader to develop the potential ideas, to unfold the significance out of the folds of the book.

Development was the key, then, the mystery in the process of photography. Oliver Wendell Holmes, who was a master at mixing cool scientific explanation with spiritual wonder (and who described photography as "a divine gift, placed in our hands nominally by science, really by that inspiration which is revealing the Almighty through the lips of the humble students of Nature" [1861, 28]), in the late 1850s described the process of development as the very incarnation of an invisible soul into a visible image. The glass plates in the camera, he suggested, performed a supernatural magic informed by chemistry:

> Such a ghost we hold imprisoned in the shield we have just brought from the camera. . . . No eye, no microscope, can detect a trace of the change in the white film that is spread over it. And yet there is a potential image in it,—a latent soul, which will presently appear before its judge. (1863, 5)

Here again is Fox Talbot's "latent image," the same "latent soul" Whitman celebrated in all of reality, the objects "latent with unseen existences" (*LG* 150). For Holmes, the development paper, when sensitized, seems as if it "has a conscience, and is afraid of daylight," and out of this dark secretive urging, the "*negative* is now to give birth to a *positive*,—this mass of contradictions to assert its hidden truth in a perfect harmonious affirmation of the realities of Nature." The ultimate transformation is the perfect "copy of Nature" that emerges on the latent paper "out of the perverse and totally depraved negative." The negative is for Holmes a horrifying reversed vision of reality seemingly "wrenched" into being by "some magic and diabolic power," but the wondrous transformation of this "depraved negative"—where "its light is darkness, and its darkness is light"—into a positive image of harmonious nature suggested to Holmes a larger spiritual truth:

> Perhaps this world is only the *negative* of that better one in which lights will be turned to shadows and shadows into light, but all harmonized, so that we shall see why these ugly patches, these misplaced gleams and blots, were wrought into the temporary arrangements of our planetary life. (1859, 740–41)

Holmes's notion here is very close to Whitman's concept of "eidó-lons": "I met a seer, / Passing the hues and objects of the world, / . . . To glean eidólons" (*LG* 5). Eidólons were, for Whitman, the *images* of objects, phantomized and idealized, as opposed to the actual objects themselves; his idea may have derived from Balfour Stewart and P. G. Tait's influential 1875 book *The Unseen Universe*, in which the idea of a sort of cosmic spiritual photography is put forward: "Each organic or inorganic object on the earth makes, in the process of its growth, a deli-cate facsimile register of itself on the living sensitive ether that lies imme-diately around it" (quoted in *LG* 5). Photography was teaching the mid-nineteenth century how beauty could emerge out of the most mundane and unattractive reality simply by turning that reality into an image of itself (removed from time and framed for contemplation), and the cul-ture was responding by extrapolating the lesson: somewhere, perhaps, there were invisible photographs of our whole lives that transformed confusion into order, tawdriness into beauty, triviality into significance. The heavens could be thought of as a kind of sensitized photographic ether, imprinting infinite detail so that our small existences would not be forgotten, would be preserved in a universal album of life's wholeness.

This emerging faith in the reality of images of reality had its dangers. Holmes, more clearly than anyone else, stated one of the most striking effects that photography had on the human mind: photographs could convince us that we actually *possessed* objects through their *forms:*

> *Form is henceforth divorced from matter.* In fact, matter as a visible object is of no great use any longer, except as the mould on which form is shaped. Give us a few negatives of a thing worth seeing, taken from different points of view, and that is all we want of it. Pull it down or burn it up, if you please. (1859, 747)

Whitman sensed the danger of this disembodied possession, the way it could lead to the worship of images of things rather than the things themselves, how we might come to mistake the photo for the person. ("The well-taken photographs—but your wife or friend close and solid in your arms?" he cautions in "Song of Myself": "and what is life?" [*LG* 78].) We must never let go of what gave the form its shape, Whitman argues, and this emphasis on the material world as the source, the materi-als, of vision is what gives Whitman's brand of visionary poetics its dis-tinctive quality; as Hyatt Waggoner has argued, American visionary po-ets insist on beginning with actual vision, physical sight, then developing their spiritual insights out of what they grasp with the eyes: for Whit-man, a vision of the future is useless if it is not recognizably built out of and grounded in what is here around us now.

III. "AFOOT WITH VISION"

Whitman's faith, then, was photography's faith: any object, experience, process, when imprinted onto the blank page of the absorptive poem, would emerge in a new importance, as an organic part of the whole scheme of existence. For Whitman, as for the emerging generations of photographers who would explore the human spirit through physical images, "the unseen is proved by the seen" (*LG* 31). The act of photographing an object, like the act of including it in a poem, frames and redefines the object, makes it a sign—a re-presentation—and therefore significant. Gabriel Harrison, Whitman's friend and the photographer who took the famous 1854 daguerreotype of the poet that appears as the frontispiece to the first edition of *Leaves of Grass,* commented on this phenomenon in 1852, perhaps suggesting to Whitman the organizing image and central message for his life's work: "You cannot look upon anything in nature without being reminded of some peculiar and beautiful result if daguerreotyped; even the small blade of grass" (Harrison, 231).

"To photograph," says Sontag, "is to confer importance." She goes on to say that there is "probably no subject that cannot be beautified" and notes "the tendency inherent in all photographs to accord value to their subjects." Thus, photography has forced us all to redefine what is beautiful and what is ugly until, as Sontag says, it becomes "arbitrary" and "superficial" to "single out some things as beautiful and others as not" or to "treat some moments in life as important and most as trivial" (28). Photography has worked to democratize even the events of our lives. Whitman set out to make poetry as absorptive and nondiscriminating as photography, to cast the blank page as treated photosensitive paper, to allow the impress of experience to develop and set into the lines of a poem; the poet, like the photographer, would literally become the seer embracing the world. This attitude would be the primary source of Whitman's influence on future generations of writers, and it explains why so many realists and naturalists with an overlay of spiritual fervor have been attracted to him. Photographers like Walker Evans and photographic poets like William Carlos Williams would explore in this century the implications of Whitman's spiritual development of the intensely real image.

It is not surprising, then, to discover how many aspects of photographic seeing entered into poetry and fiction during the second half of the nineteenth century: an obsessive concern with the present moment, an equating of reality with what can be seen (if it could be recorded by a camera, it was real: a commonsense definition of reality came to be, in fact, that which could be recorded with a camera); a focusing on detail (often seen from a surprising angle or from a defamiliarizing distance or proximity); a recording of personal experience of the world; an emphasis on absorptive vision; an exploration of abrupt juxtapositions of separate moments that gained resonance by their often dissonant conjoining (photographic albums and galleries developed during mid-nineteenth-century America, creating new narrative structures of memory and history [see Trachtenberg, 1985, 1–8, and Orvell, 17–20]). Imagism grows out of the attempt by some poets to appropriate for poetry the notion of intense, fragmentary, momentary seeing; Pound's definition of the image ("that which presents an intellectual and emotional complex in an instant of time") tied the movement to photography, and he even defined poetry in chemical terms. Out of imagism emerges Williams with his photopoetics, no ideas but in things, brief present-tense-captured glimpses on which so much depends.

Again, Whitman anticipated the significance of the invention; he reached maturity just as photography began to transform sight (he was twenty when the first daguerreotypes appeared in America) and came to know some of America's leading pioneer photographers. Mathew Brady, whose photographs taught us to see war in realistic instead of heroic-romantic terms—war as bloated bodies on a field or wrecked bodies in a hospital tent, rather than as glorious deeds on horseback—and Alexander Gardner—who taught us to see the frontier in realistic terms for the first time as he photographed the railroads pushing west across the plains—both photographed Whitman often. Whitman earned his knowledge of Civil War strife through unstinting service in Washington's hospitals, but his own actual battlefield experience in the Civil War was virtually nonexistent; he learned to see that aspect of the war *through* the photographic representations of Gardner, Brady, and the other photographers who followed the troops. Similarly, he saw the West, an area that until 1879 he never actually was in, through the photographic images of Gardner. Part of the easy absorption of Whitman's poetry, his sweeping vistas and self-assured claims of having been everywhere, his catalogs of faraway places imaged as if he had tramped the ground of all of them, derive from a life lived during the heady development of photography, when it seemed that anyone's eyes were quite literally being extended around the world, where experience *could* be gained by hauling in albums of visual traces. Oliver Wendell Holmes, in his 1861 *Atlantic* essay on the cultural effects of photography, had urged Americans to recognize "the significance of the miracle which the Lord of Light is working for them" by giving everyone the opportunity to pull in through their eyes the actual visual forms of places they would never actually set foot in, but places that, through the miracle of photography, they *could* set eyes on:

The cream of the visible creation has been skimmed off; and the sights which men risk their lives and spend their money and endure sea-sickness to behold,—the views of Nature and Art which make exiles of entire families for the sake of a look at them, . . . these sights, gathered from Alps, temples, palaces, pyramids, are offered you for a trifle, to carry home with you, that you may look at them at your leisure, by your fireside, with perpetual fair weather, when you are in the mood, without catching cold, . . . as long as you like, and breaking off as suddenly as you like. (16)

We would never mistake this smug and gently ironic tone for Whitman's, but the notion, brought on by photography, of instantaneous global travel, the unifying pull of gathering the whole world around your fireside, a domesticated passage to India, is part of the same celebratory atmosphere surrounding the widespread technological developments in communication and transportation that seemed generally to be extending the human senses out into previously inaccessible regions of the world, a celebration that Whitman enjoyed leading. Like the "instant conductors all over me" (*LG* 57) that Whitman imagined at the edges of his senses, cameras were instruments intensifying and extending human sight, conducting the world into his infinitely absorptive soul: "My ties and ballasts leave me, my elbows rest in sea-gaps, / I skirt sierras, my palms cover continents, / I am afoot with my vision" (*LG* 61). Even this image, the soul as hot-air balloon, gained resonance and verification just a few years after it first appeared in 1855, when James Wallace Black, a Boston photographer, ascended over the city in a balloon in 1860 (the same year he photographed Whitman, who was visiting the city to see the 1860 edition of *Leaves* through press) and took the very first aerial photographs, revealing to humankind a whole new unifying perspective on the world, a perspective Whitman would often explore, culminating in the space travel of "Passage to India": "Have we not stood here like trees in the ground long enough?" (*LG* 420). Black's partner, John Adams Whipple, had in 1851 taken the first detailed photograph of the moon; it quickly became a familiar image, often reproduced, bringing it telescopically close to all human eyes; Whitman's astronomical images were endorsed by photographic developments as well.

Like the photographer, Whitman was "Both in and out of the game and watching and wondering at it" (*LG* 32): the photograph always served as evidence that the artist had actually been there, yet the photographic frame was simultaneously evidence that the artist, as close as he may have been, was separate, apart, detached enough to observe rather than to participate. (Photographers like Brady in the Civil War and Jacob Riis in the New York slums demonstrated that the power of the photograph resided in presenting painful experience that was at once both intimate and distant). Whitman's poetry moved with the growing portability of the invention, developing from a pre–*Leaves of Grass* rhymed and pietistic traditional verse into an open and tough line that responded to the swivel of the head on the neck ("My head slues round on my neck" [*LG* 76]) as it looked at the world; his catalogs brought reality hurtling into poetry with the same speed that photographs were cataloging reality and bringing things out of the range of any single person's sight into a shared field of vision. ("To me the converging objects of the universe perpetually flow" [*LG* 47].) As the camera and film became more portable, and as film became more photosensitive so that pictures could be taken anywhere (even, eventually, in the dark), Americans became accustomed to endless images of everything. The camera democratized imagery, suggesting that *anything* was worth a photograph.

The old hierarchy of seeing was represented by painting and sculpture, which emphasized selectivity, patience, formal structuring, and composing (and a formality of posing), which created objects that were never precisely what they portrayed but instead were distillations of reality, ideas *about* things. (Individuals didn't have portraits painted every month or two; one or two were expected to distill one's character in an approximation that transcended time. Identity was construed as stable.) But photographs allowed people to track their aging, to watch themselves change step by step as they grew old. Photographs were, precisely, *moments* along life's continuum, stuck *in* time, in fact the sticking *of* time (as opposed to painted portraiture, which was the transcendence of life's continuum). The hierarchy of selectivity and distillation in painting gave way to photography's brash informality, quickness (within a few years the length of time required for exposure dwindled from several minutes to seconds), commonness, and cheapness. What may not have seemed worth a painter's time was, for the photographer, always worth a few seconds and a few cents.

And, so Whitman's new poetry implied, what may not have been fit subject for a formal poet of classical education would slide effortlessly into the open forms of the democratic poet who is out to turn America into the greatest poem, a poem that will take the risks of inclusiveness: "What is commonest, cheapest, nearest, easiest, is Me, / Me going in for my chances, spending for vast returns." To make America the "greatest poem," as he set out in *Leaves of Grass* to do, would require a poet who would be so absorptive and nondiscriminatory that he could see that the prostitute has as much of a place in the overall pattern as the president has; the lunatic belongs as much as the scientist. It is a country "enmasse," a country that is truly a "United States," as we all are: warring and conflicting states of being (varied states) that are joined nonetheless in a wholeness, a personality, a fullness that will always be violated by ruling out any aspect of what is there. For Whitman, the "clutter" of reality that photography was revealing the world to be composed of became the stuff of his catalogs, poems embracing the vast and untidy variety of the world. The "nature" he would celebrate would be nature made "perfect in imperfection!" (*UPP* 2:89).

IV. CLUTTER

Clutter was the great new fact of life in the nineteenth century, and it is important to take a few moments to explore the cultural resonance of clutter. When we encounter descriptions of the "teeming" cities or the "masses" of immigrants, when we read of the chaotic changes brought on by industrialization and urbanization with all the resultant filth and growing anarchistic desires, what we are hearing are verbalizations of an uneasy new relationship with clutter. One of Whitman's favorite words, "crowd," works toward the same concept; it was a word applied to developing urban experiences that mixed classes, juggled hierarchies, threw people together in unlikely relationships: ferryboat rides, omnibuses, ballgames. Clutter is, after all, the loss of tidiness, order, hierarchy, the absence of things in their proper places. "Clutter" is, by definition, exactly what, for many, America in the last half of the nineteenth century seemed to be becoming: a societal chaos, a crowded confusion. In one sense, clutter is the same thing as litter: leavings, unwanted waste.

We know what Whitman felt about litter, for the word "leavings" is one of the key plays on the pun of *Leaves of Grass;* our life, Whitman reminds us, is "the leavings of many deaths" (*LG* 87), and the earth, which "gives such divine materials to men," also "accepts such leavings from them at last." For Whitman, always, the leavings, the litter, are also the leaf-ings, the new beginnings. Life emerges only from compost; to com*pose* (put together), we must first com*post* (take apart). It is litter's claim to a rightful place in the whole process that allows life to go on. Whitman sets out, then, to redefine litter, weeds, clutter—all the names we give to aspects of the whole that we want to neglect, to rid ourselves of—and to restore them once again to their essential role in the wholeness. "The greatest poet hardly knows pettiness or triviality," Whitman said in the 1855 preface; "If he breathes into any thing that was before thought small it dilates with the grandeur and life of the universe. He is a seer" (*LG* 713).

During the Civil War, clutter and debris came to have a particularly poignant association for Whitman, as he observed soldiers' limbs stacked outside surgeons' tents like so much litter and saw the bodies left on battlefields, America's youth having become the debris of war: "The *dust*

& *debris* below in all the cemeteries not only in Virginia & Tennessee but *all through the land.*" "When Lilacs Last in the Dooryard Bloom'd" reaches its climax when Whitman faces the horrifying results of the war: "I saw the debris and debris of all the slain soldiers of the war" (*LG* 336). Here Whitman's simple repetition of the word enacts the breaking apart of the soldiers into scattered fragments, repeated bits of debris; Whitman's etymological sourcebook, *Rambles Among Words,* defines "debris" as a word derived from geology "where it means masses of rock etc., detached by attrition or mechanical violence" (Swinton 283); Whitman's poignant soldier debris was the result of the worst mechanical violence the world had seen, and it broke debris off from the rock-solid national unity that Whitman had hoped for. For Whitman, "the varieties of the *strayed* dead" (*PW* 114) became the clutter of war that had to be composted back into national purpose, the awful loam out of which America's future would emerge: "The Dead we left behind—there they lie, embedded low, already fused by Nature / . . . The Southern states cluttered with cemeteries" (*LG* 665–66).

The word "clutter" derives from roots meaning "clot," and a clot is a mass of varied material stuck together; when we apply the term to blood, it refers to the body's way of using litter to heal itself. It is a word etymologically related to "clatter," a term that is to sound what "clutter" is to sight. Clatter refers to sounds that fail to strike us as sonorous, sounds that fail to have a harmonious place in the whole but insist on being there anyway. Much modern music that shares assumptions with Whitman involves an acceptance of clatter into the composition, teaching a hidden and surprising dissonant beauty in what had before been heard to be simply noise. Webster's 1847 *American Dictionary* traces the roots of "clutter" to the Welsh *cluder,* a heap; Webster defines "clutter" as "a confused assemblage" and goes on to associate it with "noise," noting that this particular sense of the word "seems allied to *clatter.*" The word "clutter" is also related to the word "cluster," the term that Whitman used to describe his idiosyncratic organization of poems in *Leaves;* the word signifies a bunching together of disparate things that gain similarity when so grouped. Whitman, quite literally, was turning clutter to cluster, both in his poetic catalogs and in the larger structural groupings of his book; one of his clusters, called *Sea-Drift,* is about his identification with clutter, litter: "Chaff, straw, splinters of wood, weeds, and the sea-gluten, / Scum, scales from shining rocks, leaves of salt-lettuce, left by the tide" (*LG* 254).

Whitman is always embracing the leavings, the pokeweed and mullein among the grass: "I too am but a trail of drift and debris" (*LG* 255). In the 1860 edition of *Leaves,* he experimented with cluttering his book with vital debris by including a long poem made up of random fragments and carrying the title "Debris" (*LG* 605–608). Whitman sought out and used various synonyms for *clutter* throughout his writings, and in his notes for a projected dictionary he begins with the word "Scoria," from the Greek for "dung," defining it as "ashes dross . . . rejected matter," and he records the verb form of it ("scorify," meaning "reduce to scoriae") (*DBN* 814). Whitman was out to salvage scoria and to underscore the value of scorification. Debris, chaff, clutter, drift, litter, leavings, scoria—Whitman's vocabulary is rich in words signifying unwanted or discarded matter, the very aspects of reality that his poetry would reclaim, put back in their place, the very aspects of reality that photographs in their nondiscriminating absorption of the world would reveal.

As we saw in Chapter 1, part of what Whitman sought in an ever-expanding dictionary was liberation from a coercive and limited nomenclature, from a set of names that forces us not to see the variety that we live in but instead to categorize and group rather than atomize and distinguish. Photography, by capturing distinct images of everything, by representing the various moments of a single life as an endless series of unique selves, was creating an accelerated lexicon of signs, a limitless dictionary of visual representations that kept alive his dream of an infinitely multiworded language. Language would be hard pressed to keep up with the giant visual vocabulary that photography brought into the realm of human awareness: that was for Whitman the challenge for the American poet, who "hardly knows pettiness or triviality" (*LG* 715).

Many of Whitman's titles—*Collect, Notes Left Over, A Backward Glance O'er Travel'd Roads, Autumn Rivulets, By the Roadside, Sea-Drift*—suggest the digressive, the overlooked, the secondary, the cast away, the rejected, pulled together again and given a newfound importance. Whitman often speaks of the advantage of opening up his writing to accidental discovery; his introductory note to *Specimen Days* and *Collect,* for example, insists on an image of randomly gathered clutter that nonetheless has significance precisely because it has no "definite purpose that can be told in a statement":

> I kept little note-books for impromptu jottings in pencil. . . . Some were scratch'd down from narratives I hear and itemized while watching, or waiting, or tending somebody amid those scenes . . . full of associations never to be possibly said or sung. . . . I leave them just as I threw them by after the war, blotch'd here and there with more than one blood-stain, hurriedly written. . . . The *Collect* afterward gathers up the odds and ends of whatever pieces I can now lay hands on . . . and swoops all together like fish in a net. (*PW* 2–3)

Oliver Wendell Holmes, looking at photographs in the 1850s and considering the changes they had brought about in human consciousness, also began to feel the pull of such random detail, freeing the imagination and dissolving the hierarchy of clear purpose:

> This distinctness of the lesser details of a building or a landscape often gives us incidental truths which interest us more than the central object of the picture. . . . We have often found these incidental glimpses of life and death running away with us from the main object the picture was meant to delineate. The more evidently accidental their introduction, the more trivial they are in themselves, the more they take hold of the imagination. (1859, 745)

Holmes's description sounds like a blueprint for Whitman's poetics: the imagination gripped by the accidental and trivial, discovering beauty "in spots that men and women do not think of and never look" (*DBN* 770). It was not just that photography was producing a vast library of images of reality, but *each photograph* was producing an image so rich in details that a single representation taught the eye to see things that it had never been trained to see before. This new art of democratic details, spawned by photography and carried over into the intense and rich detail of much American painting of the mid-nineteenth century, forced the mind of the observer to absorb reality in a new way, as M. Wynn Thomas has argued:

> By giving them equal attention, and full, appreciative consideration, the mind renders democratic justice to all the specific particulars of the scene, while integrating them into a single perception. . . . Every detail in turn bulks large in experience, each displacing an equal amount of mental space while it occupies the imagination. (102)

In Whitman's view, such luminous clutter was the harbinger of a truly democratic art, an art that was in consonance with the necessary decentering of a democratic society, a society built on "the perception that its center is everywhere, and its circumference nowhere" (Thomas 99). Late in his life, Whitman was still preaching the same lesson: "I do not think we want abbeys or Pantheons. . . . That is the idea of concentration," he told Horace Traubel; "America ought to be *diffusion*—ought to scatter. . . . Nature's method is always the method of diffusion—in her winds, skies, streams, all" (*WWC*, MS).

V. "EVERY LEAF A MIRACLE"

We can divide much of nineteenth-century American thought into two camps: those who despised clutter, clatter, and scatter and sought in some way to arrange things tidily again (or who simply gave up and mourned the loss of the tidiness), and those who welcomed the clutter, thrived on it, found in it for the first time in human history a democratic sweep of wholeness and completion. With things no longer arranged in their proper places, everything suddenly had a place of its own. This nineteenth-century struggle with clutter underlies and defines many of the works that we have come to call realistic or naturalistic; the tensions are perhaps most vividly embodied in the 1907 *The Education of Henry Adams* (Adams). Adams's various educations are a series of failures to teach him to deal with and to absorb clutter; he has been taught on the assumptions of and through the methods of order and tidiness, so when he faces the growing "supersensual chaos" of the world around him, he is increasingly confused and disheartened. For Adams, the persistent dark encounters with clutter are rendered in four incessantly used words: "chaos," "convulsion," "complexity," and "confusion." The dynamo becomes the icon of the new age of multiplicity, ushering in a cluttered "multiverse" to displace the tidy universe. Adams becomes aware of his mind as "littered and stuffed beyond hope with the millions of chance images stored away without order in the memory." He portrays himself as unadaptable to a world in which his ideas of order no longer apply, and his mind feels clogged with the litter that won't organize itself into pattern: "One might as well try to educate a gravel-pit" (1042). When he returns to the Midwest after a decade's absence, he finds everything changed:

> Agriculture had made way for steam; tall chimneys reeked smoke on every horizon, and dirty suburbs filled with scrap-iron, scrap-paper and cinders, formed the setting of every town. Evidently, cleanliness was not be be the birthmark of the new American. (1145)

The ability to accept and absorb this new clutter would be, for Adams, a major requirement of the modern mind.

It is a mind Adams knew he would never possess; his education effectively ruled out his own abandonment of the desire for order. Instead, he sees himself simply losing a grip on the accelerating world, becoming an anachronism, unable to figure out how to worship at the new altar of mechanical force. Adams comes to proclaim "that in the last synthesis, order and anarchy were one, but . . . the unity was chaos" (1091). It is a Whitmanian vision seen from the other side; for Whitman, what appears to be chaos is unity, and anarchy seen from another perspective is order. ("It is not chaos or death—it is form, union, plan" [*LG* 88].)

For Adams, though, the joining of unity and multiplicity was night-marish: "The scientific synthesis commonly called unity was the scientific analysis commonly called multiplicity. The two things were the same, all forms being shifting phases of motion." Adams had begun by offering to let the scientists be the lawgivers of history, just as Whitman had called on them to be the "lawgivers of poetry." But science finally seemed to have evanesced into its own alien vocabulary, in which words like "unity" and "synthesis" had ceased to correspond to common usage; to follow science now was to gain "nothing but a dissolving mind." A new kind of mind, Adams believed, would be required of those "born into a new world which would not be a unity but a multiple . . . where order was an accidental relation obnoxious to nature" (1138). The human mind would have to take an evolutionary jump in order to endure in the new world of chaotic force: "The mind could gain nothing by flight or by fight; it must merge in its supersensual multiverse, or succumb to it" (1141). Again, Adams sounds as if he is describing Whitman: to confront untidiness, disturbing and contradictory facts, endless barrages of countless forces, the American mind would have to come to "think in complexities unimaginable to an earlier mind. . . . Evidently the new American would need to think in contradictions" (1174–75). The new mind would have to see in the way a camera sees, absorbing all details with equal emphasis, prepared to say, with Whitman, "Very well then I contradict myself, / (I am large, I contain multitudes)" (*LG* 88). Whitman's jarring, cluttered catalogs were the sign of Adams's new mind, allowing Whitman (as Lawrence Buell has noted) "to move so fast through the circuit of forms that no catastrophe can touch him. The spirit triumphs over chaos by sheer energy" (Buell 186).

The clutter of reality was one of photography's great lessons, one of the ways it trained us to see the world anew. When we go back to the early responses to photography, we find that this aspect of the art—its insistence on clutter—is one that fascinates everyone. It is this indiscriminate quality of photographs that led many to assert in the mid-nineteenth century that photography would never be an art, would only increase respect for painting, and would never replace it; for painters *had* to be selective as they shaped the world before them, cleaned it up and edited out the extraneous details, created a hierarchy of importance by emphasizing the significant and deleting the insignificant. That selectivity, so the argument went, was art. But others, including Whitman, argued just the opposite, that it was precisely the nondiscriminating quality of photographs that made photography the perfect emerging democratic art form, the visualization of a world of equality. Holmes, for example, in a well-known passage notes:

> The very things which an artist would leave out, or render imperfectly, the photograph takes infinite care with, and so makes its illusions perfect. What is the picture of a drum without the marks on its head where the beating of the sticks has darkened the parchment? (1859, 746)

So Whitman in his *Drum-Taps* and other writings on the Civil War looked intently at the very things other artists of war had left out; he turned attention from the battlefield to the hospital, from heroism to convalescence, from scenes of intense physical courage to scenes of extended grief. Led by Brady, Gardner, and the other photographers of the war (whose technology was best suited for capturing the immediate aftereffects of a battle—the bloated dead and dismembered wounded—rather than the battle itself), Whitman opened his writing to the overlooked details, taking infinite care with the least glamorous aspects of the war. And Whitman's love of the seemingly extraneous detail was something that, oddly enough, Holmes came to celebrate when he wrote of the photograph's "charm of fidelity in the minutest detail": "The very point which the artist omits, in his effort to produce general effect, may be exactly the one that individualizes the place most strongly to our memory." Looking at a photo of his own birthplace, Holmes sees the advantage of the nondiscriminating, detail-absorbing camera over the selective brush of the painter:

> An artist would hardly have noticed a slender, dry, leafless stalk which traces a faint line, as you may see, along the front of our neighbor's house next the corner. That would be nothing to him,—but to us it marks the stem of the *honeysuckle vine,* which we remember, with its pink and white heavy-scented blossoms, as long as we remember the stars in heaven. (1861, 14)

Whitman, too, would remember a particular lilac-bush "with heart-shaped leaves of rich green, / . . . with the perfume strong I love, / . . . With every leaf a miracle" (*LG* 329). He had been at his mother's home in Brooklyn, visiting his brother George who had just been released from a Confederate prison, when he heard of Abraham Lincoln's death, and the sharp intake of his breath upon hearing the news carried into him the scent of lilacs, which would forever be part of the memory of that moment:

> I remember where I was stopping at the time, the season being advanced, there were many lilacs in full bloom. By one of those caprices that enter and give tinge to events without being at all a part of them, I find myself always reminded of the great tragedy of that day by the sight and odor of these blossoms. It never fails. (*PW* 503)

He knew that every detail of that bush was woven into his memory of the death of Lincoln; without the details, the larger memory would lose its vivid and piercing quality. "In these homely accidents of the very instant that cut across our romantic ideals with the sharp edge of reality," Holmes realized, "lies one of the ineffable charms of the sun-picture. It is a little thing that gives life to a scene or a face" (1861, 22).

VI. THE ASTONISHING SUNLIGHT

It is fitting that Oliver Wendell Holmes is the writer who captured, most convincingly, the cultural ambivalence toward what photography was ushering into our consciousness. R. W. B. Lewis reminds us that Holmes is an "instructive guide" to the nineteenth century exactly because he failed to become its representative man; Lewis correctly portrays him as someone standing "midway between the vanishing virility of his father's Calvinism and the emerging vitality of his son's militant humanism," but someone who "because he was at the center of so many tendencies . . . managed to occupy the middle only by achieving a consistent mediocrity" (33). Like Henry Adams, Holmes was clearly attracted to ideas and experiences that his upbringing prevented him from embracing; his writing thus often takes on a tone of bemused tolerance for things he himself wants nothing to do with. In an essay on the new American poetic style, for example, Holmes gently mocks Whitman by grouping him with Timothy Dexter and others who dispense with punctuation and rhythm, make up words and spellings, "glorify without idealizing":

> I confess that I am not in sympathy with some of the movements that accompany the manifestations of American social and literary independence. . . . I shrink from a lawless independence to which all the virile energy and trampling audacity of Mr. Whitman fail to reconcile me.

But in a revealing passage, Holmes goes on to transcend his own discriminating tastes:

> But there is room for everybody and everything in our huge hemisphere. Young America is like a three-year-old colt with his saddle and bridle just taken off. The first thing he wants to do is to *roll*. He is a droll object, sprawling in the grass with his four hoofs in the air; but he likes it, and he won't harm us. So let him roll,—let him roll! (1891, 237–38)

Holmes's argument that America is large and can contain vast varieties of style and experience is a bit ironic, since only a few pages earlier he had complained about Whitman's poetic stance precisely because it was too accepting:

> He accepts as poetical subjects all things alike, common and unclean, without discrimination, miscellaneous as the contents of the great sheet which Peter saw let down from heaven. He carries the principle of republicanism through the whole world of created objects. He will "thread a thread through [his] poems," he tells us, "that no one thing in the universe is inferior to another thing." (1891, 234)

The difference, of course, is that Whitman accepts "without discrimination," where Holmes accepts discriminatingly, tolerantly allowing but certainly not embracing experience that he personally finds distasteful. He maintains a hierarchy, charitably allowing some aspects of experience to enter in on the lower rungs of the hierarchy where others might not allow them to appear at all. But Whitman's form of acceptance, Holmes makes clear, leads to clutter—to "all things alike, common and unclean," "miscellaneous."

Holmes's biblical reference, however, revealingly compounds his ambivalence; he ascribes to Whitman Peter's vision from God of the "great sheet": "Wherein were all manner of fourfooted beasts and creeping things of the earth and fowls of the heaven." In the Bible, a voice from above tells Peter to consume this motley, but Peter demurs, saying, "I have never eaten anything that is common and unclean." The voice upbraids Peter: "What God hath cleansed, make not thou common." And then Peter interprets the vision: "Unto me hath God shewed that I should not call any man common or unclean" (10 Acts). Holmes, in a backhanded way, makes Whitman the recipient and enactor of God's democratic vision, the teacher of acceptance of the totality of God's creation. Holmes is uncomfortable with the common and unclean, though at some level he also knows he should not be, and so he is fascinated with Whitman while at the same time he is careful to distance himself from him.

What is finally most revealing about Holmes's reaction to Whitman is that his description of the poet matches precisely his own description of photography; both Whitman and photography are, for Holmes, harbingers of a new aesthetic of democratic wholeness. Both, to use Holmes's terms, carry "the principle of republicanism through the whole world of created objects." What most attracted Holmes to photography was something that clearly disturbed him as well, as his vocabulary of fear suggests:

> There is such a frightful amount of detail, that we have the same sense of infinite complexity which Nature gives us. A painter shows us masses; the stereoscopic figure spares us nothing,—all must be there, every stick, straw, scratch, as faithfully as the dome of St. Peter's, or the summit of Mont Blanc, or the ever-moving stillness of Niagara. The sun is no respecter of persons or of things. (1859, 744)

Here we have again a version of Peter's vision of the sheet from heaven; the sun, like God, is no respecter of persons or of things; it shines on everything equally, not granting its warmth according to a predetermined hierarchy. Whitman admired the sun for just that quality: "Not till the sun excludes you do I exclude you" (*LG* 387). Holmes (like many

others in mid-nineteenth-century America) called photographs sunpic-
tures or sunpaintings, for whatever the sun touched could (and eventually, it seemed, *would*) become etched in a photograph; no matter how
painful the thing recorded, the "honest sunshine" never blinked (1863,
12). "Photography," literally light writing, came to be the common
word for the new art, and in some essential ways this term applies directly to Whitman's poetics, a poetry that strove to name whatever the
sun lit:

> As they emit themselves facts are showered over with light . . . the
> daylight is lit with more volatile light. . . . Each precise object or condi-
> tion or combination or process exhibits a beauty. (*LG* 721)

"Does the daylight astonish?" asks Whitman, affirming the miraculous
in the commonplace; often he explicitly carves his images out of their
reflected light, as when he views a black man in "Song of Myself": "The
sun falls on his crispy hair and mustache, falls on the back of his polish'd
and perfect limbs" (*LG* 40). The sun highlighted and made powerful
those very things that society ignored and rendered powerless; the sun
was the cosmic democrat, turning every moment before our eyes into a
scene of infinite miracle:

> We hear of miracles.—But what is there that is not a miracle? What
> may you conceive of or name to me in the future, that shall be beyond
> the least thing around us?—I am looking in your eyes,—tell me then, if
> you can, what is there in the immortality of the soul more than this
> spiritual and beautiful miracle of sight? . . . I open two pairs of lids,
> only as big as peach pits, when lo! the unnamable variety and whelming
> splendor of the whole world come to me with silence and with swift-
> ness.—In an instant make I fluid and draw to myself, keeping each to
> its distinct isolation, and no hubbub or confusion, or jam, the whole of
> physical nature, though rocks are dense and hills are ponderous, and
> the stars are away off sextillions of miles.—All the years of all the beings
> that have ever lived on the earth, with all the science and genius, were
> nobly occupied in the employment of investigating this single minute
> of my life. (*NUPM* 106–107)

This absorptive inclusiveness, of course, finds its poetic manifestation
in Whitman's cataloging technique, a representative randomness of detail, suggesting the possibility that literally anything could enter the
poem and only add to, never detract from, its overall beauty and fullness
of celebration. Photography seemed to have the same impulse to catalog,
make images of, all of reality, every detail. When Holmes looked
through his endlessly growing collection of photographic images, he was
fascinated by how he could leaf through the world with abandon, losing
any sense of predetermined direction, how he could move about "with-

out following a *valet-de-place,* in any order of succession,—from a glacier to Vesuvius, from Niagara to Memphis,—as long as you like, and breaking off as suddenly as you like" (1861, 16). Examining a photograph of Broadway in 1861, Holmes actually begins to catalog his reactions, as if the photograph has taught him the variety of detail in any moment that undermines strict order, chronology, and hierarchy: "But what a wonder it is, this snatch at the central life of a mighty city as it rushed by in all its multitudinous complexity of movement!" If we assign each of his ecstatic sentences its own line, we end up with a Holmesian Whitman poem, cataloging Mannahatta:

> There stands Car No. 33 of the Astor House and Twenty-Seventh Street Fourth Avenue line.
> The old woman would miss an apple from that pile which you see glistening on her stand.
> The young man whose back is to us could swear to the pattern of his shawl.
> The gentleman between two others will no doubt remember that he had a headache the next morning, after this walk he is taking.
> Notice the caution with which the man driving the dapple-gray horse in a cart loaded with barrels holds his reins, one in each hand.
> See the shop-boys with their bundles, the young fellow with a lighted cigar in his hand, as you see by the way he keeps it off from his body, the *gamin* stooping to pick up something in the midst of the moving omnibuses, the stout philosophical car-man sitting on his cart-tail.
>
> (1861, 17)

Holmes's description goes on and on; the "multitudinous complexity" of the "hundreds of objects" in this "fearfully suggestive picture" have released something in him, a desire to name and identify "all things alike, common and unclean, without discrimination, miscellaneous"—the very thing he attacked Whitman for thirty years later, when he chastised Whitman for accepting such commonplace things as "poetical subjects." But as for photographic subjects, the "one infinite charm" was the idea that "a perfect photograph is absolutely inexhaustible":

> In a picture you can find nothing which the artist has not seen before you; but in a perfect photograph there will be as many beauties lurking, unobserved, as there are flowers that blush unseen in forests and meadows. (1859, 744)

Holmes finds the same thing in photographs—a lurking, unobserved beauty—that Whitman finds in the world, where "ten million supple-wristed gods are always hiding beauty in the world—burying it every where in every thing" (*DBN* 770).

VII. "TO PHOTOGRAPH A TEMPEST"

But as always for Holmes, there were limits to his enthusiasm for variety. Just as he had been both attracted to and bothered by the "frightful amount of detail" in each individual photograph, so was he uneasy about the insatiable appetite of the whole enterprise of photography: "The field of photography is extending itself to embrace subjects of strange and sometimes fearful interest." Holmes looked in fascinated horror at Brady's Civil War battlefield scenes, "views which the truthful sunbeam has delineated in all their dread reality." They offered chastening lessons: "Let him who wishes to know what war is look at this series of illustrations." But for Holmes, the scenes were too painful, too real, and they finally needed to be excluded from the album of our familiar sight: "We buried them in the recesses of our cabinet as we would have buried the mutilated remains of the dead they too vividly represented" (1863, 12–13). The new images were too radical, too vivid, in their representation; they too violently overturned the visual constructions of war that artists over the years had offered to help us contain the chaos. They created, as Alan Trachtenberg has noted, "a potential fissure within Holmes's system of belief" as "the seeable represented the unspeakable" and led to a questioning of the worth of the war itself (1985, 10), so these images needed to be tucked away, like dark secrets.

Too vivid a representation—here is where Holmes and Whitman part ways in their enthusiasm for photography. Whitman took the war photographs of Brady and Gardner and enfolded them in words, absorbing them fully into *Leaves of Grass* and *Specimen Days:* "Faces ghastly, swollen, purple . . . / . . . the dead on their backs with arms toss'd wide" (*LG* 320–21). It was primarily through photographs that Whitman and the rest of America learned to see war in nonheroic terms, and it was through photographs that Whitman experienced the battlefield bloodshed; his absorption of the scenes into his poems was not easy, for it tested his theory of openness to experience, his desire to face unflinchingly the whole of reality: "I saw the bloody holocaust of the Wilderness & Manassas / I saw the wounded & the dead, & never forget them / (Ever since have they been with me—they have fused ever since in my poems:—) / They are here forever in my poems" (*LG* 682).

The real power of Whitman's Civil War writings, especially the glowing prose of *Specimen Days,* is in his evocation of the aftermath of war, its lingering deaths and haunted memories. Once, late in his life, when talking about why writers fail effectively to capture the battle scenes of war, Whitman appealed to a photographic analogy:

> My experiences on the field have shown me that the writers catch very little of the real atmosphere of a battle. It is an assault, an immense noise, somebody driven off the field—a victory won: that is all. It is like trying to photograph a tempest. (*WWC* 2:53)

In the twentieth century, photography would become quick enough and portable enough to photograph that tempest, to make us see the terror of combat in ways we had never before conceived of it, but in the 1860s photography still required tripods, developing wagons, and careful preparations; it lent itself to capturing the harrowing still results of the battle, not the transient close-up action of battle itself (see Trachtenberg 1985, 1–3). Whitman's remarkable attempt to turn the war inside out, to bring America to the hospital that its war had created ("America, already brought to Hospital in her fair youth" [*C* 1:69]), to recenter the war on what had previously been its marginal and ignored aspects (the amputation and infection and diarrhea) was in large part the result of being taught, along with the rest of America, to see the war in just this ghastly way: the teachers were the Civil War photographers, and we still feel the silent bleak power of their lessons in the thousands of surviving photographs. War would never again look the way artists had taught us for hundreds of years to see it, though the old habits of seeing would die hard; Theodore Davis, the Civil War illustrator, commented on how people's trained expectations were continually disappointed by the stark reality of war photographs, how the public wanted to be shown visual images of heroism of the sort they had been taught to look for. People, he said, "seem to have an idea that all battlefields have some elevated spot upon which the general is located, and that from this spot the commander can see his troops, direct all their manoeuvres and courteously furnish special artists an opportunity of sketching the scene" (quoted in Thomas 204). This hierarchical image of battle was, under the force of photography, giving way, and the tidy and ordered imagery of war was being replaced by the uncontrollable clutter of actual battle. It was another way that Henry Adams's ordered universe was being displaced by a chaotic "multiverse," and as more and more horrifying battle scenes became effectively photographed in the twentieth century, the battlefield itself was revealed to be chaos, filth, and clutter, not order, discipline, and command. And still, after all the blistering horrors of twentieth-century wars, the most harrowing photographs of all remain the images of aftermaths: the concentration camps, the streets of Hiroshima, the naked and burned Vietnamese child with her mouth frozen in a scream. Those are the images, like the images of Andersonville and the Civil War hospitals in Whitman's time, that make us question what we really are.

5

Whitman and Photographs of the Self

> It is like trying to photograph a tempest.
> Whitman (*WWC* 2:53)

Whitman was referring to Civil War battles when he talked of photographing a tempest, but there was another tempest that photography came to reveal to Whitman, and that was the ceaseless tumult of life, the ravages of *tempus* recorded on the human face. Before photography, no one had seen a full series of accurate images of a single life; photographs taken of the same person over a long period of time revealed that life itself was something of a tempest, an irreversible process of aging and dying. As an old man, Whitman was part of the first generation of humans who could observe themselves as young people, who could examine traces of themselves along a visual continuum leading directly up to the image of themselves in the present. This revelation was immediately seen at the advent of photography as one of its most revolutionary aspects.

Whitman was among the first generation, then, to become fascinated, as by now we all are, with photographic images of the self. From the early 1840s (within a couple of years after the daguerreotype process first came to America) until within a year of his death, Whitman sat-for photographers, collected and commented on the results, admired certain poses and disliked others, tolerated the middling ones, and burned some of the bad ones. Toward the end of his life, he and his friends began thinking about publishing a book or album containing a selection of his photographs, images that had made the "good gray poet" something of a celebrity. The album was never completed, but during his last years Whitman sifted through the clutter of photos scattered about him in his

Camden room and peered carefully at that lifetime of images, trying to read what they told him of himself.

Some of the photos were clearly personal mementos, not part of Whitman's various schemes for self-advertisement and self-iconography. Others were simply not pleasing to him; they sometimes revealed aspects of himself he did not like to admit were there, and for a poet who celebrated the fullness and wholeness of an endlessly diverse self, such feelings were dangerous and puzzling. Then there were the images that he chose to have reproduced, some by the hundreds, some in his books, images that he would sanction as the authentic Whitman, that would form the public face out of which emerged the voice in the poems. We now have around 130 remaining photographic images of him—there were once no doubt many more—but even these form a remarkably full photographic record for someone who died before photography reached its truly portable phase. It was around the time of Whitman's death that roll film and small cameras came into existence, quickly democratizing the act of photography, moving it out of the hands of skilled masters into all of our hands, making image making far easier than even he could have imagined.

Whitman's adult lifetime of photographs forms at once the most intimate and most public record of any nineteenth-century writer. To look at this impressive series of images is to wonder whether we are seeing one of the great narcissistic acts of the century—an obsessive turning in, a fascination with his own uniqueness—or one of the most public acts, an exfoliation of the self through filmic images out into the world, a replication of the self analogous to the publication of his poems, an attempt to become the representative American. As with his best poetry (a poetry that defined the self as infinitely absorptive as it turned out to the world to embrace the vast contradictions of experience, then pulled that variety firmly into the self to hold it, contain it, caress it, and unify it), his photographic project seems at once an attempt to define the self by sharing it with the world, but also by casting it into a represented image so that he could contemplate it, dwell on it, look outward into his own eyes.

I. "THE LAUGHING PHILOSOPHER"

One of Whitman's favorite photographs of himself was a George Cox portrait that Whitman entitled "The Laughing Philosopher." We don't know why Whitman chose this allusion to Democritus, the laughing philosopher—perhaps only because Cox's photo captured an angle on Whitman that made him look both sage and jolly—but it turned out to be an appropriate appellation. Democritus was in fact

Figure 2. Early 1840s. Daguerreotype. Photographer unknown: perhaps John Plumbe, Jr. Bayley Collection, Ohio Wesleyan University.

Figure 3. July 1854. Steel engraving by Samuel Hollyer of daguerreotype by Gabriel Harrison (original daguerreotype lost). Used as frontispiece for 1855 *Leaves of Grass*. Charles E. Feinberg Collection.

129

Figure 4. 1859. Steel engraving by Schoff from a painting by Charles Hine. Used as frontispiece for 1860 *Leaves of Grass*. Charles E. Feinberg Collection.

Figure 5. 1864? Photograph by Alexander Gardner, Washington, D.C. Charles E. Feinberg Collection.

130

Figure 6. 1867? Photograph
by Mathew Brady, Wash-
ington, D.C. Charles E.
Feinberg Collection.

Figure 7. 1869? Photogra-
pher unknown: perhaps
William Kurtz. Bayley Collection, Ohio Wesleyan
University.

131

Figure 8. 1871? Woodcut engraving by William J. Linton of George C. Potter photograph. Charles E. Feinberg Collection.

Figure 9. 1881? Photograph by Charles E. Spieler, Philadelphia. Used as frontispiece for *Complete Poems and Prose of Walt Whitman 1855 . . . 1888*. Charles E. Feinberg Collection.

Figure 10. 1887. Photograph by George C. Cox, New York. This photo was named by Whitman "The Laughing Philosopher." Charles E. Feinberg Collection.

much on the American mind as photography and photographic portraits began to change the way humans perceived the world; he had become the accidental prophet of photography, because he had, in 400 B.C., talked of films. When Oliver Wendell Holmes tried to bring some perspective to the photographic revolution in 1859, twenty years after the daguerreotype first appeared in the United States, he began with a discussion of the Laughing Philosopher:

> Democritus of Abdera, commonly known as the Laughing Philosopher, probably because he did not consider the study of truth inconsistent with a cheerful countenance, believed and taught that all bodies were continually throwing off certain images like themselves, which subtile emanations, striking on our bodily organs, gave rise to our sensations. . . . Forms, effigies, membranes, or *films,* are the nearest representatives of the terms applied to these effluences. They are perpetually shed from the surfaces of solids, as bark is shed by trees. . . . Under the action of light, then, a body makes its superficial aspect potentially present at a distance, becoming appreciable as a shadow or as a picture. . . . These visible films or membranous *exuviae* of objects, which the old philosophers talked about, have no real existence, separable from their illuminated source, and perish instantly when it is withdrawn.

Holmes goes on to imagine Democritus's reaction to the very idea of the daguerreotype:

> If a man had handed a metallic speculum to Democritus of Abdera, and told him to look at his face in it while his heart was beating thirty or forty times, promising that one of the films the face was shedding should stick there, so that neither he, nor it, nor anybody should forget what manner of man he was, the Laughing Philosopher would probably have vindicated his claim to his title by an explosion that would have astonished the speaker. (1859, 738)

But over two thousand years later, the Laughing Philosopher, in a later incarnation, would be captured in a photograph, in the guise of Walt Whitman, who, in choosing to label his photograph "The Laughing Philosopher," playfully acknowledged a deep and transhistorical identity with Democritus. Whitman and Democritus share many assumptions; the opening to "Song of Myself" can in fact be read as Whitman's succinct version of Democritus's atomic theory: "every atom belonging to you as good belongs to me." Democritus was the originator of Greek atomism, the idea that atoms and the void are the only elements of reality, that all things we perceive as "difference" are only "modifications in the shape, arrangement, and position of atoms" (Lloyd 447). Democritus thus postulates what for Whitman would become the essentials of a democratic reality, an infinite variety made up of an overriding unity, a unity that is always changing shape in an ecstatic composting catalog of infinitely various forms of ongoing life. Democritus also is the first philosopher to offer a full account of the physical basis of sensation; he was fascinated, as was Whitman, with the "curious mystery of the eyesight" (*LG* 714). For Democritus, the images or films emitted by all physical objects have a physical presence; these images are met by parallel images emitted by the eye, and the air between the object and the eye is momentarily imprinted with what we see. Just as for Whitman, the poet is the one who traverses for all people "the path between reality and their souls" (LG 714), so is that which we see always for Democritus a melded image of what is out there and what is in the self.

"Appearances, now or henceforth, indicate what you are!" commands Whitman in "Crossing Brooklyn Ferry": "You necessary film, continue to envelop the soul!" (LGV 224). The film that envelops the soul is what creates appearance, is what "reality" is and why reality is for Whitman the crucial starting point; objects in the world are the "dumb beautiful ministers" (LGV 225) whose souls are told only when the poet brings words to them and penetrates the film by describing it accurately. When Whitman in this poem says he was "struck from the float forever held in solution" and thus "received identity by my body" (LGV 221), he suggests that identity itself is like a photograph: the striking of the individual out of the cosmic float is the creation of self-as-representation, a soul incarnated as image. The self for Whitman, struck like an engraving, impressed into reality, and separated from others, is the basal representation that allows for and is confirmed by all subsequent representations: photographs of ourselves confirm that we have been struck from the float, just as every photograph strikes us once again from the float of our temporal existence. We are souls enveloped by film.

For Holmes and Whitman, then, as for most observers of photography in its first fifty years, photographs were more than images: they were actual magical presences. This sense of photographs still persists, of course; Susan Sontag discusses how photographs have actually been able to "usurp reality" because "a photograph is not only an image (as a painting is an image), an interpretation of the real; it is also a trace, something directly stenciled off the real, like a footprint or a death mask." Sounding much like Democritus, Sontag defines a photograph as "never less than the registering of an emanation (light waves reflected by objects)—a material vestige of its subject in a way that no painting can be" (154).

From the time Whitman as a young man first saw photographs up until the time he died, he was overwhelmed by the power of the photographed face. As a young man, he wandered the great daguerreotype galleries in New York where he felt himself watched by the "material vestiges" of hundreds of faces peering out from the walls, and as an old man in his house in Camden he sifted through the clutter of photographs on the floor of his room—photos of his friends and of himself—and carefully examined each one, caressing the image of life that he found there. If Whitman's test for art was, as he said in Democratic Vistas, the ability to "breathe into" material creation "the breath of life, and endow it with an identity" (*PW* 419), then no art was more perfect in Whitman's eyes than portrait photography.

II. THE "HEART'S GEOGRAPHY'S MAP"

In his poetry, from the beginning, Whitman was obsessed with faces, with what he called in the 1840s "that masterpiece of physical perfection, the human face" (quoted in Rubin 158). One of the original twelve *Leaves of Grass* poems was the long catalog of faces variously named over the years "Poem of Faces," "Leaf of Faces," and finally simply "Faces." Harold Aspiz has offered a convincing reading of this poem as a phrenological study, and certainly Whitman's fascination with faces owes much to phrenology, though phrenology was more concerned with the shape of the skull than with the particulars of the face. In this poem, Whitman gives us "Faces of friendship, precision, caution, suavity, ideality," and he gives us faces "bitten by vermin and worms," faces like "a dog's snout sniffing for garbage." As he presents this gallery of faces, Whitman reads them as a tangle of often-grotesque present reality that masks the potential, the fully realized soul that lies latent in and justifies each face: "Do you suppose I could be content with all if I thought them their own finale?" The poem embodies, then, Whitman's incessant desire to capture the flux of the actual world around him but to see that reality always as suggestive of an ideal that will eventually emerge from it; some of the faces the poet sees, like the "old face of the mother of many children, . . . her face is clearer and more beautiful than the sky," are simply closer to ideal fulfillment than others.

The many faces in this poem may well derive from Whitman's frequent tours of New York daguerreotype galleries; writing about his visit to John Plumbe's gallery in 1846, he sounds the very note that would generate the poem: "What a spectacle! In whatever direction you turn your peering gaze, you see naught but human faces! There they stretch, from floor to ceiling—hundreds of them." The poem simply moves the gallery outdoors: "Sauntering the pavement thus, or crossing the ceaseless ferry, faces and faces and faces, / I see them and complain not, and am content with all." In Plumbe's gallery, Whitman catalogs the "great legion of human faces" that surround him, describing characters that would later occupy prominent places in his poem:

> Here is one now—a handsome female, apparently in a bridal dress. . . .
> Another, near by, is the miniature of an aged matron, on whose head many winters have deposited their snowy semblance.—But what a calm serene bearing! How graceful she looks in her old age! (*GF* 2:114)

Whitman came to believe, looking at these daguerreotypes, that it was "hardly possible to conceive any higher perfection of art, in the way of transferring the representation of that subtle thing, *human expression,* to the tenacious grip of a picture which is never to fade!" (quoted in Brasher 215).

Whitman often presents his own face in his poems in vividly photographic portrayals. "Song of Myself," illustrated from the beginning with the wonderfully shadowed Gabriel Harrison daguerreotype, presents the poet's face—lit and shaded by the play of the sun upon it—as part of the worshipped "spread of my own body": "Sun so generous it shall be you! / Vapors lighting and shading my face it shall be you!" (*LG* 53). He wants the reader, via the poem and portrait, to look deeply into his face: "I carry the plenum of proof and every thing else in my face"; "Listener up there! . . . / Look in my face while I snuff the sidle of evening" (*LG* 55, 88), and he in turn looks deeply into all faces, including his own: "In the faces of men and women I see God, and in my own face in the glass" (*LG* 87). A great variety of faces is the gift that New York gives him in abundance, and it is a gift he can never have enough of: "you give me forever faces; / . . . Give me faces and streets . . . / Give me interminable eyes" (*LG* 313).

The faces in Whitman's poems become more pervasive and haunting in the Civil War poems, where soldiers' faces again and again look into his own as he peers into and remembers face after face ("I think this face is the face of the Christ himself" [*LG* 307]; "I draw near, / Bend down and touch lightly with my lips the white face in the coffin" [*LG* 321]; "His eyes are closed, his face is pale, he dares not look on the bloody stump" [*LG* 311]; "Found you in death so cold dear comrade, . . . / Bared your face in the starlight, . . . / Long there and then in vigil I stood" [*LG* 304]). All these faces stay in the memory like an album of photographs of the lost and dead, a poetic echo of the Brady and Gardner and O'Sullivan photos of the Civil War dead. Photographs had become an organic part of the human memory; Whitman's letters record how often he exchanged photos with his soldier-friends who survived, externalizing and holding memories and identities by means of such portraits.

Whitman's most direct poetic statement about the power of the photographic face is "Out from behind This Mask," a poem first published in *Two Rivulets* in 1876. It is a remarkable piece, though it has received little critical attention. The poem is subtitled "(To Confront a Portrait.)," and originally Whitman made it clear that the poem referred to W. J. Linton's woodcut of George Potter's 1871 photograph of the poet (see Figure 8), which had appeared in the 1876 *Leaves.* But Whitman set the poem floating free of this portrait in *Leaves,* so that the subtitle not only invites the reader to hear the poem as a poetic statement literally confronting the Linton/Potter portrait, but also as a kind of general tutorial on how we should confront any portrait, any photograph of a face. It thus becomes Whitman's one extended poetic meditation on the power of portrait photography.

The poem clearly finds its origins in Whitman's own overwhelming initial reactions to the daguerreotypes he saw as a young reporter in New York:

> . . . it is little else on all sides of you, than a great legion of human faces—human eyes gazing silently but fixedly upon you, and creating the impression of an immense Phantom concourse—speechless and motionless, but yet *realities*. You are indeed in a new world—a peopled world, though mute as the grave. . . . It is singular what a peculiar influence is possessed by the *eye* of a well-painted miniature or portrait.—It has a sort of magnetism. . . . For the strange fascination of looking at the eyes of a portrait, sometimes goes beyond what comes from the real orbs themselves. Plumbe's beautiful and multifarious pictures all strike you . . . with their *naturalness,* and the *life-look* of the eye—that soul of the face! In all his vast collection, many of them thrown hap-hazard, we notice not one that has a dead eye. (GF 2:116–17)

Just two years before the first edition of *Leaves,* Whitman wrote again about being haunted by the multitude of faces in a daguerreotype gallery, this time Jeremiah Gurney's establishment:

> A thousand faces? They look at you from all parts of the large and sumptuously furnished saloon. Over your shoulders, back, behind you, staring square in front, how the eyes, almost glittering with the light of life, bend down upon one, and silently follow all his motions. . . . How many of these, whose faces look upon us, are now away in distant regions? How many are dead? (quoted in Rubin 283)

It is exactly the riveting eyes of his own portrait, with their ability to glitter with the light of life, to carry the *"life-look,"* that Whitman wants to emphasize in the poem. The effect of the eyes is heightened by the fact that he is separated from us by death; just as he intensifies the effect of many of his poems by addressing them to readers who will be reading them long after the poet is dead, so does he use his portraits to add to the sense of a conquering of space and time: though he is not of our time or place, still he speaks to us through the time-conquering medium of poetry, and he looks at us (and we look at him) through the time-conquering medium of the photograph. It is fitting, then, that the poem is written as if the portrait itself is speaking:

1
Out from behind this bending rough-cut mask,
These lights and shades, this drama of the whole,
This common curtain of the face contain'd in me for me, in you for
    you, in each for each,
(Tragedies, sorrows, laughter, tears—O heaven!
The passionate teeming plays this curtain hid!)
This glaze of God's serenest purest sky,
This film of Satan's seething pit,
This heart's geography's map, this limitless small continent, this
    soundless sea;
Out from the convolutions of this globe,
This subtler astronomic orb than sun or moon, than Jupiter, Venus,
    Mars,
This condensation of the universe, (nay here the only universe,
Here the idea, all in this mystic handful wrapt;)
These burin'd eyes, flashing to you to pass to future time,
To launch and spin through space revolving sideling, from these to
    emanate,
To you whoe'er you are—a look.

2
A traveler of thoughts and years, of peace and war,
Of youth long sped and middle age declining,
(As the first volume of a tale perusèd and laid away, and this the
    second,
Songs, ventures, speculations, presently to close,)
Lingering a moment here and now, to you I opposite turn,
As on the road or at some crevice door by chance, or open'd window,
Pausing, inclining, baring my head, you specially I greet,
To draw and clinch your soul for once inseparably with mine,
Then travel travel on.

                                                          (LG 381–83)

The opening stanza is syntactically a reprise of the opening paragraph of
"Out of the Cradle Endlessly Rocking"; the inverted, cumulative piling
on of originating clauses creates a suspense as we await the base clause,
the subject and verb that will settle the deluge of clauses into a unified
order. In "Out of the Cradle," the base clause is "I sing," and the singing
"I" literally emerges *out of* the various natural voices that give rise to it:
the sounds of the sea and the mocking bird and the words aroused by the
various sights and experiences of nature and family that created the "I"
that can only now sing a reminiscence of them by embodying them. Just
as "Out of the Cradle" opens with repeated "Out of" and "Out from"
and "From" clauses, so also does "Out from behind This Mask." Yet a
base clause never does emerge in this poem; there is, after all, no "I" to
emerge, no subject that can sing or do anything; for behind the mask of

the portrait is only "a look." The first stanza insistently remains a sentence fragment, doing nothing, simply staying still, like the portrait, in an unchanging state of casting out a look. As we confront the portrait, after all, it is only ink and paper, just as are the words of Whitman's poems: poems and portraits can carry life only if readers and lookers respond to them by bringing life to them, instilling them with spirit and meaning. In the original version of "A Song for Occupations," Whitman had mourned the loss of life when living poems were embodied in a book: "I was chilled with the cold types and cylinder and wet paper between us. / I pass so poorly with paper and types. . . . I must pass with the contact of bodies and souls" (*LGV* 84). Similarly, he had warned, as we have seen, about coming to love images more than the life they represented: "The well-taken photographs—but your wife or friend close and solid in your arms?" (*LG* 78). The danger of art, Whitman argued, was that it made us worship the images of reality rather than pointing us back to the reality that the art is only signaling.

As *Leaves* grew, however, Whitman gained more faith in the ability of the cold types to carry life, to embody an identity, and much of the radical success of his book was his development of what C. Carroll Hollis has called "the most successful metonymic trick in poetic history" (252): "Camerado, this is no book, / Who touches this touches a man, / . . . I spring from the pages into your arms" (*LG* 505). Whitman thereby developed a complex strategy for forcing the reader into an athletic struggle with his poems, challenging the reader to be active not passive, to enter into the creative act, to bring the poem to life, not to sit back and wait for the author-ity to pour meaning into the vessel-reader. The portraits of himself that he included in his books were part of his strategy, printed faces fixing the reader with a gaze, fragments of ink casting out a look that the reader would have to energize, bring to life. It was all part of Whitman's radical democratic aesthetics, what Alan Trachtenberg (paraphrasing Karl Mannheim) has called "the ecstasy of identifying with the physical point of view of another, seeing through the other's eyes into one's own, as the psychological basis of a truly democratic culture" (1989, 68). Photographs of himself allowed Whitman to see into his own eyes (a necessary act of democratic self-regard), and they encouraged readers to see through his eyes into their own, to imagine what thoughts lay behind the mask (a necessary act of democratic identification).

Preparing the final edition of *Leaves,* Whitman worked long and hard on his choice of portraits, wanting to make sure each one "has its place: has some relation to the text"; he wanted "all the pictures [to] have a significance which gives them their own justification . . . whether the fortunate (or unfortunate) reader sees it or fails to see it" (*WWC* 2:536). Even the inclusion of portraits, then, was a challenge to the reader to work, to struggle for meaning, to respond. Whitman's strategy often involved casting his words in fragments, inviting the reader to supply the verb, to form the syntactic bond that would activate the whole process of the poem every time the poem was encountered, confronted. To confront a portrait, then, was for Whitman similar to confronting a poem: both required an active responder, what Whitman called an "athletic reader."

The second stanza of the poem, then, works toward the union of poet/poem/portrait and reader, and Whitman moves toward that union through a typically complex syntactic strategy. The base clause of the second stanza is "I turn to you," but Whitman casts it in an inverted form: "to you I opposite turn." By such an inversion, Whitman accomplishes several effects. First, the "I" emerges only after the "you" has been manifested; only when the you—the active reader, the energetic confronter—engages the portrait or poem fully—"here and now," in this exact place at this exact time—will the "I" that is contained there come alive, suddenly and quickly "turn" and "greet" and "draw" and "clinch" and "travel travel on" in a sequence of confronting, joining, and departing (a sequence that is characteristic of, among other things, any successful act of reading—it is, after all, the basic overall movement of "Song of Myself" as the poet confronts and challenges us, cajoles us into a union, then departs "as air"). Whitman bids the reader to have an encounter with his portraits (and by implication his poems) every bit as intense as the encounters he, in the 1840s, had with those various galleries of photographed faces he was always energized by. By inverting the clause, too, Whitman manages to juggle the words so that the "you" and "I" stand together, separated by no intervening action or conjunction, thus accomplishing a linguistic effect not easy to achieve, a moment of magical joining between the "you" and "I" so that we can effectively hear the clause as "*into* you I opposite turn"; that is, in this act of confronting a portrait, our active engagement allows the "I" to turn, for a moment, into you, into us: the opposites are resolved and embraced. Only by such active union, by our giving the ink voice and breath again in our time and place, can the poet enter our present and we enter the poet's past. It is the active conspiracy that Whitman is always trying to beguile his reader into: "What is more subtle than this which ties me to the woman or man that looks in my face? / Which fuses me into you now, and pours my meaning into you?" (*LG* 164).

So Whitman offers a maze of participles in the poem, words that hold the verbs' active qualities in potential, waiting for the reader to offer up the necessary copulative verb that will bring the potential to actuality; the portrait face is described as bending, teeming, flashing, revolving, sideling, declining, lingering, pausing, inclining, baring—doing all it can to lean toward the observer, pour forth an offer for union, wait patiently for a response. In this way the poem is similar to "A Noiseless Patient Spider," another post–Civil War poem that offers up what appears to be an extended sentence that also turns out to be a fragment filled with participles seeking a copulative, seeking something to join and catch and give completion:

> And you O my soul where you stand,
> Surrounded, detached, in measureless oceans of space,
> Ceaselessly musing, venturing, throwing, seeking the spheres to
>   connect them,
> Till the bridge you will need be form'd, till the ductile anchor hold,
> Till the gossamer thread you fling catch somewhere, O my soul.

Just as the spider/soul in this poem, exploring "the vacant vast surrounding, / . . . launch'd forth filament, filament, filament, out of itself, / . . . ever tirelessly speeding them" (*LG* 450), so do "These burin'd eyes, flashing to you to pass to future time" seek "To launch and spin through space . . . a look" (*LG* 382). In both poems the poet is waiting for the reader who will complete the act, turn the fragment to a complete sentence: in "A Noiseless Patient Spider," the active responder would serve as the "ductile anchor" that would hold so that the "gossamer thread" flung by the soul would firmly "catch somewhere"; in the portrait poem, the search is for a "you" that will allow the portrait poem to "draw and clinch your soul for once inseparably with mine" (*LG* 383). The photographic portrait, then, becomes another image for the poet portrayed in "To a Stranger," always on the lookout for the partner who would complete any moment: "Passing stranger! you do not know how longingly I look upon you, / You must be he I was seeking, or she I was seeking" (*LG* 127). "Out from behind This Mask" originally appeared in *Two Rivulets,* part of a cluster of poems having to do with joinings of subjects and objects; the cluster opened with "Two Rivulets," where the streams of the title image are pictured as "Two blended, parallel, strolling tides, / Companions, travelers, gossiping as they journey" (*LGV* 655). So in the portrait poem, the reader and poet are portrayed as two travelers who become blended through the medium of the portrait, their individualities flowing into a common ocean.

"Out from behind This Mask" begins with a line that echoes "So Long!," the poem Whitman chose as the concluding statement of *Leaves of Grass:* "From behind the screen where I hid I advance personally solely to you" (*LG* 505). Whitman, of course, claimed to be the poet of indirection, and certainly his claims that he is "far different from what you suppose" (*LG* 123) relate to the portrayal of his portrait in this poem; whenever Whitman wrote about photographs, the imagery of veils and masks entered in, as in his notes for a poem on a photograph of himself taken by William Kurtz: "Veil with the lids thine eyes, O soul! / . . . Mask with the lids thine eyes" (*NUPM* 1400; see Figure 7). This imagery does not, however, suggest the impossibility of direct confrontation, but rather encourages the removal of barriers, urges the removal of the veil or of the type and paper that separated Whitman from his onlooking reader: the magic of a good portrait or poem for Whitman is that the veil can be pierced with a significant look, and the two rivulets can merge. As Marcus. A. Root noted in his influential 1864 textbook on photography (*The Camera and the Pencil*), "As the first step towards obtaining a good portrait, the photographer should penetrate, by whatever means at his command, the fleshly mask, which envelopes the spiritual part of his model, and ascertain his real type and character" (439). To pull the "expression" of "the true and dominant character" of the subject out from behind the "fleshly mask," says Root, is the "absolute essential" of portrait photography (439, 442).

Whitman's poem proceeds beyond the conventional face–mask metaphor to a remarkable series of metaphors for the face: it is a curtain behind which dramas are always going on, passions acted out that are hidden to the public by an unchanging facade; it is a glaze or film hiding the serene heaven or seething hell that lies behind; it is a map, a continent, a sea, the earth, a planet, the universe. The most striking metaphor is the face as "This heart's geography's map," as if in the contours and lines of the face itself can be read the true nature of the heart; in this trope, the face is now seen as an accurate guide, not a disguising veil or misleading glaze. As the series of images builds, the distance between the face and what lies behind it dwindles; the drama metaphor, with its histrionic emphasis on cut-out masks, heavy curtains, and acted-out roles, culminates in a line in which the syntax separates the speaker and reader as much as the imagery does: "This common curtain of the face contain'd in me for me, in you for you, in each for each" (*LG* 382). Each contained phrase holds a verbal mirror (me/me, you/you, each/each) that hopelessly isolates us all from each other. But when the imagery shifts to the "heart's geography's map," the emphasis moves toward possible understanding and union; if there is a map, then we can learn to read it, to follow the signs, to come to know a foreign country, explore a continent, travel the sea. The imagery expands wildly from theater to heaven to hell to continents and seas, to planets, to the universe, only to contract miraculously in the striking phrase, "all in this mystic handful wrapt." Like Blake seeing the world in a grain of sand or Dickinson avowing that the brain is wider than the sky, Whitman condenses the universe into the head in a powerful and physically constricted image, reminding us that though the brain is the size of our balled fists pressed together, it can contain the universe. And out from this compressed vastness, this infinity hovering behind the map/face, the eyes ("only as big as peach pits," as Whitman notes elsewhere) launch and spin a look out through time and space, right into our eyes, whoever and wherever we are—the look itself a space traveler and time traveler, "revolving sideling" toward us. Again Whitman astonishes with the odd juxtaposition of words: "revolving," "launching," and "spinning" suggest the vast traveling through the universe, and also hint at the actual physical motion of the eyeballs, while "sideling" familiarizes and domesticates the look, offering it up as a furtive glance, approaching us obliquely (as Whitman's looks usually do—"I am a man who, sauntering along without fully stopping, turns a casual look upon you and then averts his face" [LG 14]).

The second stanza, then, as we have seen, enacts the joining of his look to ours, pulling the "you" to "I," breaking out of the separating and mirrored isolation of the first stanza into the "opposite turning" of this union, drawing and clinching us, then averting his face and traveling traveling on. This stanza incorporates much of what Whitman came to find most intriguing about photographic portraits, the way they captured and created a pause along life's endless traveling and change. Life is a long speeding and declining, as youth evanesces into age; any photograph of ourselves becomes an occasion for reflection on life's ceaseless journey. In the 1870s, Whitman considered abandoning Leaves of Grass, calling it complete, and opening a second volume, to contain poems of the spirit instead of poems of the body; so here he viewed his life as a written work, with one volume completed and a second final one begun. Just as he draws our soul and clinches it to his, then moves on, so does a photo draw the soul—via the eyes and face—into a film, clinch it there, then remain a steady and unchanging map while the soul in its body travels on, speeding through youth, declining through middle age. The incessant traveling that this poem ends on is what a lifetime of photographs reveals about ourselves, a series of looks that record the soul's journey through this world by mapping the changing contours of the face. To view a lifetime's photographs of ourselves is to see how fleeting these permanent images really are. And Whitman, again, was of the first generation ever able to observe themselves age, to watch themselves—in a series of accurate images—"travel travel on."

III. "THE OUT LOOK OF THE FACE IN THE BOOK"

Whitman's belief that the various photographs he chose for inclusion in Leaves of Grass "have a significance which gives them their own justification . . . whether the fortunate (or unfortunate) reader sees it or fails to see it" is, of course, a challenge to the reader to discover the significance of, to see the interplay between the photographic and the verbal representations of Whitman in the book. To begin such an investigation, we might focus on two photographs that serve as a frame of sorts: the 1854 engraving of a daguerreotype that opens the first edition of *Leaves* and the 1881 profile photograph that Whitman chose to open his culminating *Complete Poems and Prose of Walt Whitman 1855 . . . 1888.* Both are open-collar photos, both are unorthodox poses, and both demand a redefinition of the image of "poet" (see Figures 3 and 9).

There is a theory of photographic portraiture which holds that the more studiolike and muted the background of a portrait is, the more emphasis there is on the individual importance of the subject. The suggestion inherent in a neutral backdrop is that this person does not have to be *placed* in order to understand his or her significance; there are enough cues in the very face, the clothes, the demeanor, to read the significance. The less distinguished the subject, the more an environment is needed to give significance to the person, and the more emblematic the person then becomes—more important for being *representative* of a place and a time than for one's individual importance. Thus, we have the well-known Lewis Hine photographs of anonymous faces of immigrants at Ellis Island or of steelworkers in Pennsylvania towns, faces that, while they may be memorable individually, tend to be so precisely because they are immediately suggestive of a group of people. There was a great deal of discussion in the nineteenth century about photographic backdrops and the social standing that various backgrounds suggested; some commentators even argued for a "plain, spotless, even background" as a kind of classless, democratic mode appropriate for portraiture in America (see Orvell, 90–91).

The daguerreotype Whitman used as the frontispiece to the first edition of *Leaves* is perhaps the most familiar image of him—hat on, shirt open, head cocked, arm akimbo. He stands against the most democratic of backgrounds, a vast blank page. But while there is no visible background, the pose (and the fact that the portrait remains anonymous, unnamed) invites us to read this figure symbolically, to place it in a social context that makes sense of the figure and, in so doing, to question traditional assumptions about what a poet can be, where a poet can come from, and how a poet can be portrayed. The portrait is Whitman's announcement of his first poetic pose: the worker/poet, his physicality signaled by the costume, by the suggestion of outdoors (he has his hat on, after all). Whitman referred to the photo as "the street figure" (*WWC* 2:412), thus suggesting an urban background.

The portrait, perhaps the first daguerreotype ever used as a frontispiece for a book of poems, makes its point in a number of ways: it is in sharp contrast to the expected iconography of poets' portraits, which conventionally emphasized formality and the head instead of this rough informality in which the center of the portrait is the torso, where we see arms, legs, body, all serving to diminish the centrality of the head, or at least to put the head in its place. Poets' portraits in the nineteenth century indicated that poetry was a function of the intellect, a formal business, conducted in book-lined rooms where ideas fed the head through words. Whitman, of course, was out to undermine this conception, to move poetry to the streets, to deformalize it, tear it away from the authority of tradition, and to insist that poetry emerged from the heart, lungs, genitals, and hands as much as from the head. He wanted the representative democratic poet to speak in his poems, so he omitted his own name from the title page to his book, instead letting the representative portrait speak to authorship: a representative democratic person, living life in the world, experiencing life through the five senses, a self that found authority in experience, that doffed its hat to no one, that refused to follow the decorum of removing the hat when indoors or even when in books. In 1850, Mathew Brady had published his *Gallery of Illustrious Americans*, containing a dozen daguerreotype portraits of what he called "representative" Americans—presidents, senators, generals, even a poet (William Ellery Channing)—and Alan Trachtenberg has shown how Whitman offered his own 1855 image as a different kind of "illustrious American," redefining Brady's notions and rejecting his "emphasis on established leaders and dignitaries," proposing a new conception of "illustrious" that was more democratically representative (Trachtenberg 1989, 69), allowing access to parts of the body and to parts of society that had up to that point been considered anything but illustrious.

Since there were as yet no methods for reproducing photographic images, Brady's "illustrious American" daguerreotypes were distributed as lithographs (by Francis D'Avignon), and part of their effect, as Trachtenberg has noted, results from the necessary transformation of the photographic image to a lithograph engraving, a process that produced "a general likeness in place of the original vibrancy and presence": "the daguerrean image is drained of its vitality in the processed picture, product of the engraver's interpretation." Such compromises were inevitable, given the available technologies; daguerreotypes offered a new vitality and accuracy to portraiture, but when mass duplication was needed, that vitality and accuracy gave way to "a formal look preserved and popularized by lithography" (Trachtenberg 1989, 46). But Whitman worked against this effect; instead of seeking an engraving that pretended to be a copy of a daguerreotype, he had Samuel Hollyer—a young British engraver visiting the United States who would after the Civil War settle in New Jersey and become one of the finest portrait engravers in the country—engrave Gabriel Harrison's daguerreotype in a way that did not *disguise* but rather *emphasized* the artificial and constructed nature of the lithographed image. While Hollyer's engraving renders Whitman's face and upper torso in photographic detail, its intensity of realistic detail begins to fade toward the bottom of the image; Whitman's legs are rendered with less and less detail until they diminish to simple sketch lines, then fade into the blankness of the paper itself. The image advertises its constructedness.

What has not been noticed about this familiar and overread image is that it is Whitman's first gesture at creating the organizing metonymy of *Leaves of Grass:* the book as man, the pages and the ink as identical to the poet himself. We can imagine that if Whitman had had the means, he might have made his portrait in the 1855 *Leaves* a pop-up figure, literally springing from the page ("I spring from the pages into your arms," he announces in 1860). The effect of Hollyer's engraving in fact suggests this, for the background of the unframed portrait is literally the page itself: this author lives in his book. Hollyer intensifies this effect by adding the odd oval shading around the barely sketched-in legs, suggesting a dent in the page, a hole out of which the poet literally emerges into ink, springing out of the page into the reader's eyes. The legs are not truncated in this portrait; rather they simply disappear into (or appear out of) the dark dent in the paper, and we witness the poet rise on the page, through the ink lines into an illusion of presence, a presence captured by Hollyer's careful rendering of the detailed face of the daguerreotype. The image allows Whitman to play on the relationship between photograph and engraving, suggesting an analogous relationship between poet and poem, each a reflection of the other.

Whitman undermines, then, the expectations that his readers would bring to an engraving in this context; this is anything but the conventional image of the poet on the frontispiece of a book. He offers us an image of self-assurance, informality, physicality, manners, and dress unbefitting the anticipated environment of poetic pages. This image of the poet is just as much out of place in the tradition of poetry books as the poetry itself is, and thus the image effectively announces Whitman's new American poetic project, with all its ironies and its dissolving tensions between "poetry" and "work," between "poet" and "working man."

During the same year this daguerreotype was taken, Soren Kierkegaard wrote about the "leveling down" process of the democratic art of photography; his comments now sound almost as if they were pointed at Whitman and as if Whitman were defiantly responding. "With the daguerreotype," Kierkegaard said, "everyone will be able to have their own portrait taken—formerly it was only the prominent; and at the same time everything is being done to make us all look exactly the same—so that we shall only need one portrait" (quoted in Sontag 207). Sontag notes these democratic underpinnings of photography and comments on the resultant problems:

> In the mansions of pre-democratic culture, someone who gets photographed is a celebrity. In the open fields of American experience, as catalogued with passion by Whitman and as sized up with a shrug by Warhol, everybody is a celebrity. No moment is more important than any other moment; no person is more interesting than any other person. (28)

Whitman was aware of this dilemma, and his response to it was not a simple one. In some ways, he would embrace and celebrate the problem, offering up his own daguerreotype as the representative single portrait, hoping his "simple separate person" would suggest the "En-Masse," that in singing "One's-Self" he would be of necessity chanting the "Modern Man." Sontag argues that recently photography has left Whitman's ideal behind: "Instead of showing identity between things which are different (Whitman's democratic vista), everybody is shown to look the same" [47]. But for Whitman, of course, the hope was that the individual, while woven into the social fabric, would never be swallowed up in the "En-Masse"; colorful individuals made up the communal whole, their diversities precisely the quality that would prevent the country from collapsing into a bland uniformity. "I have allow'd the stress of my poems from beginning to end to bear upon American individuality and assist it," Whitman remarked in the 1880s, "as a counterpoise to the leveling tendencies of Democracy" (PW 2:276). Whitman's faith in the power of photography, to be sure, was not that it would make everyone look the same, but rather that it offered the democratic possibility of giving equal emphasis to everyone's distinctness; R. W. B. Lewis notes this aspect of photography in the nineteenth century:

> The instrument of Daguerre could achieve in art what the hopeful sought for in life: the careful and complete differentiation of the individual in time and space, the image of the single person in all his rugged singularity. (19)

Whitman's nameless portrait, then, while certainly representative of the new democratic man—informal, self-assured, unconventional, independent—was also unmistakably a single, separate individual; no one would mistake *this* person for someone else. Whitman would continue to return to this originating image his whole life; it remains in the final edition of *Leaves*. Many of his friends, particularly his friends later in life when his image had become more saintly and ethereal, did not appreciate

Figure 11. Illustration from *Ballou's Pictorial Drawing-Room Companion* (December 27, 1856), 400. University of Iowa Libraries.

the early image: William Sloane Kennedy expressed hope "that this repulsive, loaferish portrait, with its sensual mouth, can be dropped from future editions, or be accompanied by other and better ones that show the mature man, and not merely the defiant young revolter of thirty-seven, with a very large chip on his shoulder, no suspenders to his trousers, and his hat very much on the side" (248). Earlier friends who more commonly celebrated Whitman's revolutionary aspect tended to read it quite differently; Whitman remembers that William O'Connor admired it "because of its portrayal of the proletarian—the carpenter, builder, mason, mechanic." What all these reactions have in common is that they read the image as a social sign, a representative image of class and attitude. Whitman, however, as much as he may have been attracted to the image of himself as a true Jacksonian artisan, tended to resist the typological readings and thus disagreed with O'Connor's characterization, emphasizing instead the photo's casual qualities: "I like it because it is natural, honest, easy: as spontaneous as you are, as I am, this instant, as we talk together" (*WWC* 3:13).

Whitman clearly was in command of his image, and he manipulated it to garner the greatest effect. If we look at the first two known daguerreotypes of Whitman, for example, we see a well-dressed young man, identifiable as a "Broadway swell," one of the standard types seen sauntering the streets of New York. As John Kasson has noted in his study of "bodily management in public" in nineteenth-century America, the two poles of male deportment were the Bowery tough and the dandy, and an 1856 magazine engraving illustrates the contrasting styles nicely: the two portraits look like slightly intensified versions of Whitman's 1840s and 1850s portraits (see Figures 2, 3, and 11). As he published *Leaves of Grass,* Whitman had transformed himself from the fashionable swell to the common tough, "swagger[ing] along the street, shouting and laughing with his companions, his hat on one side" (Kasson 123). And yet if we look closely at the first daguerreotype of Whitman and then again at the 1854 engraved daguerreotype, we see that his hat, even the cocked angle of the hat, looks the same. What has changed is his body: the delicate hands passively holding the cane have become the fisted hand on the hip; the neat suit with the dandy tie has been shed for the open shirt, with the dark undershirt replacing the dark tie as the neck ornament. It is all style, and by the 1860s he would alter it again, reassuming the tie and the suit, but now wearing them much more casually, the overall image too "shaggy" (as Whitman referred to his early 1860 photos) to be mistaken as a dandy. Yet the 1859 Schoff engraving based on Charles Hine's painting of Whitman, which served as the frontispiece for the 1860 *Leaves* (see Figure 4), is another dandified image, dramatically different from the more rugged Whitman that appears in photographs around this time.

We can get an idea of how vital the questions of style were to Whitman by reading a late reminiscence by one of his old newspaper friends, who recalled Whitman's image in the late 1850s:

> This city was comparatively small then, and Walt Whitman was as conspicuous a citizen as any—knew everybody and everybody knew him. He was a marked figure on Broadway—a most manly man, as vigorous and virile as his own poetry. His very personality impressed itself upon all passers-by, and men, and even women, turned around to look at him. He was almost the first to make the now fashionable fad of the flannel shirt in Summer his all the year round convenience and comfort. . . . His ordinary wear was a neat suit of workingman's clothes. Brady, then famous as a photographer, was the first to capture Whitman, and thereafter every photographer in town displayed colored pictures of Walt. (*WWC* MS)

The writer also comments on a gaudy silk tie that Whitman wore, and reading this piece in 1891, the poet is upset that his image would be so misrepresented: "It is all untrue—all of it. I never wore a tie—or rarely—& if I did, it was a black silk one. I dressed in black anyway at that time." He didn't really wear gray, he goes on to say, until "from 1860 to 65," though "perhaps it had its suggestion earlier" (*WWC* MS). To the end of his life, then, he was conscious of his image and his manipulation of it.

The 1854 daguerreotype, then, was to serve as a guide to the attitude the reader should take when approaching *Leaves,* a relaxed and natural posture, a spontaneous exchange (not a rehearsed lesson). In fact, Whitman worried that the image might undermine this quality by its threatening air of rough arrogance: "The worst thing about this is, that I look so damned flamboyant—as if I was hurling bolts at somebody—full of mad oaths—saying defiantly, to hell with you!" That would create the opposite effect from what Whitman hoped to achieve, an intimate encounter with the reader, a meaningful embrace. Whitman characteristically created a kind of legend out of the facts surrounding the picture:

> The steel came from a photo—the photo from what would be called a chance. . . . I was sauntering along the street: the day was hot: I was dressed just as you see me there. A friend of mine—Gabriel Harrison . . .—stood at the door of his place looking at the passers-by. He cried out to me at once: 'Old man!—old man!—come here: come right up stairs with me this minute'—and when he noticed that I hesitated cried still more emphatically: 'Do come: come: I'm dying for something to do.' This picture was the result. Many people think the dominant quality in Harrison's picture is its sadness: even Bucke has said something of the kind—and others too. (*WWC* 2:506–507)

Whitman's friends tended to prefer another daguerreotype taken that same day, a calmer, hatless one that some of them came to call the "Christ-likeness," an image that many saw as capturing a transcendent gaze, Whitman's eyes looking at us but also through us, lit by divine insight. (The photo is still used when an image of Whitman as a divine is desired, as on the cover of George Hutchinson's recent book about Whitman's prophetic role playing and his employing of elements of nineteenth-century American ecstaticism, called *The Ecstatic Whitman: Literary Shamanism and the Crisis of the Union.*) Whitman, however, preferred the rougher, more physical image, and he never had the ecstatic image engraved, nor did he use it in any of his books.

When Whitman decided on a photographic frontispiece for his retrospective volume of collected poems and prose, he chose a profile shot (see Figure 9), noting that one thing a profile does is to make the face unfamiliar to oneself; we seldom see ourselves in profile, and most of our portraits tend to imitate the angles on ourselves that we normally observe in the mirror. By putting a face in profile, we heighten the features, but we also make it slightly alien, less personal and less familiar (eyes of a face in profile, of course, are never looking at the viewer). For Whitman it was crucial that the profile portrait of himself was looking *out,* away from the spine of the book, away from the book itself, inviting the reader to follow his gaze out into the world, not to rest within either the book or the self: "It is appropriate: the looking *out:* the face *away* from the book. Had it looked *in* how different would have been its significance." And that gaze out into the world, with unfamiliar eyes, from the poems to what is around us, became for Whitman as good an emblem as any for the distinctive quality of American poetry, for the identifying tone of our emerging poetry, a poetry that would look to nature and experience for its authority, not to the past and to tradition: "I am after nature first of all: the out look of the face in the book is no chance" (*WWC* 2:460).

The profile of American poetry, Whitman suggested with this portrait, is a face looking out into the world, seeking words out of experience instead of out of books, attaching the filaments of language to *things* more than to ideas, discerning and describing the unfamiliar, or the familiar in an unfamiliar way. This photo and another (that he came to call the "Lear" photo) taken at the same session were the first pictures he had had taken since the Civil War in which he does not wear a coat; the shirtsleeves informality harkened back to his 1854 daguerreotypes and to the Gardner "night-dress" photos of the mid-1860s (see Figure 5). The profile portrait thus echoes Whitman's self-image from his more robust earlier days, and he sees it as "so thoroughly characteristic of me—of the book—falls in line with the purposes we had in view at the start." And he stood firm on the use of the image despite the objection, even ridicule, of his friends. The photo in fact was even more generally unpopular than the 1854 daguerreotype: "I think I am the only one who likes it," Whitman said, but went on to justify its use in a number of ways:

> What does it express? . . . it says nothing in particular—suggests, what? Not inattention, not intentness, not devil-may-care, not intellectuality: then what is it? . . . It is truth—that is enough to say: it is strong—it preserves the features: yet it is also indefinite with an indefiniteness that has a fascination of its own. I know this head is not favored, but I approve it—have liked it from the first. (*WWC* 2:520–21)

Whitman even altered the title of his book so as to avoid a possible joke; Horace Traubel looked uneasily at the portrait as he prepared to take it to the printer and Whitman asked, "What's the matter?" Traubel explained, "I was thinking that if we put above this portrait 'Walt Whitman Complete' they'll laugh at us" (*WWC* 2:412). Traubel reports that Whitman laughed, said he had already thought of that, and went on to change the title. The portrait, in significant ways, does contrast with the 1855 image: where the 1855 pose emphasized "Walt Whitman Complete" by including torso and limbs, the 1880s pose does signal a diminishing sense of physicality; and where the 1855 pose is literally confrontational, challenging in its direct stare at the onlooker, the 1880s shot looks away, as if the poet's interests have shifted from direct encounter with the reader to a search for something beyond the book and perhaps, in keeping with the theme of the later poetry, beyond this life. Still, Whitman insisted on containing both images within the book; the 1880s pose never displaces the 1850s one: it only complicates the image by contradicting it while joining it, clashing with it while echoing it in its informality. As such, the two photos work to suggest the changes that a lifetime of photos records in a life full of contradictions but still strung on a single identity: if a lifetime of photos teaches us anything, it is that life is a series of contradictions and echoes.

IV. "MEN WHO SAW FURTHER THAN THEIR CAMERAS"

The threat of conformity, the loss of differentiated American crafts and trades, the emergence of a "single commercial class," were major anxieties for Whitman in the post–Civil War years, as M. Wynn Thomas has recently demonstrated. It is fitting, then, that Whitman would look to the still highly skilled craft of photography with its colorful group of artisan-operators as a remaining source of differentiated identity; it was a trade, after all, whose major purpose was precisely to offer Americans images of their differentiated identity. The major economic shift in America that Whitman was reacting to was, as Thomas has demonstrated, "the breaking up of the artisanal class, under the impact of metropolitan capitalism" (85), leading to the loss of Whitman's strong democratic vision of a nation of individualistic, self-supporting artisans, skilled workers in a variegated but classless union. Throughout his life, Whitman sought out representatives of this vision: "I resolved at the start to diagnose, recognize, state, the case of the mechanics, laborers, artisans, of America—to get into the stream with them—to give them a voice in literature" (*WWC* 2:142). But Whitman's adult life was spent watching the artisanal vision die into a hopeless division and subdivision of labor, an increasing specialization resulting in some artisans moving into positions of massive entrepreneurial wealth while others slipped into less favored positions as disenfranchised salaried employees of growing manufacturing conglomerates.

We have seen how Whitman's love of baseball was initially wrapped up in the sport's origins among artisanal guilds, but no group of workers better illustrated this evolution than the photographers Whitman knew. They were colorful nonconformists, men of diverse interests who learned their craft well and went into business for themselves; they were one of the last groups of artisans to develop a new craft, one learned through a long apprenticeship. But these artisans' ultimate success in photography finally depended more on their business acumen and marketing skills than on their artistic skills; some of the finest photographers went bankrupt, some quit, while others not as talented became major commercial successes. In 1863, Holmes began his *Atlantic Monthly* essay on photography by noting how quickly the new techniques, new art, and new skills had transformed themselves into a capitalistic enterprise:

"Few of those who seek a photographer's establishment to have their portraits taken know at all into what a vast branch of commerce this business of sun-picturing has grown" (1863, 1).

Someone like John Plumbe, one of Whitman's favorite daguerreotypists, was himself a kind of entrepreneurial pioneer, a traveler on the frontier who made maps and wrote books about his explorations, an advocate of the transcontinental railroad who fought tirelessly for the idea, eventually a prospector following the gold rush to California. Along the way, he became an early commercial success, setting up one of the first chain store operations in America, opening galleries in thirteen different cities, from the East Coast out to Dubuque; he was a master advertiser who even marketed what turned out to be a fraudulent method to duplicate daguerreotypes (the supposedly revolutionary Plumbeotype turned out to be little more than an engraving of the daguerreotype). He was one of those artisans who made the transition to businessman quite easily, but he was dead before the Civil War, a bankrupt suicide who had given up his business success to follow his Western dreams of railroads and gold; in Whitman's mind he no doubt remained the model of the rugged but skilled new democratic man, despite the toll that America's new commercial spirit had taken on him.

Gabriel Harrison was out of the same mold, a man not narrowly defined by his photographic skills: a writer, actor, painter, and stage manager as well as a photographer. Whitman liked him because he was as "wild and unpruned as nature itself" (quoted in Rubin 283), and he no doubt approved of Harrison's resistance to the forces of overorganization and conformity creeping into the photographic craft by mid-century; Harrison singlehandedly fought the formation of the American Daguerre Association, an attempt by the emerging elite of photography to set standards of good taste. Harrison argued that all tastes must be represented: "Let the corner stone of the institution be democratic" (quoted in Welling 86). He remained for Whitman one of the true artisan-heroes of the era.

But Whitman's great photographic artisanal hero was Alexander Gardner. This wild-looking Scotsman, with his long beard, intense eyes, and rugged good looks, had originally come to America to take part in a utopian community scheme on the Iowa frontier. He ended up instead working in Mathew Brady's New York studio, and he became the manager of Brady's successful Washington, D.C., studio before leaving to begin his own competing studio. He was a good businessman, but he never gave himself over to the corporate mentality that eventually undid people like Brady; Gardner did not hesitate to close up his studio in 1867 when the opportunity arose for him to go West with the Union Pacific railroad and, riding in his horse-drawn darkroom, to turn the frontier into accessible images. Whitman admired the way his artistic genius took precedence over his business concerns: "Gardner was a real artist—had the feel of his work—the inner feel, if I may say it so: he was not a workman—only a workman (which God knows is a lot in itself, too!)—but he was also beyond his craft—saw farther than his camera—saw more" (*WWC* 3:346). Gardner *looked* like the kind of democratic artist Whitman endorsed: "Gardner was large, strong—a man with a big head full of ideas: a splendid neck" (*WWC* 3:234). The neck, pivot of the head, was always crucial for Whitman's art; as a poet, he depended on perceiving the world when his "head slues round on my neck" (*LG* 76), and the best photographer, too, would have to have a strong neck, since it was the result of the swivel of the head that the panorama of the world was brought into the brain. And Gardner's portraits of Whitman are the ones that most emphasize Whitman's neck, his beard closely trimmed and collar wide open. They are strong photos, the most informal ones taken of the poet (he recalled one reporter commenting that "Whitman had been photographed in his night-dress"), and they were his favorites, reminding him of the period of his life when he was "physically at my best, mentally, every way." Both Gabriel Harrison and Gardner had photographed Whitman as something of an artisan-poet, a poet in shirtsleeves, a poet of physical strength who riveted attention with his eyes, not with his elegance.

After the Harrison and Gardner photos, Whitman's portraits tended to become more formal, and the photographers who took them tended to be the more established big business operators. The famous Mathew Brady photographs generally portray a more refined Whitman (see Figure 6). Brady was another photographer whom Whitman admired; his bravery at Bull Run—where he was nearly killed and wandered lost through the woods for days after the battle, all in the service of getting his photographs—clearly made him something of a hero to Whitman as he was to many Americans. But Brady became an emblematic victim of the post–Civil War urge to capitalize, incorporate, and expand; trying to cash in on his Civil War photos and expand his string of studios, he ran out of capital and by the 1870s was well into a long physical, mental, and financial decline; he died in poverty just a few years after Whitman's death.

After the war, Whitman was photographed by some of the most successful commercial photographers in the country, the photographers of the gilded age who created obscenely opulent studios catering to the rich and famous; they were in large part responsible for creating the very celebrities they then catered to. Jeremiah Gurney ran a "photographic palace" on Broadway, developing an intricate system of sidelights to wash out the wrinkles from his sitters' faces, bringing back youth to their images. George G. Rockwood helped develop the *carte-de-visite* fad that turned people cheaply into images of themselves, that served as the nation's first real trading cards, and that created a market for the selling and trading of images of identity. He also prided himself on an assembly-line efficiency that allowed him to photograph over 113,000 sittings by the early 1880s. The flamboyant Napoleon Sarony, dressed in his Hussar uniform, ran the most famous gallery in the world in the 1870s; he was a celebrity selling cabinet cards of other celebrities, forty thousand of whom he photographed and publicized by making their portraits available to an adoring public learning to be consumers of images of fame. Frederick Gutekunst, like Sarony a photographer of celebrities, boasted the largest collection of cabinet cards of the famous. He was the master at mechanizing the photographic process and developing methods of photoduplication that made possible mass consumption of desired images; his Philadelphia gallery contained giant presses that allowed for massive runs of photos, a service Whitman often used in the later years, ordering thousands of copies of photos of himself. Whitman had surprisingly little to say about the skills of these men; they were more like corporate bosses than skilled artisans, ruling over vast empires of machines and employees, producing commercial products that they marketed skillfully, creating a mass demand for images. Whitman, who by the 1880s had become something of a celebrity himself, had business dealings with them, ordering the most effective images of himself to include in his various printings of *Leaves;* he occasionally noted having a "pleasant time" when going to be photographed at their elaborate studios, but he never felt the affection for any of them that he felt for the early, more rugged artisans of the craft of photography, the men like Harrison and Gardner who seemed actually to care for, read, and think about *Leaves of Grass.* Even in the means of production of the images of his own face, Whitman could read the disturbing changes in American society, changes that would make him question just what the Civil War had been fought for, changes that made him question the direction America was going in; he had come to worry a great deal about what he called "the wounds and diseases of peace" in America's age of material corruption (*PW* 2:430).

This was the era Marx identified as the moment of the "birth and decline" of the individual, and America's photographers both manifested the phenomenon and helped create it, as their mass-produced images of individuals began to blur distinctions, creating types and styles to be emulated, until one's own picture could never easily be seen as truly one's own picture. Toward the end of his life, as he examined his own photographic portraits, Whitman questioned some of the easy assumptions about identity that his poetry had been built on: he had in some ways become a very different person from the poet who began *Leaves,* and he had in some ways become the creation of others—in the sales-rooms of Gutekunst's and Sarony's and Cox's studios, after all, Whit-man's white-bearded ancient poet-prophet image was in some demand.

V. "CATCHING LIFE ON THE RUN"

Photography brought to narcissism a new depth, a new inten-sity. If the myth of Narcissus has its roots in ancient taboos against seeing one's own reflection, then photography was in its very origins the shat-tering of taboos, the invitation to dwell on one's own image. One of the first responses to the invention of photography was to call it a "miracu-lous mirror" (Newhall 97), miraculous because it allowed for mirrored moments to be preserved, frozen, held onto. Humans were thus granted a distinctly modern Narcissus role, dwelling not only on their present reflection, but on the reflection of the process of change that their lives enacted. Humans could begin to reflect on their past reflections, dwell on the images of the dead, track their own growth and decline. Photog-raphy taught many lessons in the nineteenth century, but none was more revelatory than the demonstration that life was an incessant process, a shifting action: photographs, as they captured and held fleeting mo-ments, offered the only stasis, but it was a permanence that simply un-derscored change. Tiresius prophesied that Narcissus would have a long life if he never looked on his own features, and photography brought the prophecy home with a vengeance; by the end of the nineteenth century, for the first time, humans were able to look in a miraculous mirror at a series of images of themselves quickly growing old; by the end of one's life, there would be a stack of paper mirrors that compressed that life into a brisk shuffle of aging. Recently a national arts granting agency made a large grant to a photographer to photograph his own aging, to take weekly pictures of himself in the same pose against the same back-ground, so that eventually we would have for the first time a detailed record of the aging process. It is a dream as old as photography itself, and it is a project that Walt Whitman came closer to accomplishing than any other member of that first generation of Americans whose adult lives were lived after the advent of the photographic image.

To return for a moment to Whitman's 1854 daguerreotype, we can see that his decision to use that portrait as the frontispiece to his first edition of Leaves is bound up with the emerging awareness of the nature of iden-tity that photography brought: instead of a timeless formal portrait of himself, Whitman presented himself as a brash, changing (some would say shifty) informal being whose transformations would be tracked not only in the growth of his book, but in the gallery of photographic por-traits that he would use to illustrate himself in the various editions. (He would continue to reprint the 1854 daguerreotype in many succeeding editions and juxtapose it with later photographs to emphasize that his book recorded a life process—shift, change, aging—rather than attempting a permanent embodied meaning.) Usually his name did not appear on the title page of his books; the visual image, the eyes in an ever-aging face looking out into the world, stood for the poet more than the authority of a deceptively permanent and never-changing name. For Whitman (at least the pre-1870 Whitman), the soul was an accumulating transit through the world, an absorptive embodiment of palpable experience: "Was somebody asking to see the soul? / See, your own shape and countenance, persons, substances, beasts, the trees, the running rivers, the rocks and sands" (*LG* 23). Like an endless roll of film, the soul was a connected string of impressions ("glories strung like beads on my smallest sights and hearings" [*LG* 160]), a collection of the traces of the experiences that the lenses had opened themselves to. The self (and the song of the self) was the album composed of the resultant photos, a life's experiences strung like beads on the soul.

As we cast back to the mid-nineteenth century, when Americans began to come to grips with the new reality that photography was developing before their eyes, we find that it was this aspect of the new discovery that generated the most awe. In 1862, as *cartes-de-visite* became the American rage, *Scientific American* called them "a blessing to the world" and began to imagine for the first time just what might be revealed in the coming generation:

> One of the most interesting results of the ease and cheapness with which photographs are produced is the prompting which it will give many persons to have their likenesses taken frequently during their lives. What would a man value more highly late in life than this accurate record of the gradual change in his features from childhood to old age? . . . First, the new-born babe in his mother's arms; then, the infant creeping on the floor; next the child tottering by the mother's apron; then the various phases of boyhood, till the sprouting beard tells of the time when the plans and hopes of life began to take form and purpose; another portrait with softer locks and eyes is now coupled with the series, and the stern warfare with the world begins; the features henceforward grow harder and more severe; lines slowly come into the forehead and grey hairs mingle with the locks; the lines grow deeper and the head whiter, till the babe is changed into the wrinkled and grey old man, so different but still the same! (reprinted in Gilbert 82)

Around the same time, Oliver Wendell Holmes was ruminating, as we have seen, over the revolution in perception that "sun-painting" had brought about, and he dwelled on the same phenomenon, imagining the sometimes awful truth that photographs were about to demonstrate:

The new art is old enough already to have given us the portraits of infants who are now growing into adolescence. By-and-by it will show every aspect of life in the same individual, from the earliest week to the last year of senility. We are beginning to see what it will reveal. Children grow into beauty and out of it. The first line in the forehead, the first streak in the hair are chronicled without malice, but without extenuation. . . . Family-traits show themselves in early infancy, die out, and reappear. . . . Each new picture gives us a new aspect of our friend; we find he had not one face, but many. (1861, 14)

Whitman's generation was the first to actually look back on its youth in a distant mirror. The power of photography, Whitman said, was in its "knack of catching life on the run, in a flash, as it shifted, moved, evolved" (*WWC* 3:23). Vast realms of reality became for the first time represented, turned into representations, and the changing, shifting, evolving face of every individual over time was part of the new pile of images photography brought into consciousness.

Turning once again to Holmes's penetrating early comments on the cultural effects of photography, we find his uneasy realization that portrait photography was the genre that was going to excite a democracy; a democratic people would find images of their own faces far more fascinating than photographs of the far reaches of the world:

We . . . will not quarrel with the common taste which prefers the card-portrait. The last is the cheapest, the most portable, requires no machine to look at it with, can be seen by several persons at the same time,—in short, has all the popular elements. Many care little for the wonders of the world brought before their eyes by the stereoscope; all love to see the faces of their friends. (1863, 8)

For Holmes, though, portrait photography was ultimately anything but democratic; stripped of the painter's ability to fabricate, photographs revealed what Holmes believed to be the natural class distinctions of the subjects:

The picture tells no lie about them. There is no use in their putting on airs; the make-believe gentleman and lady cannot look like the genuine article. Mediocrity shows itself for what it is worth, no matter what temporary name it may have acquired. (1863, 9)

Holmes's reaction to the growing mass of photos of common people was an odd mixture of smug satisfaction at his own obvious superiority to the masses and perverse fascination with the unfamiliar realms of experience such photos brought to him; he could now study carefully faces he would not otherwise have encountered: "The weakness which belongs to the infirm of purpose and vacuous of thought is hardly to be disguised, even though the moustache is allowed to hide *the centre of expression."* Even the dregs of humanity posed for photos, and Holmes at least found comfort in the knowledge that the lowest classes were offering up only their own ugliness and not compounding it with the awful techniques of cheap painters: "We still feel grateful, when we remember the days of itinerant portrait painters, that the indignities of Nature are no longer intensified by the outrages of Art" (1863, 9).

But after such discriminating and discriminatory tirades, Holmes settles into a perceptive analysis of one of photography's most radical lessons:

> We have learned many curious facts from photographic portraits which we were slow to learn from faces. One is the great number of aspects belonging to each countenance with which we are familiar. Sometimes, in looking at a portrait, it seems to us that this is just the face we know, and that it is always thus. But again another view shows us a wholly different aspect, and yet as absolutely characteristic as the first; and a third and a fourth convince us that our friend was not one, but many, in outward appearance, as in the mental and emotional shapes by which his inner nature made itself known to us. (1863, 9–10)

Holmes goes on to discuss how photos teach us a certain "tone" in a human expression that for the first time reveals just what we mean when we refer to "family likeness." Holmes's insatiable medical curiosity leads him to express his anxiousness for a whole generation to pass so that photography can finally yield up "a precise study of the effects of age upon the features," so that for the first time we can "study of the laws of physical degeneration" (1863, 10). "Nature," he notes, "is very exact in the tallies that mark the years of human life," for the "sun is a Rembrandt in his way, and loves to track all the lines in these old splintered faces" (1863, 9–10).

VI. "EVOLUTIONARY OR EPISODICAL"?

It is probably something of a cruel irony that Whitman was the first person to illustrate, fully and dramatically, such a process of aging through photographs. And as he tried to puzzle out the meaning of the process that the photos revealed, his concerns were deeper than just determining the effects of age on his features; his photos seemed to him to track an identity, to capture in the changing contours of his face the sweeping changes in his life. In 1891, less than a year before his death, Whitman described his cluttered Camden room, with the floor "half-cover'd by a deep litter of books, papers, magazines, thrown-down letters and circulars, rejected manuscripts, memoranda"; on the table was an additional "jumble of more papers," including "many photographs, and a hundred indescribable things besides." His room, he said, had become "a sort of result and storage collection of my own past life." As he sifted through the rubble, as he sorted the photographs of himself and composed narratives of his life (he was, when he wrote this description, just completing a short autobiographical sketch, "an old remembrance copy"), he was struck by the process of change, of growth, and decline that those photographs traced; they were themselves a "storage collection" of his life, and they suggested to him "a sort of result" (*PW* 701–702). Whitman performed, via his photographs, a self-examination of the kind that Holmes foresaw, the great variety of "outward appearances" tracking "the mental and emotional shapes by which [the] inner nature made itself known to us" (1863, 10).

Certainly no writer in the nineteenth century saw more of his faces than Whitman. (Mark Twain had more photos taken, but many of the most familiar ones were in the twentieth century.) "No man has been photographed more than I have" (*WWC* 2:45), he once said, and many contemporary observers agreed with his assessment: Horace Traubel in 1889 raised the question to William Douglas O'Connor and Richard Maurice Bucke: " 'I wonder if Walt is not the most photographed man that ever lived?' William said, 'It looks to me as if he was.' Bucke said: 'There's no doubt of it' " (*WWC* 4:260). At times Whitman seemed fatigued with the profusion of images: "I have been photographed, photographed, photographed, until the cameras themselves are tired of me." Looking at the hopeless clutter of photographs scattered around him in his Camden room in the late 1880s, unable to identify the dates and circumstances of many of them, Whitman lamented, "I have been photographed to confusion" (*WWC* 2:454). "I've been taken and taken beyond count," he said, "taken from every side—even from my blind side" (*WWC* 2:45). At times he made it sound as if photographers had hounded him into sitting for them and had used him mercilessly: "They have photographed me all ages, sizes, shapes: they have used me for a show-horse again and again and again" (*WWC* 2:446). His photographs, reproduced and widely distributed by various photographers and by Whitman himself, had made him something of a celebrity: "My head gets about: is easily recognized" (*WWC* 3:532). But the sheer number of images again and again bothered him; he seemed to have lost touch with the selves they represented, almost as if some of the self-images were of strangers: "Can a man by searching find God?" he asked one day: "Can a man by searching find the origin of a picture of himself?" (*WWC* 4:393).

Stumbling upon photos of himself he had forgotten had been taken, he joked: "I meet new Walt Whitmans every day. There are a dozen of me afloat. I don't know which Walt Whitman I am" (*WWC* 1:108). Different photographers brought out different angles, shadowed different features and highlighted others, until the number of miraculous mirrors began to add up at times to a bewildering fragmentation of self:

> What a study it all is—this of portraits: no two of them identical: every interpreter getting another view. What amazing differences develop in the attempt of a dozen observers to tell the same story . . . there are as many views as there are people who take them. (*WWC* 2:45)

This "confusion" of Whitmans created something of a jocular identity crisis, but his tone often turned more serious as he thought about what all these images over the years suggested about the wholeness of his life: "It is hard to extract a man's real self—any man—from such a chaotic mass—from such historic debris" (*WWC* 1:108). While he knew that "the man is greater than his portrait" (*WWC* 1:108), he also knew that his photographs over a lifetime were adding up to something, were capturing a persisting quality that had never before been seen in human experience: "The human expression is so fleeting—so quick—coming and going—all aids are welcome" (*WWC* 5:478). When Horace Traubel suggested that "a photograph is a fragment [but] a painted portrait may be a whole man," Whitman rejected the implied slight to photography; he saw that photography affirmed his belief that identity was not some transcendent quality but rather was an embodied process: "I am getting more and more in spirit with the best photographs, which are in fact works of art" (*WWC* 4:434).

At times it was as if Whitman wanted to see his various photographs in a composite form, like the English scientist Francis Galton's experiments in the 1870s and 1880s; Galton built on the growing realization that photography was transforming identity into a process, and he sought ways to make the fragmented nature of individuated portraits yield a transcendent identity. His composites, as Miles Orvell has noted, were formed "by combining individual portraits into a single homogenized facial image": "By photographing an individual as many as twenty times and printing a single composite print at the end, Galton argued that he would avoid the hazard of the single image and would arrive at an averaged expression that was the sitter's true self" (92). The variety of discrete and partial images could be melded into one true and whole image. In a similar way, Whitman carefully read and interpreted his photos, looking for clues to their individual and momentary significance and also looking for ways the single images added up to a totality, ways the "elements" formed a "compound": "I guess they all hint at the man" (*WWC* 6:395; 2:156). Most of the photos, he believed, were "one of many, only—not many in one," each picture an image that was "useful in totaling a man but not a total in itself" (*WWC* 3:72). Each photo was like a word in a giant lexicon, one small fragmented representation of a giant self: the poet kept working to lift the diffusion into wholeness, prevent it from slipping into dispersion.

Earlier we examined Whitman's metaphor equating a photograph of his face to "This heart's geography's map" (LG 382), and as he examined his photographs he applied the metaphor, trying to read the images like a map, a series of visible shorthand signs cast on paper that would guide him to the nature of his invisible heart. Late in his life, the photographs became an equivalent for his earlier fascination with phrenology; he was always looking for an external map to interior and invisible regions, for a way the physical shape could suggest spiritual contours. When, in "Song of Myself," he imagines that his "palms cover continents," he is offering up a vision of continental phrenology, his hands (and the poems that emerge from those hands) reading the character of a country through the contours of the land that formed that character (just as later he would claim he found the "law of [his] own poems" in the jagged contours of the Rocky Mountains [PW 1:210]). So in thinking of his photographs, he conceived of the image of his face as "this limitless small continent" (LG 382), a landscape on a different scale to be mapped and read. Sitting with a hundred images of his face surrounding him, Whitman was still reading heads, still looking (as he had forty years before) for positive qualities and traits in his physiognomy, and he was sometimes confused by the conflicting signals the various images of himself returned to him.

Particularly toward the end of his life, he was insistent about certain qualities that he felt should and should not be discerned in public images of himself, and he was fascinated with and at times disturbed by some of the qualities that appeared in images he hoped to keep private. We have seen how entranced Whitman was when he first entered the large New York daguerreotype galleries in the 1840s, how he found a "strange fascination" in "looking at the eyes of a portrait," a fascination, he said, that "sometimes goes beyond what comes from the real orbs themselves." Wandering through a daguerreotype gallery in 1846, he mused, "We love to dwell long upon them—to infer many things, from the text they preach—to pursue the current of thoughts running riot about them" (GF 116–17). Forty years later, the gallery of faces he would be dwelling on would be a legion of himself, and he maintained his curiosity about the text that his own fixed and gazing eyes preached over the years. Alan Trachtenberg talks of how Mathew Brady's galleries had "answered a need, for breaking out of the confinement of the self, through transaction with images," a reassuring company of photographic compatriots that offered a solution to Alexis de Tocqueville's sobering analysis that "not only does democracy make every man forget his ancestors, but it hides his descendants and separates his contemporaries from him; it throws him back forever upon himself alone and threatens in the end to confine him entirely within the solitude of his heart" (Trachtenberg 1984, 246). Whitman, alone in his room with his lifetime of photographs, suggests that photography also gave to the lonely democratic man a whole set of ancestors, all of them early versions of the self, in whose faces he could trace his own lines.

There was no doubt for Whitman that his portraits tracked a life *in* time and demonstrated that life was a process of continuity and change. And he even began to wonder whether the photos finally demonstrated that life was "evolutional or episodical," a unified sweep of a single identity or a jarring series of new identities: "Taking them in their periods is there a visible bridge from one to the other or is there a break?" (*WWC* 4:425). Whitman tried to maintain the faith that his photos finally were like the catalogs in his poems, an infinite and contradictory variety that piled up a wild randomness that created a unity, a form and a plan, a happiness; *Leaves of Grass* was modeled on the procession of a life from the starting through the parting, and it set out to embrace the shifting moments of change into an overarching identity: "It is not chaos or death—it is form, union, plan—it is eternal life—it is Happiness" (*LG* 88). Whitman looked at his photos and said, "We judge things too much by side-lights: we must have a care lest we pause with the single features, the exaggerated figures, individuals, facts—losing thereby the ensemble" (*WWC* 1:283). But Whitman's reactions to his photographs reveal that he maintained his doubts about the ensemble, the wholeness, the unity; his photos often spoke to him instead of fragmentation, disunion, and conflicted emotions.

VII. "THE TERRIBLE DOUBT OF APPEARANCES"

While in his poems Whitman could often look directly and honestly at dark hidden elements of himself, when he looked at his photos he was at times horrified by hints of emotions and qualities he found there and tried to turn away from them. In "A Hand Mirror," Whitman orders himself to "Hold it up sternly" and to see beyond the external "fair costume" to "within" where there are "ashes and filth," where a "slave's eye . . . / A drunkard's breath, unwholesome eater's face, venerealee's flesh" and a rotted physiology (remarkably prophetic of his own autopsy) look back at him, demonstrating "Such a result so soon—and from such a beginning!" (*LG* 268–69). It is as if in looking into the mirror, he sees possible processions of his life unfold like a series of photographs (the hand mirror was, in fact, the earliest and most common metaphor for the photograph [Trachtenberg 1989, 60–61]), and each procession leads him to an unwanted end. There is a similar sudden con-fession in "Crossing Brooklyn Ferry," in which the poet blurts out the existence of his "guile, anger, lust, hot wishes I dared not speak" and admits to "wayward, vain, greedy, shallow, sly, cowardly, malignant" behavior (*LG* 163).

But in actual photos of himself, he was concerned about the appear-ance of anything negative; he did not want to exude any hint of despair. Looking at one photo, he asked, "Does it look unkind? No man has any excuse for looking morose or cruel: he should do better. . . . That is so important to me: to not look downcast—cloud up things." He let Horace Traubel have that particular photo, but only with the proviso that "If you should ever use this portrait in any way—for this, that—be sure to say Walt Whitman was not a glum man despite his photographers" (*WWC* 3:378). Again and again he would talk about this morose or downcast quality that so often crept into the photos. Looking at another photo, Whitman asked, "Do you think it glum? severe? I have had that suspicion but most people won't hear to it . . . I don't want to figure anywhere as a misanthropic, sour, doubtful: as a discourager—as a put-ter-out of lights" (*WWC* 3:14). Looking at yet another photo, he told Traubel that "it can't be said to be worth while: it's empty: lacks any positive characteristics." And he concluded: "It has no value: I think we'd best dismiss it" (*WWC* 4:38). He had a large investment in publish-ing a series of photographs that tracked his life in such a way that the various images added up to a positive and unified statement. Thus, he carefully selected the photos that would be circulated and published, but when he looked at *all* the photos—including the ones that did not fit the program—he felt less secure in his unity of purpose.

Graham Clarke argues that when we look at the photographs of Whit-man "en masse," we can "see the extent to which they reflect the distinc-tion between the public and the private and how, in turn, the 'private' photographs question the larger public image Whitman adopts." Clarke goes on to categorize "two groups of image [*sic*], the public and the private—each part of a single process in which 'identity' is the central subject" (135–36). This dichotomy is not nearly as pronounced as Clarke would have it, though, since most of what he calls "public" photos are simply formal portraits, while most of the "private" photos are informal shots, taken late in Whitman's life when the portability of equipment and other technological advances (requiring less light for exposure) allowed for home photography. That Whitman's Camden home was more clut-tered than the backdrop of a photography studio leads Clarke to claim that the "at home" photos "split open the Whitman myth," revealing the poet as "the product of his habitat, not the maker of it" (as he appears to be in the formal "sealed frame of the constructed photographic space" where he is freed "from any historical context" [148]). But such an analysis ignores the way that Whitman was working hard to make his cluttered and closed life *very* public, part of his final mythic incarnation as the aged and impoverished prophet-poet. Many of his late poems, the prose of *Good-Bye My Fancy,* and the numerous letters and newspaper pieces that he oversaw the publication and distribution of all testify to his desire to manipulate this old, sick, private self every bit as much as he manipulated his earlier versions of self. The appearance of a public–private division, then, is more a function of the state of photography at given periods of his life than an intentional result. Rather, Whitman spent a good deal of time *deciding* which of his photos would be public and which would remain private: some of his most formal poses revealed something private, a darker side, that he believed had to be kept from the public eye. Some of his informal poses, on the other hand, exposed an intimate side that he pondered making public.

For Whitman, the public and the private were inseparable, and the variety of his photographs underscores the easy slippage he made from one realm to another. While individual photos may initially be intended as private documents, after all, they are (as long as they exist as objects in the world) always potentially public. While Whitman did destroy some photographs, he kept most, even those that he disliked. And as friends gathered around him in Camden, he shared some of his private ones with them, thus beginning a process that guaranteed that they would eventually be made very public, as his executors carefully preserved the images in order to make them generally accessible.

At times, Whitman debated whether or not some of the unpublished photos should become public images. The most revealing cases involve the relatively few photos he had taken of himself with others, always with much younger men or with children, most of which were tucked away as private documents and some of which embarrassed his friends: the photos with Peter Doyle, Harry Stafford, Bill Duckett, and Warren Fritzinger represented emotions and relationships that tested the line between public and private, and these photos remain some of the most interesting images of the poet in his wavering private–public pose (see Figures 12–15). If these photos most clearly document the Calamus-relationships he believed to be the foundation of an emerging democracy, it is telling that he chose to keep them private (even though most of them are formal studio portraits): he never used them in his books as illustrations or suggestions of a new kind of democratic affectional relationship.

Horace Traubel and Thomas Harned, who became two of Whitman's literary executors, along with W. D. O'Connor, who immortalized Whitman as "The Good Gray Poet" but who later distanced himself from him, all had some deep and uneasy reactions to one particular photograph that Whitman liked a great deal. This is a photograph of Whitman with his young former-Confederate soldier friend, Peter Doyle (see Figure 12). The photo was taken in Washington, D.C., in the late 1860s, one of two extant photos taken at the same session. In one, Doyle rests his arm on Whitman's shoulder, but in the one that bothered Whitman's friends, Whitman and Doyle sit in chairs facing each other, smiling and looking in one another's eyes. In 1889, in Whitman's Camden home, Traubel picked up the picture from a box and described it as "a rather remarkable composition: Doyle with a sickly smile on his face: W. lovingly serene: the two looking at each other rather stagily, almost sheepishly." What happened in the room as Whitman and his friends looked at the photo is revealing: Whitman, Traubel tells us, "laughed heartily the instant I put my hands on it," and Harned began to mimic and mock the look on Doyle's face, causing Whitman to retort: "Never mind, the expression on my face atones for all that is lacking in his. What do I look like there? Is it seriosity?" Harned's answer is astonishing: "Fondness, and Doyle should be a girl." Clearly, Harned has sensed a homoerotic quality in the photo that he finds perverse and very discomfiting. Whitman shakes his head at Harned's remark and laughs, defending Doyle as "a master character": "Tom, you would like Pete—love him: and you, too, Horace" (WWC 3:542–43).

The next year, Traubel finds the picture again (now on the floor) and this time describes it as "the two sitting looking gazing into each other's eyes"; Traubel's emendation is telling, for he clearly sees more than a look, something intimate, expressive of desire, requiring him to correct the neutral "looking" to the more suggestive "gazing." Traubel then writes that it is "a picture which O'Connor described to me as 'silly-idiotic,'" though Whitman insists on calling it "first-rate." Whitman then exclaims, according to Traubel, "Dear Pete! Many's the good day (night) we have known together!" (WWC MS; see also WWC 7:265). Traubel's parenthetical "night" is also suggestive; since Traubel in this manuscript is recording Whitman's words, he almost never uses parentheses, and it is difficult to imagine how Whitman could speak a parenthetical word. It is probable that Whitman said "night," but that Traubel thought he'd better record "day" and at least contemplate for a while which way he should present the statement when he published it. (Since Traubel never published these notes, it is impossible to say.) Traubel apparently is uneasy about the implications of Whitman's many good nights with Doyle, just as he is about the "sheepish" look on Whitman's and Doyle's faces, and he is struck by how negatively Harned and O'Connor react to the photo: it was an icon of male–male affection that some of Whitman's friends clearly felt was dangerous to make public, for fear that it would confirm what many already suspected of Whitman,

Figure 12. 1869? Photograph of Whitman and Peter Doyle by M. P. Rice, Washington, D.C. Charles E. Feinberg Collection.

Figure 13. Late 1870s. Photograph of Whitman and Harry Stafford. Photographer unknown. Edward Carpenter Collection, Sheffield (England) Library.

168

Figure 14. 1886. Tintype of Whitman with Bill Duckett. Photographer unknown. Charles E. Feinberg Collection.

Figure 15. 1890. Photograph by John Johnston of Whitman with Warren Fritzinger on Camden, New Jersey, wharf. Charles E. Feinberg Collection.

that his *Calamus* poems spoke of a physical as well as a spiritual union between males. The photograph, as a trace of reality, seemed to Whitman's friends *too* physical, too telling in the bodily proximity and erotic gaze that it recorded. So after Whitman's death, when Traubel issued a collection of Whitman's letters to Doyle and called it *Calamus,* he carefully chose the *other* photograph of the two friends—the safer, more casual one—to be engraved as the frontispiece, presenting the book as the record of a loving but spiritual friendship. Whitman himself never could figure out what to do with the photograph; he argued with his friends about their uneasy reactions to it, but he finally never published it; nor did he destroy it. Instead, he left it for posterity, a private image that is still flowering into public meaning.

Whitman's photographic images often gave him pause, much like the occasional pauses we hear in *Leaves* where he faces "the terrible doubt of appearances," realizes that "we may be deluded," that the life images the photographs caught may be "only apparitions, and the real something has yet to be known" (*LG* 120). "Of the Terrible Doubt of Appearances," from *Calamus,* is one of many statements Whitman made near the end of the 1850s doubting the apparent reality of physical forms. This was a time, we know, of deep personal conflicts for him, and it was the time also that he was beginning to be surrounded by photographic portraits in the massive galleries of New York; he began more and more to wonder about "That shadow my likeness that goes to and fro seeking a livelihood, chattering, chaffering," and he began to "question and doubt whether that is really me" (*LG* 136). The *Calamus* poems—often read as the most intimate of Whitman's writings, the place where he turns to "paths untrodden" (*LG* 112) to speak of private manly attachments—are a key point in any discussion of Whitman as public and private poet. Whitman insisted the *Calamus* poems were his most political statement, precisely because they turned the private public, exposed the self's affections to communal scrutiny and offered them up as the key to democratic love.

Even though he kept his Calamus photos out of public view, many of the *Calamus* poems can be read in terms of the new photographic awareness that he (and the rest of America) was developing, can be read as if the photos themselves spoke: "Behold this swarthy face, these gray eyes, / This beard"; "Passing stranger! you do not know how longingly I look upon you" (*LG* 126, 127). Like the photo galleries Whitman visited as a young man—where he felt all those "human eyes gazing silently but fixedly" upon him, "speechless and motionless" faces "but yet realities" (*GF* 116)—his poems became a gallery of real voices, beckoning and addressing the reader, human presence captured on paper. But poems, like photos, only allowed a superficial closeness; Whitman was careful to add the caution: "To begin with take warning, I am surely far different from what you suppose" (*LG* 123). The photos cast the private face as a public icon and did what Whitman, using the language of photography, said *Leaves* set out to do: "to cast into literature not only his own grit and arrogance, but his own flesh and form, . . . to stamp a new type of character, namely his own, and indelibly fix it and publish it, not for a model but an illustration, for the present and future of American letters and American young men" (*LG* 777–78). But once cast as a public face, the image began to mask emotions and thoughts that conflicted with the projected image; the face became a "curtain" more than a window, and Whitman was aware of "The passionate teeming plays this curtain hid!" (*LG* 382).

As Whitman tried to read his own photographs, he wondered and worried about how much conflicted difference showed through the composed exterior. If, as he proclaimed in *Calamus*, he wanted to "Publish my name and hang up my picture as that of the tenderest lover, / The friend the lover's portrait" (*LG* 122), then he was extremely sensitive to any hints in the photos of something not tender but tough, something not loving or loveable: he most liked the photos where he appeared "strong enough to be right and gentle enough to be right, too. . . . It would be no consolation to me to be a giant with the love left out" (*WWC* 2:412). He worried about one picture that suggested to a woman that "Walt Whitman was a sensualist." Whitman recalled that "she said she'd rather have a picture that had more love in it." Then Whitman looked at the photo again and rescued it by reading some tenderness into it, by embracing this former self as his own offspring: "It's a little rough and tumble, possibly, but it's not a face I could hate" (*WWC* 2:273). He was worried about how "unaccountable" it was that "this repellent 'something,' " a negative quality like severity, could steal into a photograph; yet, he realized, "we know how elusive such things are" (*WWC* 3:110). At times he would joke about the lack of tenderness: "Is that the picture of a tough? Maybe I am not sensitive—maybe I am a tough—maybe the people who don't like toughs, don't like me" (*WWC* 1:276). At other times, as when he first saw a picture of himself taken as a young man, he was not convinced that tenderness was even an accurate part of the self he saw: "That benignity—it puzzles me: . . . that is a mistake: such benignity, such sweetness, such satisfiedness—it does not belong. I know it often appears—but that's the trick of the camera, the photographer" (*WWC* 4:151).

Tricks of the camera and photographer were things Whitman disliked; the power of photography for him was its cold realistic eye; it portrayed what was there, not what the artist wanted to see there. In this he agreed with Holmes: "If you wish to see the very look your friend wore when his portrait was taken, let not the finishing artist's pencil intrude within the circle of the vital knot of expression" (1863, 9). To touch up was to undo exactly what the photo did best: present things as they are, revealing "flaws" and "imperfections" as necessary parts of the whole composition. Whitman would cry out in exasperation when someone touched up one of his photos: "Why didn't the fellow let the thing alone as we sent it? It's the old story of the artist trying to improve on nature again" (*WWC* 2:475). His aesthetic principles were often expressed in terms of photography; he railed against "the people who think they can improve on God Almighty's work—who put an extra touch on here, there, here again, there again, until the real man is no longer recognizable" (*WWC* 1:398). In this way photography served to endorse Whitman's belief in organic form, a form that emerges from the very rhythm of the experience—untouched, unfussed with, unformed from without: to watch the latent image emerge as the photo developed was to witness the unfolding of a form that was organically bound to the experience it represented. Even if photography was "perhaps a little too chemically definitive" and too much involved with "a mechanism," Whitman always held to his belief that photography "has this advantage: it lets nature have its way" (*WWC* 4:124–25).

In letting nature have its way, photography handed to Whitman a puzzling and endlessly fascinating clutter of images of himself, images more conflicted and ultimately more illuminating than any painted portrait; for built into painted portraits were meaning and unity of impression. Built into a lifelong series of photographs were fragmentation and change, and it was in reading that fragmented and shifting process of his life, that crowd of former selves, that Whitman finally prevented himself from resting in a simplistic summary of his identity; his photographs helped turn the moments of his life into something of a democracy, a democracy of various versions of the self in time, each claiming equal status, each insisting on its own identity even while clearly merging into the overall process of the life: simple, separate selves, yet part of the life's "En-Masse." To the end, his photographs helped keep the self a mystery, helped quite literally keep him alive as he traced his heart's geography's map.

Photography, then, gave Whitman a basis for his democratic poetics. It allowed him to conceive of his own life as a kind of democratic crowd, a contradictory series of separate selves joined mysteriously into an overarching unity, an identity, just as it offered him a sanction to perceive reality itself as democratic, a fullness and a wholeness composed of all the necessary details, the clutter that composed the complete image. It is fitting that Whitman was looking at photoengravings when he announced, "Art will be democratized" (*WWC* 2:107).

VIII. SALUTING THE WORLD

We have seen how the terminology of what we now call "photography" was a matter of some contention during the middle years of the nineteenth century. Holmes preferred "sun-painting," and there was a confusing proliferation of words for the various processes of what eventually would settle into the single concept of "photographs": daguerreotypes, Plumbeotypes, ambrotypes, calotypes, tintypes, sun pictures, heliographs. There was a battle for lexical hegemony among proponents of the various terms just as there were legal and marketing battles among proponents of the various processes and claims that the terms indicated. Marcus A. Root, a Philadelphia photographer who coined the term "ambrotype," wrote in the late 1850s one of the most influential early books on photography, *The Camera and the Pencil,* in which he argued

> that Heliography, "Sun-sketching," is a *correct general name* for the art in all its varieties; while Photography, "Light-sketching," with all its derivatives, is a *misnomer,* since it is not light, but *actinism,* which is the producer. "Heliochart," "Sun-paper," is the proper title of what is now called a photograph. (Root xviii)

Root goes on to quote authorities who support the inaccuracy of the term "photography," though he resigns himself to the idea that even only twenty-five years after the advent of sun sketching, the lexical battle may already have been lost: "It is not to be hoped (I presume) that this error will ever be amended in the popular speech" (Root xviii).

Some of the terms did not exist long enough even to make it into Webster's or Worcester's dictionaries during Whitman's lifetime, although "sun-picture" did enter Webster's 1864 dictionary as a synonym for "photograph," and Root's "ambrotype" (literally an "immortal impression") received its own technical definition, as did "calotype" ("beautiful impression"). "Actinism," one of Root's favorite terms, also entered the 1864 Webster's, as the "power in the sun's rays by which chemical changes are produced, as in photography." For Root, "actinism" was a mix of the scientific and the mystical; he traces the word's etymology (from the Greek for "sunbeam") and describes it as one of the three "elements" of "the solar beam," the first two being light and heat, the third being "actinism" or "power of the ray." Actinism is "a chemical force, of which one of the principal functions is to decompound and alter the arrangement of the particles in whatever it touches"; this quality allows it "to pierce through the earthy covering to the seed" and thus to become the agent of germination. It is a force closely allied to what Whitman called "composting," the force that breaks things down into elements so that new forms can emerge:

> As a decompounding force, actinism effects some change in the atomic arrangement of every body whereon it falls, be it the firmest rock or the softest wood or leaf. Were it not, then, for *counteracting* and *reparative* agencies in the economy of creation, this delicate-seeming power, though the tender nurse of the vegetable infant, would eventually crumble into ruins the total frame-work of the universe! (Root 64–65)

It is this gentle but all-powerful portion of the sunbeam, then, that allows for pictures to be made, breaking down the subject it falls on in order to form a new likeness.

When "photography" had first appeared in Webster's dictionary (in 1847), it had been cross-indexed with Root's preferred "heliography," and at the time Webster endorsed Root's choice. (His 1847 definition of "heliography" privileged the word, noting that the "name is preferable to that of Daguerreotype.") Almost as if some force like actinism itself were at work on the language, the dictionary was churning and composting the burgeoning new words associated with the revolutionary new process, gradually settling on the new standard usages. Whitman, reading his dictionaries, settled on "photography," too; in his own writings, he never was tempted with any of the ubiquitous but short-lived alternatives—he would generally favor the popular choice over the authoritative or the technically correct. So, though in his 1855 version of the poem that would eventually be called "A Song for Occupations" Whitman singled out "The implements for daguerreotyping" (*LGV* 94), by the 1881 edition he had dropped the reference, aware that the term had already become obsolete. *Leaves* would become a wordbook of American democratic usage, and its continuing contemporary tone derives in part from Whitman's intuitive sense of how the American language was evolving, of which words would remain and which would be left behind.

At the time Whitman was working on his 1860 edition of *Leaves,* Root was defining in detail for the first time the artistic nature of photography, claiming "that Heliography is entitled to rank with the so-named Fine Arts" (19). He saw four major uses of photography. The first great use was to offset "the order of nature," to respond to the sad fact that "families are dispersed, by death or other causes; friends are severed." Photography could keep "our loved ones, dead or distant, our friends and acquaints, however far removed . . . within daily and hourly vision." Thus, photography allows for "domestic and social affections and sentiments" to be "conserved and perpetuated" by the image's "literal transcripts of features and forms": "How can we exaggerate the value of an art which produces effects like these?" (26–27). The photographs Whitman collected of his Civil War soldier-friends served precisely this function for him, as did the friendship photos he had taken of himself with his postwar young male friends.

This was photography's more intimate use, to memorialize loved ones; but photography had a more public use, Root said, to keep "the great and the good, the heroes, saints, and sages of all lands and all eras" close by us, "within the constant purview of the young, the middle-aged, and the old" (27). These were the photos that inspired by example, that prompted admiration and patriotism more than intimate affection. Some of Whitman's formal poses seem to be his attempt to leave such images of himself, the sage of America who would take his iconic place next to his heroes Lincoln and Jackson and Washington. But his use of photographs finally always blurred the very distinction that Root attempted to make, for it is precisely Whitman's "representative" nature that makes him intimate. He is the hero and sage because he celebrates "social affections and sentiments," because he continually revealed himself to be no more than any and all of us are. Thus, his more intimate poses were also public, portraying the warmth and affection that would bind a democracy into a Union; and his more formal poses could reveal a morose and very private side that seemed to undermine his public role as a representative of hope.

Root's third function of photography was the educative one, its ability to increase "the knowledge and happiness of the masses." This aspect of photography is the one Whitman tried to capture in his poetry. Root notes, "What, heretofore, the traveller alone could witness (and travelling was out of the reach of ninety-nine hundredths of mankind), even the humblest may now behold, substantially, without crossing his own threshold" (28). Root's catalog of the "natural scenery, grand, beautiful, or picturesque, of every quarter of the globe" that photography makes available to "even the lowliest of the community" sounds like a précis for Whitman's "Salut au Monde!" which allows the poet access to the scenes of the world:

> . . . the noblest edifices, secular and religious, of the most highly civilized lands; together with the weird, fantastic piles, reared by semi-barbaric peoples to the "strange gods;" the multitudinous reliques still remaining of the skill and the power, the pomps and the glories of the most celebrated regions of the ancient world; the localities, on either continent, where conflicts have been waged, or events have occurred, which have acted powerfully on the destinies of nations, and perhaps have turned the currents of the world's history into new channels; the inhabitants of every zone, from the Arctic to the Antarctic Circle, with their costumes and their exterior ways of life; the finest existing speci-

mens of art, ancient and modern, of foreign countries or our own; the most exciting, impressive, and awful acts or scenes which may occur anywhere at any moment—a thunder-storm, a tempest at sea, a great battle, in the very heat and fury of its crisis . . . (28)

Root here demonstrates a sudden urge to catalog when he describes the vast democracy of global seeing that photography opened up to anyone with eyes; it is the same urge we saw Holmes succumb to when he tried describing the variety of detail that a photograph captured. Whitman's quick visionary jumps in a poem like "Salut au Monde!" (in which there are distinct groups of images corresponding to every category in Root's catalog, as if he is trying to capture in words all the realms photography had opened) are part of the same urge, part of the energetic sweep of multitudinous detail that endless stacks of photographs were demonstrating. So, in "Salut," Whitman begins by asking himself what he hears, and the ensuing catalog is brief; but when he asks himself at the beginning of Section 4 what he *sees,* he generates nine long additional sections of quick-jump scenes, catalogs rolling out of his anaphoric "I see." In Whitman's lifetime, technology had extended sight far more than hearing, and his poetry was generated by that new technology.

So Root's fourth use of the art of photography is its aesthetic one; photography, he says, "is destined to do much for the improvement of the other fine arts and their professors" (29). It will teach the portraitist to paint better portraits, the landscape artist to paint more accurate landscapes, and it will increase accuracy of impression for all artists. It will supply "reliable sketches" of machines, architecture, and people for book illustrations. Root does not foresee the way that photography would also generate a new kind of poetry, paced and organized and worded differently than any poetry before it, but that is exactly the lesson Whitman learned from the new mode of representation. He would not write *about* photography so much as he would write *with* and *from* photography, discovering how to transform its new way of seeing to words, how to take its visual representations and find linguistic forms that were equally suggestive of detail, completeness, cluttered wholeness.

This was Whitman's great cultural achievement: many writers incorporated cultural events and technological developments into their work by describing them, but few had the genius to throw out the old ways of describing and to discover new ways generated *out* of the new forms and actions and tools that the national culture was defining itself with. His challenge was not to write about a new national culture with forms derived from the past, but rather to "word the future" with a poetry that was truly in rhythm with the burgeoning dictionaries, the emerging national sport, the fading autochthonous cultures, and the stunning new technologies of representation. If he could use these cultural acts as writing *tools* more than writing subjects, his faith was that he could create a poetry of native representations, one that would be experienced as distinctly American.

Bibliographic Notes

PREFACE AND INTRODUCTION

Texts Cited

Erkkila, Betsy. *Whitman the Political Poet* (New York: Oxford University Press, 1989).

Hollis, C. Carroll. *Language and Style in Leaves of Grass* (Baton Rouge: Louisiana State University Press, 1983).

Swinton, William. *Rambles Among Words: Their Poetry, History and Wisdom* (New York: Charles Scribner, 1859).

1. WHITMAN AND DICTIONARIES

Texts Cited

Burkett, Eva Mae. *American Dictionaries of the English Language Before 1861* (Metuchen, NJ: Scarecrow, 1979).

Cmiel, Kenneth. *Democratic Eloquence: The Fight over Popular Speech in Nineteenth-Century America* (New York: Morrow, 1990).

Dressman, Michael Rowan. "Walt Whitman's Plans for the Perfect Dictionary," in Joel Myerson, ed., *Studies in the American Renaissance, 1979* (Boston: Twayne, 1979), 457–74.

Simpson, David. *The Politics of American English, 1776–1850* (New York: Oxford University Press, 1986).

Swinton, William. *Rambles Among Words: Their Poetry, History and Wisdom* (New York: Charles Scribner, 1859).

Warren, James Perrin. *Walt Whitman's Language Experiment* (University Park: Pennsylvania State University Press, 1990).

Webster, Noah. *An American Dictionary of the English Language* (New York: S. Converse, 1828).

An American Dictionary of the English Language (Springfield, MA: G. & C. Merriam, 1847).

An American Dictionary of the English Language, rev. Chauncey Goodrich and Noah Porter (Springfield, MA: G. & C. Merriam, 1864).

A Note on Sources Concerning Whitman and Dictionaries

Given Whitman's fascination with lexicography, surprisingly little attention has been paid to his relationship with dictionaries and dictionary makers. Michael Dressman's revealing essay entitled "Whitman's Plans for the Perfect Dictionary" (in Joel Myerson, ed., *Studies in the American Renaissance, 1979* [Boston: Twayne, 1979]) is the best sustained study; Dressman lays out the various Whitman manuscript materials dealing with his own plans for compiling a dictionary. Whitman's involvement in the writing of William Swinton's *Rambles Among Words* has been a topic of some controversy in Whitman studies for thirty years now; the place to begin is C. Carroll Hollis, "Walt Whitman and William Swinton: A Co-operative Friendship," *American Literature* 30 (1959), 425–49. More recently, James Perrin Warren has offered further rationales supporting Whitman's authorship; see "Whitman as Ghostwriter: The Case of *Rambles Among Words,*" *Walt Whitman Quarterly Review* 2 (Fall 1984), 22–30. Edward Grier chose to include large sections of *Rambles* in his edition of Whitman's *Notebooks and Unpublished Prose Manuscripts,* giving the material a dubious canonical standing as Whitman's work.

David Simpson, *The Politics of American English, 1776–1850* (New York: Oxford University Press, 1986), is an outstanding historical overview of the development of the American language in the context of American culture and literature; Simpson has several insightful comments about Whitman's language concerns. J. L. Dillard, *Toward a Social History of American English* (New York: Mouton, 1985), tracks, in a way Whitman would have admired, the multitudinous dictions and accents that have formed the American version of English. James Perrin Warren, *Walt Whitman's Language Experiment* (University Park: Pennsylvania State University Press, 1990), is a compendious study of Whitman's "real grammar," his relationship to nineteenth-century proponents of the organic theory of language, and his various theories of language and how they structure his poetry. Of particular relevance is Warren's study of Whitman's "Loan Words and Word Formations in *Leaves of Grass,* 1855–1856" (34–69), with its enumeration of Whitman's attempts to expand the language. Kenneth Cmiel's lively *Democratic Eloquence: The Fight over Popular Speech in Nineteenth-Century America* (New York: Morrow, 1990) contains a particularly illuminating discussion of the Webster–Worcester dictionary war and emphasizes the similarities rather than the differences between the two competing sides (see especially chap. 2, "The Democratic Idiom").

As for Whitman's own personal dictionaries, his notes reveal that he primarily referred to various editions of Webster's (he quotes definitions from Webster and passages from Webster's introductory essay on the history of English), but he also owned at least one copy of Worcester: Joel Myerson owns a title page to Worcester, *Universal and Critical Dictionary of the English Language* (Boston: Wilkins, Carter, 1849) that is signed by Whitman.

2. WHITMAN AND BASEBALL

Texts Cited

Adelman, Melvin L. *A Sporting Time: New York City and the Rise of Modern Athletics, 1820–70* (Urbana: University of Illinois Press, 1986).

Berthold, Dennis, and Kenneth M. Price, eds. *Dear Brother Walt: The Letters of Thomas Jefferson Whitman* (Kent, OH: Kent State University Press, 1984); foreword by Gay Wilson Allen.

Bieler, Stephen. "Poem to Be Named Later," *CoEvolution Quarterly* (Summer 1983), 94.

Bucke, Richard Maurice, ed. *Calamus* (Boston: Laurens Maynard, 1897).

Clark, Michael. *Dos Passos's Early Fiction, 1912–1938* (Selingsgrove, PA: Susquehanna University Press, 1987).

Crosby, Ernest. *Plain Talk in Psalm & Parable* (Boston: Small, Maynard, 1899).

Frost, Robert. *Selected Prose of Robert Frost,* ed. Hyde Cox and Edward Connery Lathem (New York: Collier, 1968).

Furness, Clifton Joseph. "Walt Whitman Looks at Boston," *New England Quarterly* 1 (1928), 353–70.

Gipe, George. *The Great American Sports Book* (Garden City, NY: Doubleday, 1978).

Gold, Michael. "3 Schools of U.S. Writing," *New Masses* 4 (September 1928), 13–14.

Goldstein, Warren. *Playing for Keeps: A History of Early Baseball* (Ithaca, NY: Cornell University Press, 1989).

Grella, George. "Baseball and the American Dream," *Massachusetts Review* 16 (Summer 1975), 550–67.

Grobani, Anton. *Guide to Baseball Literature* (Detroit: Gale Research, 1975).

Guttmann, Allen. *Sports Spectators* (New York: Columbia University Press, 1986).

Horowitz, Mikhail. *Big League Poets* (San Francisco: City Lights, 1978).

Melville, Herman. *Selected Poems of Herman Melville,* ed. Robert Penn Warren (New York: Random House, 1970).

Mencken, H. L. *The American Language* (1919; rev. New York: Knopf, 1937).

Messenger, Christian K. *Sport and the Spirit of Play in American Fiction* (New York: Columbia University Press, 1981).

Noverr, Douglas A., and Lawrence E. Ziewacz. *The Games They Played: Sports in American History, 1865–1980* (Chicago: Nelson-Hall, 1983).

Rader, Benjamin G. *American Sports: From the Age of Folk Games to the Age of Spectators* (Englewood Cliffs, NJ: Prentice-Hall, 1983).

Roe, Charles A. "Walt Whitman, Schoolmaster: Notes of a Conversation with Charles A. Roe, 1894," ed. Horace Traubel. *Walt Whitman Fellowship Papers,* no. 14 (April 1895), 81–7.

Spalding, Albert G. *America's National Game* (New York: American Sports, 1911).

Thomas, M. Wynn. *The Lunar Light of Whitman's Poetry* (Cambridge, MA: Harvard University Press, 1987).

Traubel, Horace, Richard Maurice Bucke, and Thomas B. Harned, eds. *In Re Walt Whitman* (Philadelphia: David McKay, 1893).

Twain, Mark. *Mark Twain's Speeches* (New York: Harper & Brothers, 1923).

Voigt, David Quentin. *American Baseball* (Norman: University of Oklahoma Press, 1966).

America Through Baseball (Chicago: Nelson Hall, 1976).

Williams, Jonathan. *The Empire Finals at Verona* (Highlands, NC: Jargon 30, 1959).

Woolf, Virginia. "American Fiction," in *The Moment and Other Essays* (New York: Harcourt, Brace, 1948).

A Note on Sources Concerning Whitman and Baseball

Albert Spalding's comments are taken from his book *America's National Game* (New York: American Sports Publishing, 1911), a biased but fascinating history of baseball. More reliable histories of baseball's beginnings are Harold Seymour, *Baseball: The Early Years* (New York: Oxford University Press, 1960) and David Quentin Voigt's *American Baseball* (Norman: University of Oklahoma Press, 1966). Arthur Bartlett's *Baseball and Mr. Spalding* (New York: Farrar, Straus, & Young, 1951) contains useful information and anecdotes about the 1888–89 worldwide baseball tour. For a detailed debunking of Spalding's Doubleday creation myth and for an accurate genesis of baseball see Robert W. Henderson, *Ball, Bat and Bishop: The Origin of Ball Games* (New York: Rockport Press, 1947). Irving A. Leitner, *Baseball: Diamond in the Rough* (New York: Criterion, 1972) offers a good collection of photographs of early baseball artifacts; a (mis)quotation from Whitman serves as the epigraph for this book, the only use I've found of Whitman in baseball literature. (This quotation is the concluding monologue in the recent movie about minor-league baseball, *Bull Durham*.) One of the most delightful and useful compendiums of baseball history and facts is Bill James, *The Bill James Historical Baseball Abstract* (New York: Villard, 1986). Gene Karst and Martin J. Jones, Jr., provide indispensable biographical information in their *Who's Who in Professional Baseball* (New Rochelle: Arlington House, 1973). And Daniel Okrent and Steve Wulf offer some key narratives in *Baseball Anecdotes* (New York: Oxford University Press, 1989).

Some of the recent books that examine the larger cultural resonance of baseball include Leverett T. Smith, *The American Dream and the National Game* (Bowling Green, OH: Bowling Green University Popular Press, 1975); Wiley Lee Umphlett, *The Sporting Myth and the American Experience* (Lewisburg, PA: Bucknell University Press, 1975); David Q. Voigt, *America Through Baseball* (Chicago: Nelson Hall, 1976); Steven A. Riess, *Touching Base: Professional Baseball and American Culture in the Progressive Era* (Westport, CT: Greenwood, 1980); Benjamin G. Rader, *American Sports: From the Age of Folk Games to the Age of Spectators* (Englewood Cliffs, NJ: Prentice-Hall, 1983); Melvin L. Adelman, *A Sporting Time: New York City and the Rise of Modern Athletics, 1820–70* (Urbana: University of Illinois Press, 1986); and Warren Goldstein, NY: *Playing for Keeps: A History of Early Baseball* (Ithaca, NY: Cornell University Press, 1989). Riess's, Adelman's, and Goldstein's books are particularly valuable for their careful study

182   BIBLIOGRAPHIC NOTES

of the economic and class backgrounds of early baseball clubs and players. John
F. Rooney, Jr., in *A Geography of American Sport* (Reading, MA: Addison-Wesley, 1974), tracks the geographical origins of baseball players, demonstrating the
western migration of baseball talent and interest in the last decades of the nineteenth century. Allen Guttmann, *Sports Spectators* (New York: Columbia University Press, 1986) offers a history of sports crowds from antiquity to the present, with an emphasis on the social strata of the various kinds of spectators. Two
books that, though they don't deal with baseball, have helped me put the sport
in the context of post–Civil War corporate mentality are M. Wynn Thomas,
The Lunar Light of Whitman's Poetry (Cambridge, MA: Harvard University Press,
1987); and Alan Trachtenberg, *The Incorporation of America* (New York: Hill &
Wang, 1982).

Herbert Bergman of Michigan State University has edited all of Whitman's
extant journalism; I am grateful to Professor Bergman for furnishing me copies
of several uncollected newspaper pieces, including "Baseball—The Eastern District Against South Brooklyn," *Brooklyn Daily Times,* June 11, 1858. (Since few
of the articles in the *Times* were signed and since the paper had two reporters,
we can only make conjectures about authorship.)

3. WHITMAN AND AMERICAN INDIANS

Texts Cited

Allen, Gay Wilson. *The Solitary Singer* (New York: New York University
Press, 1955).
Clark, Leadie M. *Walt Whitman's Concept of the American Common Man* (New
York: Philosophical Library, 1955).
Drinnon, Richard. *Facing West: The Metaphysics of Indian-Hating and Empire-Building* (New York: Meridian, 1980).
Emerson, Ralph Waldo. *Selected Writings of Ralph Waldo Emerson,* ed. William H.
Gilman (New York: Signet, 1965).
Friend, Joseph H. *The Development of American Lexicography, 1798–1864* (The
Hague: Mouton, 1967).
Kenny, Maurice. "Whitman's Indifference to Indians." *Greenfield Review* 14
(Summer–Fall 1987), 99–113.
Lane, Margaret. *Frances Wright and the "Great Experiment"* (Totowa, NJ: Rowman & Littlefield, 1972).
Least Heat Moon, William. *Blue Highways* (Boston: Little, Brown, 1982).
Mendelsohn, Maurice. "Whitman and the Oral Indian Tradition," *American Dialog* 7 (Summer 1972), 25–28.
Merwin, W. S. *Regions of Memory,* ed. Ed Folsom and Cary Nelson (Champaign:
University of Illinois Press, 1987).
Neihardt, John G. *Black Elk Speaks* (New York: Pocket Books, 1972).
Ortiz, Simon J. *From Sand Creek* (Oak Park, NY: Thunder's Mouth Press, 1981).
Pearce, Roy Harvey. *Savagism and Civilization: A Study of the Indian and the American Mind* (1953; rev. Berkeley: University of California Press, 1988).
Perlman, Jim, Ed Folsom, and Dan Campion, eds. *Walt Whitman: The Measure
of His Song* (Minneapolis, MN: Holy Cow!, 1981).

Rubin, Joseph Jay. *The Historic Whitman* (University Park: Pennsylvania State University Press, 1973).

Schevill, James. "A Changing Inventory: For Walt Whitman," *American Dialog* 5 (Spring–Summer 1969), 30–31.

Sigourney, L[ydia]. H. *Select Poems* (Philadelphia: U. Hunt & Son, 1843).

Simpson, David. *The Politics of American English, 1776–1850* (New York: Oxford University Press, 1986).

Snyder, Gary. *Earth House Hold* (New York: New Directions, 1969).

Turtle Island (New York: New Directions, 1974).

The Real Work: Interviews and Talks, 1964–1979 (New York: New Directions, 1980).

Swinton, William. *Rambles Among Words: Their Poetry, History and Wisdom* (New York: Charles Scribner, 1859).

Taft, Robert. "The Pictorial Record of the Old West: IV. Custer's Last Stand— John Mulvany, Cassilly Adams and Otto Becker," *Kansas Historical Quarterly* 14 (November 1946), 361–90.

Turner, Frederick Jackson. *The Significance of the Frontier in American History* (1893; rpt. New York: Ungar, 1963).

Williams, William Carlos. *In the American Grain* (1925; rpt. New York: New Directions, 1956).

Wilson, Norma. "Heartbeat: Within the Visionary Tradition," *Mickle Street Review*, no. 7 (1985), 14–23.

A Note on Sources Concerning Whitman and the Indians

Two books that have fundamentally shifted assumed Western cultural perspectives about the relationship of Euro-Americans to native tribes are Richard Drinnon, *Facing West: The Metaphysics of Indian-Hating and Empire-Building* (New York: Meridian, 1980); and Richard Slotkin, *Regeneration Through Violence: The Mythology of the American Frontier, 1600–1860* (Middletown, CT: Wesleyan University Press, 1973); I am deeply indebted to both. Robert F. Sayre, *Thoreau and the American Indians* (Princeton, NJ: Princeton University Press, 1977), demonstrates the centrality to Thoreau's thought of questions concerning the Indians and suggests directions for realigning our study of "classic" American authors. These books have all built on Roy Harvey Pearce's seminal study *Savagism and Civilization: A Study of the Indian and the American Mind* (1953; rev. Berkeley: University of California Press, 1988).

Slotkin does mention Whitman, but only in passing; at one point, he loosely associates Whitman with the Indians:

> Chanticleer Whitman's "barbaric yawp" sounding like Indian war cries full of bloodlust and sexual threat over the rooftops of the assaulted town, was perhaps more dramatically effectual [than *Walden*] as a statement of identification with the Indian character and spirit of the wilderness and the erotic impulses of the subconscious mind. (534)

And Asebrit Sundquist glances at Whitman's use of Indian women in *Pocahontas & Co.: The Fictional American Indian Woman in Nineteenth-Century Literature*

(Atlantic Highlands, NJ: Humanities Press International, 1987). In the major studies of the relationship of American Indians to Anglo-American writers and to Anglo-American literature, however, Whitman is virtually ignored. See Ray Allen Billington, *Land of Savagery, Land of Promise* (New York: Norton, 1981); Albert Keiser, *The Indian in American Literature* (1933; rpt. New York: Octagon, 1970); Elemire Zolla, *The Writer and the Shaman: A Morphology of the American Indian* (New York: Harcourt, Brace, Jovanovich, 1973); Louise K. Barnett, *The Ignoble Savage: American Literary Racism, 1790–1890* (Westport, CT: Greenwood, 1975); and Pearce, where Whitman is never mentioned, and Drinnon, where "Facing West from California's Shores" serves as epigraph and furnishes the title, but where Whitman's own views of Indians are never explored. Donald D. Kummings, in his bibliography of work done on Whitman since 1940 (*Walt Whitman, 1940–1975: A Reference Guide* [Detroit: Gale, 1983], x), notes the strange paucity of comment on Whitman's attitudes toward Indians, and he views the failure to deal with the subject as one of the major oversights of Whitman criticism.

As I note in this chapter, Whitman's view of the American Indian in some ways never progressed much beyond that of Frances Wright, the freethinking author of *A Few Days in Athens* (1822), whom Whitman heard speak and whose work he absorbed; he called her "one of the best in history" and recalled how he "fell down before her": "I never felt so glowingly toward any other woman" (quoted in Allen 30). In her *Views of Society and Manners in America* (1821), which Whitman no doubt knew well, she offers the usual equivocation of early-nineteenth-century white liberal attitudes: a sadness about the inevitable loss of the native, "the wasting remnant that must soon disappear with the receding forest," but a recognition of—even an enthusiasm for—the necessity of that loss:

> The falling greatness of this people, disappearing from the face of their native soil, at first strikes mournfully on the imagination; but such regrets are scarcely rational. The savage, with all his virtues, and he has some virtues, is still a savage. . . . The increase and spread of the white population at the expense of the red, is, as it were, the triumph of peace over violence. (quoted in Lane 11).

On her travels, she came upon an Indian sitting, pensive, on the shores of Lake Erie. She was surprised to find his "countenance had much in it of dignity and savage grandeur" as he seemed to muse "upon the fallen strength of his tribe." Wright feels a momentary regret "that even this conquest of the peaceful over the savage arts, should have been made at the expense of this wild race," but the feeling passes as she recalls that it is all for the best: "for the well-being of man, how glorious the change, which has turned these vast haunts of panthers, wolves and savages, into the abode of industry, and the sure asylum of the oppressed." Wright's own utopian scheme, her community of Nashoba, set up to free slaves and educate them, as well as to test out her advanced theories of free love and affection, was itself carved out of cheap land in Tennessee from which the Chickasaw Indians had recently been cleared. Whitman's similar progressive ideals dominate his writing, and he was usually comfortable celebrating how America was "enacting to-day the grandest arts, poems, &c., by beating up the wilderness into fertile farms" (*PW* 369).

4 AND 5. WHITMAN AND PHOTOGRAPHY, WHITMAN
AND PHOTOGRAPHS OF THE SELF

Texts Cited

Adams, Henry. *Novels, Mont Saint Michel, The Education* (New York: Library of America, 1983).
Brasher, Thomas L. *Whitman as Editor of The Brooklyn Daily Eagle* (Detroit: Wayne State University Press, 1970).
Buell, Lawrence. *Literary Transcendentalism* (Ithaca, NY: Cornell University Press, 1973).
Clarke, Graham. *Walt Whitman: The Poem as Private History* (London: Vision Press, 1990).
Gilbert, George. *Photography: The Early Years* (New York: Harper & Row, 1980).
Harrison, Gabriel. "The Dignity of Our Art," *Photographic Art Journal* 3 (April 1852), 230–32.
Hollis, C. Carroll. *Language and Style in Leaves of Grass* (Baton Rouge: Louisiana State University Press, 1983).
Holmes, Oliver Wendell. *Over the Teacups* (Boston: Houghton Mifflin, 1891).
"The Stereoscope and the Stereograph," *Atlantic* (June 1859), 738–48.
"Sun-Painting and Sun-Sculpture," *Atlantic* (July 1861), 13–29.
"Doings of the Sunbeam," *Atlantic* (July 1863), 1–15.
Hutchinson, George. *Ecstatic Whitman: Literary Shamanism and the Crisis of the Union* (Columbus: Ohio State University Press, 1986).
Kasson, John. *Rudeness and Civility: Manners in Nineteenth-Century Urban America* (New York: Hill & Wang, 1990).
Kennedy, William Sloane. *The Fight of a Book for the World* (West Yarmouth, MA: Stonecroft, 1926).
Lewis, R. W. B. *The American Adam* (Chicago: University of Chicago Press, 1955).
Lloyd, G. E. R. "Leucippus and Democritus," in *Encyclopedia of Philosophy*, ed. Paul Edwards (New York: Macmillan/Free Press, 1967), 4:446–51.
Miller, Edwin Haviland, ed. *The Artistic Legacy of Walt Whitman* (New York: New York University Press, 1970). Gay Wilson Allen's essay "The Iconography of Walt Whitman" appears on pp. 127–52.
Newhall, Beaumont. *Latent Image: The Discovery of Photography* (1967; rpt. Albuquerque: University of New Mexico Press, 1983).
Orvell, Miles. *The Real Thing: Imitation and Authenticity in American Culture, 1880–1940* (Chapel Hill: University of North Carolina Press, 1989).
Root, Marcus Aurelius. *The Camera and the Pencil, or The Heliographic Art* (1864; rpt. Pawlet, VT: Helios, 1971).
Rubin, Joseph Jay. *The Historic Whitman* (University Park: Pennsylvania State University Press, 1973).
Scholnick, Robert. "Whitman and the Magazines: Some Documentary Evidence," *American Literature* 44 (May 1972), 222–46.
Sontag, Susan. *On Photography* (New York: Farrar, Straus, & Giroux, 1977).

Swinton, William. *Rambles Among Words: Their Poetry, History and Wisdom* (New York: Charles Scribner, 1859).

Thomas, M. Wynn. *The Lunar Light of Whitman's Poetry* (Cambridge, MA: Harvard University Press, 1987).

Trachtenberg, Alan. "Brady's Portraits," *Yale Review* 73 (Winter 1984), 230–53.

"Albums of War: On Reading Civil War Photographs," *Representations* 9 (Winter 1985), 1–32.

Reading American Photographs: Images as History—Mathew Brady to Walker Evans (New York: Hill & Wang, 1989).

Welling, William. *Photography in America: The Formative Years, 1839–1900* (New York: Crowell, 1977).

A Note on Sources Concerning Whitman and Photography

Earlier studies that are still useful include Richard Maurice Bucke, "Portraits of Walt Whitman," *New England Magazine* 20 (March 1899), 33–50; Sadakichi Hartmann, *A Note on the Portraits of Walt Whitman* (New York: Sparrow, 1921); and Jeanette Gilder's recollections of Whitman's sittings for Cox and Gutekunst in *Critic*, n.s. 7 (April 23, 1887), 207–208, and n.s. 12 (October 12, 1889), 179. Basic histories of nineteenth-century American photography include Robert Taft, *Photography and the American Scene: A Social History, 1839–1889* (New York: Macmillan, 1939); Beaumont Newhall, *The Daguerreotype in America* (New York: Dover, 1976); Beaumont Newhall, *The History of Photography from 1839 to the Present Day* (New York: Museum of Modern Art, 1949; rev. 1964); William Welling, *Photography in America: The Formative Years, 1839–1900* (New York: Crowell, 1977); and Peter Pollack, *The Picture History of Photography* (New York: Abrams, 1969). Information on Brady and Gardner is available in James D. Horan, *Mathew Brady: Historian with a Camera* (New York: Bonanza, 1955); and Josephine Cobb, *Mathew B. Brady's Photographic Gallery in Washington, Columbia Historical Society Records,* vols. 53–56. A particularly useful analysis of Brady's significance is Alan Trachtenberg, "Brady's Portraits," *Yale Review* 73 (Winter 1984), 230–53; Trachtenberg's essay, "Albums of War: On Reading Civil War Photographs," *Representations* 9 (Winter 1985), 1–32, offers many useful insights into the problems of reading historical photographs. Much of this material is included in his *Reading American Photographs* (New York: Hill & Wang, 1989). Useful information on George Cox is in Marchal E. Landgren, "George C. Cox: Whitman's Photographer," *Walt Whitman Review* 9 (March 1963), 11–15. On Whitman and Eakins, see Gordon Hendricks, *The Photographs of Thomas Eakins* (New York: Grossman, 1972), esp. 9–10, 109–14; Lloyd Goodrich, *Thomas Eakins: His Life and Work* (New York: Whitney Museum, 1933), 121–24; and William Innes Homer, "Who Took Eakins' Photographs?" *ARTnews* (May 1983), 112–19. General information about early Philadelphia photography can be found in Kenneth Finkel, *Nineteenth-Century Photography in Philadelphia* (New York: Dover, 1980). William White's back-cover comments in the *Walt Whitman Review* over the years concerning specific photographs have been helpful.

Susan Sontag's endlessly suggestive meditation *On Photography* raises numerous points of convergence between Whitman's poetics and the poetics of photography; in trying to see how photography helped form Whitman's poetics, I work backward from her observation that American photographers have responded to "the Whitmanesque mandate to record in its entirety the extravagant candors of actual American experience" (29). Miles Orvell's fine essay "Reproducing Walt Whitman: The Camera, The Omnibus and *Leaves of Grass*," *Prospects* 12 (Cambridge University Press, 1988), 321–46, is reprinted as "Whitman's Transformed Eye" in his *The Real Thing: Imitation and Authenticity in American Culture, 1880–1940* (Chapel Hill: University of North Carolina Press, 1989), 3–29; Orvell persuasively argues for how what he calls "omnibus structures," urban constructs like daguerreotype galleries and exhibition halls, taught Whitman "a way to contain within the bounds of the artwork the rich particularity and clashing contradictions of American life" (322); one of the most useful of Orvell's many insights is his notion of how daguerreotype galleries allowed Whitman the freedom to stare at human faces and offered him "an organizational model for *Leaves of Grass* . . . a way of gathering into one whole the plurality of peoples and types that composed America" (331): panoramas, expositions, galleries, etc., were all "cultural forms" invented to accommodate the growing "accumulation of discrete particulars . . . into amalgamating wholes" (332–33). Graham Clarke, " 'To Emanate a Look': Whitman, Photography and the Spectacle of the Self," in Ian F. A. Bell and D. K. Adams, eds., *American Literary Landscapes* (New York: St. Martin's, 1988), 78–101 (reprinted in revised form in Clarke, *Walt Whitman: The Poem as Private History* [London: Vision, 1990], as "Public Faces and Private Icons: Walt Whitman's Photographic Images," 127–53), argues that still photos are antithetical to Whitman's more "filmic" sensibility and proposes a dichotomy between Whitman's public and private poses. Dana Brand, *The Spectator and the City in Nineteenth-Century American Literature* (Cambridge: Cambridge University Press, 1991), usefully extends Sontag's ideas about the *flâneur* and illuminates the nature of Whitman's urban gaze.

Whitman's comments on photographs and photographers can be found scattered in all seven published volumes of Horace Traubel, *With Walt Whitman in Camden* (vols. 1–3, 1906–14; rpt. New York: Rowman & Littlefield, 1961; vol. 4, Philadelphia: University of Pennsylvania Press, 1953; vols. 5–7, Carbondale: Southern Illinois University Press, 1964–92); J. Johnston and J. W. Wallace, *Visits to Walt Whitman in 1890–1891* (London: Allen & Unwin, 1917); William Sloane Kennedy, *Reminiscences of Walt Whitman* (London: Alexander Gardner, 1896); Whitman's newspaper pieces in Cleveland Rodgers and John Black, eds., *The Gathering of Forces*, 2 vols. (New York: Putnam, 1920); Whitman's various notebooks in Edward Grier, ed., *Notebooks and Unpublished Prose Manuscripts*, 6 vols. (New York: New York University Press, 1984); William White, ed., *Daybooks and Notebooks*, 3 vols. (New York: New York University Press, 1978); and in Whitman's letters in Edwin Haviland Miller, *The Correspondence*, 6 vols. (New York: New York University Press, 1961–77). See also Thomas L. Brasher, *Whitman as Editor of The Brooklyn Daily Eagle* (Detroit: Wayne State University Press, 1970); and Joseph Jay Rubin, *The Historic Whitman* (University Park: Pennsylvania State University Press, 1973), for Whitman's comments on early photographers and studios.

The original inventory of Whitman photographs is Henry S. Saunders's *Whitman Portraits* (Toronto: Privately made, 1922), supplemented and expanded by Ed Folsom, ed., *'This Heart's Geography's Map': The Photographs of Walt Whitman*, special double issue of the *Walt Whitman Quarterly Review* 4 (Fall/Winter 1987). The first essay to explore the relationship of Whitman to photographers and to investigate in detail the significance of visual representations of Whitman is Gay Wilson Allen's essay, "The Iconography of Walt Whitman," in Edwin Haviland Miller, ed., *The Artistic Legacy of Walt Whitman* (New York: New York University Press, 1970), 127–52.

Index

Numbers in bold type indicate illustrations.

Cambridge Studies in American Literature and Culture.

Continued from the front of the book